Early reader praise for *I Am Perfectly Flawso*

"Now and then you read a book and wonder i the authors' wall. Or maybe they read all your c them were my shrink, but they knocked on many oı ıı, the danger of any pretense that perfection has been achieved.'

"And I love the net-net: 'We define Flawsomism . . . as adopting the mindset of continuous improvement while embracing your imperfections along the way.'

"Besides acknowledging that 'we learn from failure,' I loved the language. Hey, I'm a writer. Just think about 'The wrinkle of laughter, the silver strands of wisdom.'

"Thank you Tom & Michele for a yummy and meaningful read."

— James Flaherty, Author of
EMBRACE YOUR AGE: You can be better than ever

"*I Am Perfectly Flawsome* is a great resource for those looking to learn more about the impact of self-doubt, imposter syndrome, and perfectionism on our minds, bodies, careers, and lives. Whether you're looking to learn for your own personal development or to support your colleagues, friends, and loved ones who may be suffering from the vicious cycle that these behaviors and beliefs thrust upon us, this book will provide you with insights that will greatly improve your personal and professional life."

— Angela L.M. Stopper, Ph.D., CLO and Director
of People & Organization Development, UC Berkeley

"After having worked with both Tom and Michele and having read *I Am Perfectly Flawsome*, the book is, ironically, perfect. If you suffer from imposter syndrome, you need to drop what you're doing and read this book. It will save you from this debilitating and crippling condition."

— David M. Schneer, PhD/CEO Merrill Research

"This very important book by Michele Molitor and Tom Collins spoke directly to me. Most of us have lived with the idea that perfectionism is the standard in everything we do, both personally and professionally, and the authors dispel this thought in a very compelling way. I think if more of us can model the 'striving for excellence' approach instead, our relationships, businesses and lives will be that much better off.

"I wish I had these ideas in hand years ago; however, it is never too late to start. The references to the Japanese art and philosophy of Kintsugi were particularly effective and on point in defining and advocating 'Flawsome' as both a journey and a state of being that is good, right now. I feel extremely lucky and grateful that these inspiring ideas have been packaged in one place for easy access and for the strong reminder that we are all Perfectly Flawsome."

— Jeff Ottoboni, Partner, GO Advisory Group

"I did not realize how much perfectionism was a part of my daily life. 'Will it be good enough?' really means that I want to get it right and am afraid not to. I have come to understand that there is no perfect. And, I don't want perfection. I want to embrace my imperfections. They are what make me who I am. They make me flawsome!

"This is an excellent book and it's comprehensive. Not only is it chock-full of strategies that helped me become aware of how unnecessary and exhausting perfectionism is, it also gave me practical solutions, resources, journal prompts, a companion guide, and a relaxing meditation that I can use every day to do my best work and be at peace with what I am producing."

— Deborah Brown-Volkman, Career Coach, former perfectionist, and author of *Childhood Trauma, Some Rise, Some Fall*

"I loved the key tenet of this book that perfectionism is harmful at all ages. In particular, I enjoyed reading Chapter 9 that many aspects of our emotional well-being improve with age. As a recent author at age 63, I loved reading the many success stories of Tom & Michele's older clients and how they overcame perfectionism."

— Greg Davis, retirement planning coach and author of *CHECKMATE: Tips & Lessons to Help You Make the Right Moves to Achieve Happiness!*

"The last twenty years have been quite a journey for me. Two major career changes left me with a serious case of imposter syndrome both times that took many years to overcome. The timing of reading this book couldn't have been better. I'm transforming myself and career once again, but this time it's different. I'm approaching this major change with a sense of excitement and anticipation, rather than cringing with thoughts of, 'What the hell am I doing?'

"The tools and insights provided in *I Am Perfectly Flawsome* have helped me to see my flawsomeness as an asset rather than something to be ashamed of!"

— Thomas Petty, WordPress Security Specialist, thomaspetty.com

"I love that Tom and Michele give the reader both permission and reasons for not striving for perfectionism. As a perfectionist myself in the past, it took a lot of effort for me to allow myself to be good enough without fixating on perfectionism. Even though I taught Lean Principles in the past, talking about overproduction as a form of waste, when it is your own work, you tend to throw the guidance and nuggets of advice to the wind.

"I love the *I Am Perfectly Flawsome* message and the way they invite people to challenge the idea of perfectionism without coming down on them for having that idea and goal of being perfect. Well done!"

— Patrick Seaton, Chief Culture Officer, Innovative Management Tools

"I love this work! The chapter on Advanced Adulting was particularly sobering and gripping. For the past few years I've had some hard lessons dealing with aging perfectionists (a family of them), including myself. You bet I took note of the research shared highlighting that the 'risk of death was significantly greater for high scorers in perfectionism.'

"Well now, since I'm not ready to exit planet Earth, I'm so grateful to Michele and Tom for all their insights on becoming Flawsome. It's giving me new hope. I've read a boat load of self-help books and this one will go on the shelf for easy access."

— Cheryl ODonoghue, MS | Founder of Aspire2STEAM.org
& CEO of Ei Leadership Resources

"In *I Am Perfectly Flawsome*, Tom and Michele offer liberation from the tyranny of perfectionism ... and a gracious way of embracing the beautiful cracks in our identities. What a kind and loving message they are bringing to a world that desperately needs to hear it."

— David Hutchens, author of Story Dash

"*I am Perfectly Flawsome* resonated with me to the core because I have struggled with perfectionism for as long as I can remember. I used to think that being a perfectionist was a good thing, but as I got older, I realized that it was actually holding me back. It made me realize that striving for perfection was actually detrimental to my physical and mental health.

"The book is filled with valuable insights and advice for anyone who struggles with perfectionism. Tom and Michelle do a fantastic job of highlighting the dangers of trying to be perfect. Learning to accept and embrace your flaws is such a crucial step in breaking free from the chains of perfectionism.

"I want to thank the authors for providing such an important resource for people like me who have struggled with the need to be perfect. *I am Perfectly Flawsome* has helped me to release that need and just be my beautiful, flawed self. How refreshing and freeing! It's a powerful reminder that our flaws make us unique and special. I highly recommend this book to anyone who may be struggling with perfectionism. It has truly been a game-changer for me, and I'm so grateful for the wisdom and insight it has brought into my life."

— Teresa Woolard, BSc, BA, DVM, author of the upcoming book,
*Dig. Leap. Play: The Pet Lover's Guide to Discovering Your Gift,
Achieving Your Dreams, and Experiencing Joy*

"What a wonderful read! I really connected with the flawsome mind set, and knowing that excellence can still be achieved without perfectionism. As a mom of three small children, I will definitely be utilizing the tips and practical applications about increasing self esteem and breaking the perfectionist cycle. It's so important these days that we model for our kids and remind them that they are worthy and enough!"

— Kari Knitt, Operations Manager/Coach at Dignify.com

"I Am Perfectly Flawsome: How Embracing Imperfection Makes Us Better is a transformative book that offers a refreshing perspective on the pitfalls of perfectionism and the power of embracing our inherent 'flawesomeness.' The book compellingly argues that perfectionism is not only a barrier to happiness and success but also a killer of creativity and productivity. By adhering too rigidly to rules and 'the right way' of doing things, we limit our potential and stifle our capacity for innovation.

"As someone who values personal growth, this book's philosophy resonates deeply with my own practices. I, too, believe that while continuous improvement is valuable, it should not be confused with the unattainable goal of perfection. Embracing our 'flawsomeness' enhances self-esteem, fosters genuine connections, and makes us more approachable and relatable — especially important in roles like coaching, where helping others see and celebrate their progress is crucial.

"I Am Perfectly Flawsome is not just a book; it's a mindset shift that encourages us to find joy and freedom in our imperfections."

— Robbie Samuels, award-winning author of *Break Out of Boredom, Small List, Big Results,* and *Croissants vs. Bagels*

"I Am Perfectly Flawsome is a meditation on the perils and pitfalls of perfectionism, and how to avoid them. With thoughtful research and inspiring ruminations, Molitor and Collins empower us to move beyond perfection paralysis to become a truer and braver version of ourselves.

— Jacki Schklar, Writer and B2B Marketing Director

"Perfectionism encourages us to play small. To play timidly. Perfectionism heightens anxiety and fear. It robs us of trusting ourselves, our gifts, and our inherent dignity. It is so easy to unconsciously spread this insidious scripting to family (whether of origin or chosen). It's in the societal waters in which we swim. And yet there is hope!

"I Am Perfectly Flawsome shows us ways to return to our authentic self, to heal wounds lived and inherited, to cultivate greater self-trust, and celebrate our individual 'flawsomeness.'"

— Thomas Rosenberg, somatic leadership development coach

"*I Am Perfectly Flawsome*, by Tom Collins & Michele Molitor, is a sanctuary of solace, where readers can seek refuge from the relentless demands of society and the harsh judgments of the inner critic.

"Readers are encouraged to rewrite the narratives of their lives, transforming perceived flaws into sources of power and resilience.

"In the gentle guidance of the author's words, readers discover that perfection is not the destination, but rather, the journey of embracing one's perfectly flawed self. With each turn of the page, they are reminded that true beauty lies not in flawless façades, but in the courage to show up authentically, imperfections and all.

"*I Am Perfectly Flawsome* is more than a book; it is a sacred invitation to embrace the fullness of one's humanity and to celebrate the mosaic of experiences that shape each unique soul. It is a beacon of hope for anyone seeking to thrive in a world obsessed with flawlessness. It is a testament to the extraordinary power of vulnerability, and a tribute to the inherent worthiness of every individual. A must-read for all those who want to step into their perfectly imperfect power.

"I particularly loved the concept of the "Imperfect Win List" (Chapter 6). It's a brilliant way to celebrate progress, no matter how big or small. I can't wait to start mine!"

— Ioanna (Joanna) Petrochilou, Change Catalyst and Leadership Coach

"I couldn't help but chuckle at myself as I wrote this because I realized I was striving for perfection. The irony is the essence of *I Am Perfectly Flawsome*: perfectionism is often a self-imposed barrier to happiness and success.

"Through the book, Tom and Michele give us permission to explore our inner worlds and confront challenges preventing us from living authentically. They provide us with a roadmap to self-discovery, complete with checklists and thought-provoking questions that guide us through how to let go of our need to focus on flaws and embrace our true selves. Whether you're a middle school student or enjoying retirement this is a compelling book that will help you live life on your terms."

— Toby Bloomberg, Co-Founder of Diva Foodies

"I highlighted so many phrases and sections that I finally had to stop. As a (hopefully former) perfectionist, this book spoke to me in volumes. I'd MUCH rather be (truly) flawsome than (falsely) awesome.

"Soooo many different perspectives supporting the same beautiful view of "flawsomeness." I appreciated every single one: Raisman (Olympic gymnast). Oprah (nuff said). Brene Brown. Julia Cameron. Michael Jordan.

"I kept returning again and again to a quote from the authors' research interviews, this one from the 60+ age group: 'There's a huge difference between perfection and excellence.' This will now be my mantra.

"I've read and admired much about wabi-sabi in the past. As a perfectionist, this is a particularly relieving philosophy. Meaning, what we do is not all about the outcome, it's also about the search.

"We've heard this again and again, of course — it's not about the destination, it's about the journey — but *I Am Perfectly Flawsome* breaks this down in practical ways, demonstrating that perfect performance and zero defects are simply not attainable. It reminds us to have fun, and that continuous improvement is not about perfection."

— Sherri Phillips, Co-owner & COO of Deutsch Photography, Inc.

"I've spent much of my life being the grand poobah of perfectionism, holding myself up to unbelievably harsh standards I would never expect of friends and loved ones and living in constant shame of my so-called failures. I believed if people knew the real me, they would abandon me, because they'd realize how sub-par I really was.

"When I read this book, the term 'Flawsome' really resonated with me, because I've finally realized that you can be flawed and be awesome — an amazing leader, parent, sibling, spiritual leader, colleague, or friend.

"When I accepted my Flawsomeness, my healing began. I know this book will help many others like me, who struggle with trying to live up to unachievable goals. You're amazing just the way you are, even if you don't see that in yourself right now. *I Am Perfectly Flawsome* can start you on the path to liberation!"

— JaneA Kelley, Author, Educator, and Mental Health Advocate

"Whether you aim to improve your management or self-management skills, or your approach to parenting, *I Am Perfectly Flawsome: How Embracing Imperfection Makes Us Better* will give you the insight you need to make changes. Not that you need to change — you're 'flawsome' just the way you are!"

— Pamela Wilson, Chief Marketing Officer, DCS, author of
Master Content Marketing and *Master Content Strategy*

"Through their own reflections and others, Tom and Michele shed light on the roots of perfectionism in early childhood and the constant striving for an 'always out of reach high bar' to gain a sense of acceptance and belonging. The perils of perfectionism they highlight strain the psyche, leaving one in constant self-doubt and never feeling good enough. They draw on the enlightening teachings of the Japanese art and philosophy *kintsugi* which guides us to embrace our human nature and flaws — or our 'flawsomeness.'

"A must read for all who share in this struggle and are seeking a path to a more fulfilling approach to life."

— Teresa Donegan, PhD, Motivational Interviewing Trainer

"*I Am Perfectly Flawsome* showed that perfectionism isn't just a challenge for me: it's a dangerous ideal that we've let drive the bus for far too long. Their concept of 'flawsome' truly gives permission to embrace the less-than-perfect pieces of life. From Japanese philosophy to parenting to AI, this book is full of valuable ideas, important calls to action, and useful tips for eliminating perfectionism and adopting a new way of thinking. Highly recommend!"

— Lisa DeAngelis, author of the #1 New Release,
Embracing the Unknown: Exploring the Pathways to Change

"This book breaks the trance of unworthiness in a most powerful way, making it possible for readers to drop the quest for perfectionism before it takes even deeper tolls on our bodies, psyches, and relationships. Collins and Molitor are the real deal, having gone on their own extensive journeys of recovering from perfectionism, and returning with this book to show us another way to know who we are and why we matter no matter what."

— Sunni Brown, Bestselling Author of *The Doodle Revolution*,
Speaker, and Founder, Center for Deep Self Design

I Am Perfectly Flawsome

www.IAmPerfectlyFlawsome.com

I Am Perfectly Flawsome

How Embracing Imperfection Makes Us Better

Tom Collins & Michele Molitor

an imprint of
Old Dog Digital, LLC
Binghamton, NY, USA

Published by WME Books, an imprint of Old Dog Digital, LLC

ISBN: 978-1-934229-42-2 (Paperback)
        978-1-934229-43-9 (eBook)

Developmental editor: Yvonne DiVita
Cover design: Tom Collins and Michele Molitor
Page layout and interior design: Tom Collins

For special orders and bulk discounts contact:
    tom@OldDogLearning.com

Disclaimers:
  While the authors and publisher have used their best efforts
  in preparing this book, they make no representations or
  warranties regarding the accuracy or completeness of the
  contents of this book or any related, referenced, or linked
  materials. The authors and publisher specifically disclaim
  any implied warranties of merchantability or fitness for a
  particular purpose, and make no guarantees whatsoever
  that you will achieve any particular result.

  We believe all information, scientific research, and case
  studies and results persented herein are true and accurate,
  but we have not independently audited or confirmed the
  research methods, data collection, or results reported. Any
  advice or strategies contained in this book might not even be
  suitable for your situation and you should consult your own
  advisors as appropriate.

Before you start reading . . .

. . . visit this webpage for free bonus materials to help you on your journey to flawsome:

- I Am Perfectly Flawsome Guided Meditation

- Complete Book Club Readers Guide

- Reference List with live links to online research

- Bonus eBooks (*What's Causing Your Imposter Syndrome?*, by Michele; *Pivot*, by Tom)

- Self-Doubt Quiz

- Special Discount Code to assess your Top 5 Dignity Traits

www.IAmPerfectlyFlawsome.com/bonus-resources

Type in the URL or scan the QR Code —>

Contents

I Am Perfectly Flawsome

Dedications

To Yvonne —

who helps me keep living in the paradox of flawsomism
as we grow elder together.

— Tom

To my beloved family, friends, teachers, and clients who
have been an infinite well of support, encouragement, and
inspiration along my journey of becoming Flawsome.

— Michele

Foreword

When Michele invited me to write the foreword to *I Am Perfectly Flawsome*, I was instantly excited. Partly because I adore and deeply respect Michele — I have known her through her incredible contributions over many years to *YourTango*, the publishing platform focused on love and relationships that I founded nearly 20 years ago — and partly because I loved the idea of this book as I have long been fascinated by the art and beauty of *Kintsugi*.

I admire how Japanese culture has such vast wisdom for seeing the value in the brokenness, imperfection and "Is-ness" of life through this art form. I am grateful that a long time ago, some wise, wonderful Japanese people understood the powerful metaphor Kintsugi offers for embracing brokenness and imperfection. And that they developed an art form that is highly respected and has been adopted around the globe as beautiful art and philosophy, one that literally dusts the broken parts with gold. So I approached this book with my mind engaged and eager to learn more.

Then, as I started to read, I was hit hard by how much this book was FOR ME — as well as how it is a book that is required reading for business leaders and managers of teams as well as parents, aunties, uncles, teachers and other grown ups that have an out-sized influence on the lives of kids. As I am the mother to two wonderful young

"Sig" as used here is short for "sigma" which is a slang term often applied to males, as distinct from alpha males. It denotes someone who is self-confident and self-reliant, charts their own course, values independence over status, and does not seek external validation. Sometimes called an "extoverted introvert," a sigma prefers solitude or smaller, more intimate gatherings over crowded scenes or large social settings. As one article put it, sigmas are "strong leaders, innovative and creative ... but they're also very emotionally intelligent."

Applying sigma to women, the article quotes therapist Sally Baker:

"She's confident in who she is. Women are raised to be people pleasers, but if you're a sigma, you're not afraid to be your own person, and be true to yourself."

https://metro.co.uk/2022/12/02/ what-is-the-sigma-personality-and- why-you-shouldnt-claim-to-be- one-17845552/

Editor's note: You'll find sidenotes like the one above throughout the book. The authors explain why in the Introduction, pgs. 8-9.

boys, proud actual auntie to a bunch of amazing teens and young adults, and a self-appointed auntie/"sig mom" to innumerable youths in my life, I am profoundly aware for how much pressure young people are under, how vulnerable they are and how challenging their lives are — especially compared to previous generations. This book is an important one for a LOT of us.

I have long been aware that I harbored perfectionist tendencies. Thanks to Michele and Tom's own stories and experiences, their careful research, as well as the stories and insights they share from a wide swath of people, I was stopped in my tracks in the early pages.

While immersing myself in their words, I suddenly felt more understood, less alone, less confused, more validated, more empowered, and honestly, more at peace with the perfectionist tendencies that I have inherited and have perpetuated in my own life. What's clear is that perfectionism is such a crafty, sinister trait. More than a trait. It's like an entire unconscious, undermining operating system. I say "undermining" because, like so many of us who came from families who highly valued hard work and achievement, perfectionism can be a very sneaky, tricky, deceptive, and truly destructive specter in our lives. It's like a wolf in sheep's clothing with its virtuous trappings belying the danger that lurks below the surface.

As someone who was criticized quite a bit growing up, who has battled with workaholism, who, for decades, felt that she was not enough and went to extreme lengths to prove herself, I am grateful for this beautiful book. It showed me parts of myself that have been hard to see and understand but it is through that unflinching seeing and understanding, that this book has helped me take a big step toward greater wholeness. I love its honesty and actionability. I love the vast amount of research it presents in ways that are easy to understand and digest. I love how it is filled with relatable stories and anecdotes; how it offers prompts at the end of each chapter so that readers can really apply the insights and ideas that Tom and Michele offer so that growth and positive, lasting change can be made in our lives. Isn't that the point?

I realize, now, just how much I had dehumanized myself through my perfectionism. I am much more aware just how painful and ashamed I felt when I made honest mistakes. I am incredibly conscientious and an extremely hard worker and when I mess up, I am very, very hard on myself. I didn't quite realize how hard on myself I was 'til I read this book. And now I am better prepared to change these things in my life.

Additionally, I love the deep amount of care and vulnerability that Michele and Tom infused into this powerful book. In reading it, I felt that I had two wise, open, experienced and caring companions to help me go from being, well, somewhat ignorant about my perfectionistic tendencies to joyfully and gratefully embracing being ... flawsome!

Flawsome is such a powerful re-framing for how to approach our lives. And it's coming to us not a moment too soon! The statistics Michele and Tom share around the dramatic rise in perfectionism across all of society is frightening and alarming; the stats about how perfectionism has been infecting our teens is downright terrifying.

Finally, I love the practical, insightful and unexpected places this book goes — from how people and corporations completely misinterpreted *Kaizen* as a business management tool to how perfectionism is an epigenetic phenomenon to how to use Kintsugi for raising healthy, flawsome kids to how we can use wabi-sabi in all areas of our lives and more!

As the CEO of the best team ever and as a leader who understands the critical importance that our work has on our emotional well-being, mental health and life satisfaction, the misinterpretation of things like Kaizen, Lean management systems, and "Six Sigma" that has led to widespread dehumanization of workers across corporate America. I would argue this has contributed to the widespread loneliness epidemic and the mental health crisis that have swept our society — all in the foolish pursuit of institutionalized perfectionism.

No wonder the majority of people dislike their jobs.

"According to Gallup, 85% of individuals worldwide are dissatisfied with their jobs. This level of disengagement costs companies up to $550 billion annually in the United States alone and results in a 33% decrease in earnings."

Not only is it terrible for companies' bottom lines, it's clear this systemic perfectionism and dehumanization in so many businesses is negatively impacting the quality of their employees' lives. The system is currently designed to fail the people it employs — not entirely of course — but the incessant drive toward continuous improvement and perfect efficiency in corporate America are making it pretty uninhabitable for too many people.

Then, you add social media and how it has spawned a virulent comparison culture, infecting almost all of us, and especially tweens and teens, causing perfectionism to be that much more systemic and insidious.

Yeah, I'm biased but I do lead an extraordinary team and am acutely aware that my #1 job as our leader is to ensure my team knows I care about them and about us, a group of people who are drawn to work together to serve a large audience of people who benefit greatly from what we do. I wholeheartedly agree with Peter Drucker: "Culture eats Strategy for breakfast."
— Andrea

The Most Surprising Unhappy Employees Statistics And Trends in 2024, Lindner, J., https://gitnux. org/unhappy-employees-statistics/

Perfectionism thwarts creativity, joy, self-discovery, achieving meaningful growth in ourselves and in our relationships and pretty much sucks. Fortunately, it doesn't have to have dominance over us any more, thanks to Tom and Michele's passion, care, insights, advice, and actionable takeaways.

On that note and in honor of embracing being totally flawsome, I'm gonna close with a dangling participle! Oh wait. I'm not sure what that actually is. Haha! How's that for taking back power from perfectionism?! I hope you, too, take these wonderful stories and excellent advice to heart, and embrace being unapologetically flawsome.

Enjoy!

Andrea Miller,
CEO + Founder, YourTango
Host of *Open Relationships: Transforming Together*
Passionate relationships catalyst and grateful mother
Award-winning author of *Radical Acceptance: The Secret to Happy, Lasting Love*

Introduction

"I think imperfection is beauty."

— Aly Raisman

Have you ever had the experience of black-and-white thinking?

Life is either this way or that way ...

There is no grey area in between.

Perfectionism tends to land squarely in the camp of black-and-white thinking. Keeping you in a perpetual state of "it's never quite good enough" thinking.

Does this ring true for you?

It did for us.

Both individually and collectively as we set out to write this book.

We offer up these personal reflections, ideas, and research in the coming pages as part of our journey through the land of perfectionism. As we've learned over and over again, perfectionism isn't something that you defeat and then check off your list. It seems to find a way to keep tugging at your sleeve, asking you about what you're doing or creating, "Is it good enough yet?"

Captain, courageously

The beginnings of this book started with a blog post Tom wrote about embracing imperfection in our work, which itself grew out of some notes he'd scribbled and started researching back in 2016.

One of the earliest articles he found contained the quote we opened with on page 1, from Olympic gymnast Aly Raisman, "I think imperfection is beauty." She was already well-known as the Captain of the "Fierce Five" USA women's gymnastics gold medal team, plus winner of gold and bronze individual medals, at the 2012 London Olympics. And she had not yet made the team for the upcoming 2016 games in Rio.

Several other comments in that interview — and even more so the events that have unfolded in the few years since — make Raisman an ideal example for many of the lessons about imperfection we want you to absorb.

She expanded on her "imperfection is beauty" idea, connecting it to her insecurities about her body. While body insecurity isn't exclusive to women, women do face unique pressures that we'll examine along the way.

But Raisman also touched on perfectionism in her work, noting the struggle she encountered to enjoy her bronze medal, along with the two golds, let alone her disappointment in "failing" to win any medal in the All-Around. At the ripe old age of 21, she offered useful wisdom on the challenges and myths around the imperfections that come with aging.

In her book, *Fierce*, published after the 2016 team triumphs in Rio, and in her leadership through the USA Gymnastics sex abuse scandal, she provides many more

---

Top 5 Reasons You Must Embrace Imperfection in Your Work, https://masterbookbuilders.com/top-5-reasons-you-must-embrace-imperfection-in-your-work/

From a 2015 ESPN.com interview, https://www.espn.com/olympics/story/_/page/bodyalyraisman/olympic-gymnast-aly-raismanbalancing-life-gymnastics-espnmagazine-body-issue

Fierce: How Competing for Myself Changed Everything (2018), Aly Raisman

examples of accepting imperfection in herself, her work, and in others.

Raisman has become one of Tom's heroes for the way she exhibits what he calls "being and thriving despite a world around us that is full of chaos." This makes her Perfectly Flawsome.

"It Ain't a Church!"

Tom confesses that years ago, he had a sign on his office wall that scolded him daily,

"Good enough ... isn't!"

He misguidedly pointed the sign out to his kids too many times.

On the other hand, Tom has repeated in many settings a sort of reverse version. Acquired on the summer job he had during college building swimming pools, it's an equally wrong-headed jab at quality control specs. When minor mistakes or flaws happened that were easily corrected or would never be seen or noticed by anyone but themselves, he and his crew amused themselves by shouting playfully at each other, "It ain't a church!"

Of course, that might have been amusing at the time, but it still implied that perfection was out there to be sought in other settings.

At different life stages and, importantly, in different roles, Tom has been more aligned with the old Lexus slogan, "The relentless pursuit of perfection." Or the less rigid Oakland Raiders motto, "Commitment to Excellence." Or the self-deprecating Avis ad concept, "We're No. 2, so we try harder."

In high school, Tom even took the Avis concept a step further, paying careful attention to GPAs at the top of the class to position himself at No. 3. In his infinite teenage wisdom, he theorized he could get most of the upside of good grades, without the extra work and stress — along with more freedom to focus on the graduation parties, not speeches.

Throughout his career as a lawyer, he approached his work somewhere between the Raiders and Lexus. But he came to recognize, finally, that he was paying a price in other areas of his life for that relentlessness. In his work, then and now, he has learned the lesson over and over that perfection *will never be a realistic goal.*

If you'd asked Michele while she was growing up if she was a perfectionist, she would say not consciously. However, as she's gotten older, her perceived need to prove her own value and worth revealed a striving for perfection that she was unconscious of as a child.

Reflecting back on her childhood, it was riddled with self-doubt and a need for belonging. She had the uncomfortable feeling that she was on the outside looking in. These internalized beliefs kept her always striving towards perfectionism to find a sense of belonging and being enough.

This created a never-ending perfectionist high bar as she endeavored to follow in the successful footsteps of her siblings and parents in the family businesses, trying to achieve similar levels of success.

Until one day, she finally realized, "Their path is not my path, and that's ok."

It's been a double-edged sword for her. One that has helped her carve out her own path in life, but has cost her over the years in overworking and even burnout to make sure everything was "just right." All of her research, training, and work as a coach and hypnotherapist is what helped her see beyond her own deeply held limiting beliefs about never being enough, i.e., not being perfect. And thus, it has enabled her to step fully into all of who she is and in her own way.

Perfectly imperfect and utterly flawsome.

When Tom approached Michele to collaborate on writing this book together, it was an easy Yes!

Our different backgrounds and stories have both led us to this place of deeper understanding and the need to be more kind and compassionate with ourselves. While we bring different perspectives to this book, we agree that within everything, there is imperfect beauty to be found if you look closely enough.

We'll wrestle with that tension between futile perfectionism and settling for mediocrity (or worse) throughout this book. That very struggle will guide you toward a mindset that finds joy in our flawed selves and imperfect works, as well as those of other people and the world we live in, without giving up on working to improve them all.

On Golden Repair -

The bowl on the cover has great significance for our message in this book. As Tom initially set out to understand the various nuances of perfectionism, he also read more about the Japanese art and philosophy called *kintsugi* (kee-n-tsu-gee, with a hard "g"):

This art form refers to repairing broken pottery by sealing the cracks with lacquer and coating them with gold dust. As a result, the repaired piece becomes more beautiful and valuable than the original.

As a philosophy, kintsugi applies the same concepts to how we live our lives. How we grow through our mistakes and failures. And how we accept, repair, and value the resulting flawsome person we continue becoming – as well as the likewise imperfect people, places, objects, and events in our world.

"I was going to have to learn how to mend my cracks on my own, in real life. I was going to have to do the work."

— Candice Kumai, in her book, ***Kintsugi Wellness: The Japanese Art of Nourishing Mind, Body, and Spirit*** (2018)

We'll delve into kintsugi and several related ideas from Japanese culture as we journey together toward embracing imperfection and how we learn, grow, and become more flawsome for the effort.

The Road Ahead

Throughout the book you'll find our own research data and narrative responses from an online survey we ran in the summer of 2023. Michele conducted some followup interviews, as well. Our sample size is small (49 participants) and methods informal, so we are not presenting the results as scientific. We do think you'll find our results consistent with many of the peer-reviewed study findings we cite and the narrative answers especially enlightening.

Because we found some disagreement, or at least inconsistency, in the literature's treatment of the whole concept of perfectionism, the first two chapters will lay out the case for our position that perfectionism is a negative and harmful mindset in all its forms. Period.

The research is in full agreement about the mental and physical harms to the individual, as well as the societal and workplace problems caused by perfectionism. However, some researchers attempt to classify those harms as flowing from negative, toxic, or extreme perfectionism. We find that attempted distinction between positive and negative perfectionsim to be counterproductive, causing confusion and difficulty for people to follow in drawing the line between them.

Chapters 1 and 2 will contrast perfectionism with the healthy striving for excellence and show the many harms from the former.

Chapters 3 and 4 bring you the upsides of rejecting perfectionism and adopting what we call *Flawsomism*, living in its paradox of simultaneously celebrating imperfection and striving for excellence. We cover the science showing these benefits and ways to identify and work on overcoming your perfectionist tendencies, whether you're aware of them, or like us, need to dig to find their roots. We also show the benefits you bring to others and the world when you let go of perfectionism.

There's a growing body of research showing many benefits from the ability to hold what the researchers call a "paradox mindset." For more on that topic, see Tom's blog post, *Marginalia: The Power of Paradox and Fiction as Truth* (2024), https://masterbookbuilders.com/marginalia-the-power-of-paradox-and-fiction-as-truth/

Chapters 5-10 examine problems with, and solutions for, perfectionism that are specific to the workplace, women, intergenerational trauma, children, aging (or as we like to call it, "advanced adulting"), and finally the impact of AI.

Then, in the **Conclusion: The Way of the Flawsomist**, we pull all of it together and offer you a pair of questions that will guide your quest toward applying what we've learned together in your life, in your work, and in the world.

Read 'Em & Reap: 6 Science-Backed Ways Reading Puts You on the Road to Achieving More and Living Longer, Tom Collins (2019), pgs. 2-12.

Which brings up our use of the word "we" in this book. Tom has written about how a book can be viewed as a "social synapse" for connecting writers with readers and building new meanings between us.

That is our aspiration. That Tom, Michele, and you — "we" — can build upon the words and meanings we take from these pages. We can add them to what we've read and learned from others. And we can take action to achieve positive, purposeful change in our lives and our work, in our communities and our world.

One tool you can use will be the **Journal Prompts** you'll find at the end of each chapter. These prompts are there to help spur your thinking and look within yourself. Helping you perhaps to see some of the limiting beliefs or critical voices that might be creating toxic perfectionism within you.

These questions were carefully created to provide you with the opportunity to reflect upon your own habits and patterns and determine what old beliefs, behaviors, or attitudes (conscious or unconscious) you're ready to let go of once and for all. Empowering you to shine more brightly as you step more fully into your perfectly flawsome self.

In addition, the page layout of this book has been designed with wide outside margins to encourage you to write in them (we love writing in our books!). We've used a bit of the space for:

- References from our research at the point they are discussed in the text

- Explanations of something in the text that may not be familiar to everyone

- Some of our favorite inspirational quotes

But the main purpose of the wide margins is for jotting down your own thoughts, ideas, or questions and marking passages you may want to revisit later. Take full advantage to create your unique story of being Flawsome.

You will also find on the website for the book **www.IAmPerfectlyFlawsome.com** the companion guided meditation "I Am Perfectly Flawsome" that Michele has hand-crafted for you to use alongside the book. You can listen to this relaxing guided meditation anytime you need to quiet your inner critic and perfectionist so you can boldly move forward with your good works in the world.

https://iamperfectlyflawsome.com

Additionally, we offer you the companion *I Am Perfectly Flawsome Journal* created specifically for readers of *I Am Perfectly Flawsome*. Filled with inspiring quotes and questions to ponder to elevate your perfectly flawsome thinking, this journal is a way to explore and embrace your flawsomeness every day.

Now it's time for you to enjoy the reading (and writing) journey as much as we have enjoyed bringing it to you!

With Love & Gratitude,

Tom & Michele

— をんつぎ —

Chapter 1

Perfectionism and Its Variants

"The maxim 'Nothing avails but perfection'
may be spelled, 'Paralysis.'"

— Sir Winston Churchill

We believe that "Imperfect is all there is."
You may have heard a similar saying that perfection exists only in the dictionary. We have both traveled our individual journeys toward overcoming perfectionism (hence this book!), leading us to the conclusion that "imperfect is all there is" because of our lived experiences and the lessons learned from them.

This book is a culmination of those lessons learned and wisdom gathered along the way, with the intention of helping you move beyond your driving need for perfection and replace it with a healthy sense of striving for excellence instead.

An example from Tom's past:

Among my worst periods of perfectionism was when I was a young associate lawyer working to become a trial lawyer. When a labor law partner was on vacation, an appeal hearing at the Workers' Compensation Board on the eligibility of our client to receive benefits required my attention.

I felt confident about this assignment, having clerked for judges in the state and federal appellate courts after law school. In the Comp Board's less formal setting, the task seemed like a piece of cake.

See e.g. Tom's blog post, *Top 5 Reasons You Must Embrace Imperfection in Your Work* (2021), https://masterbookbuilders.com/top-5-reasons-you-must-embrace-imperfection-in-your-work/

It was a disaster.

The judge and the lawyer for the employer spoke a foreign language, filled with acronyms and alpha-numeric labels for the many forms being passed around and talked about. I had to ask for clarification, and which color-coded form they were talking about, many times.

I somehow muddled through it. But I felt like a complete idiot throughout and sick about going back to the office, let alone reporting to the partner what had happened.

And yet . . . the judge was able to translate the words I used (and we had prepared the right forms and evidence), because we won the appeal. The partner laughed with me about the whole thing.

Imperfect was, in fact, good enough.

Let's start with a common definition of what perfectionism is perceived to be, shall we? While researchers vary in their definitions, a leading textbook offers this one we find useful:

Hewitt, P. and Flett, G., *Perfectionism: Theory, Research, and Treatment* (2002), pg. 5

> "*Perfectionism* is the striving for flawlessness, and extreme perfectionists are people who want to be perfect in all aspects of their lives."

The term "flawlessness" keeps the unattainable quality of perfectionism front and center and the distinction from excellence intact.

In some contexts, it's necessary to work toward near-perfection. Brain surgery, aircraft construction, and nuclear device control software come to mind.

But even in those high-stakes areas, mistakes happen, materials break down, and the best designs prove inadequate to unforeseen circumstances. Chernobyl, the 737 Max, or the Titan sub implosion, to name just a few famous examples.

The common wisdom that "nobody's perfect" is not just true of people and our behavior.

It's true of everything.

Even the Laws of Physics appear to remain subject to an uncertainty principle, chaos theory, and randomness.

We like to say, We are all "perfectly imperfect" — or even better, "flawsome!"

So yes, strive for excellence, but do not chase perfection. Because that slogan from the 1990s Lexus campaign, "the relentless pursuit of perfection," really just condemns us to stubbornly reliving failure and disappointment. That can very easily turn into toxic perfectionism, which can have negative impacts on the body, mind, and spirit.

Also, recognize the danger of any pretense that perfection has been achieved – in yourself, in your work, or in anyone or anything else.

Indeed, as we were finishing writing this book, the news broke that mathematician Michel Talagrand had won the math equivalent of a Nobel Prize for his work on narrowing the probabilities in random event spaces. Castelvecchi, D., *Mathematician who tamed randomness wins Abel Prize* (2024), https://www.nature.com/articles/d41586-024-00839-6

"The biggest flaw lies in believing we can be, or do, or create, something that has none."

— Tom Collins

Normal vs. Neurotic

In a 2016 study, "normal" perfectionists (the prevailing understanding of perfectionism) were defined as those who can enjoy work in progress (rather than completion only), recognize and accept personal limitations, and are motivated by goals of personal excellence rather than absolute perfection.

However, "neurotic" (unhealthy) perfectionists were defined as those who have a strong fear of failure, are

Mofield, E., et al., *Perfectionism, Coping, and Underachievement in Gifted Adolescents: Avoidance vs. Approach Orientations* (2016), https://www.mdpi.com/2227-7102/6/3/21.

performance-driven, and never feel satisfied with personal performance, as it never lives up to idealized perfection.

As noted in the Introduction, we're taking a stand that ANY form of "perfectionism" is unhealthy, contrasting that with a healthy striving for excellence.

More on this in just a minute . . .

There is a multidimensional perfectionism theory to measure the degree and sources of perfectionism as well. This model identifies three different orientations of perfectionism, depending on the source and direction of the demand for flawlessness.

See e.g. Hewitt, P. and Flett, G., *Perfectionism in the Self and Social Contexts: Conceptualization, Assessment, and Association With Psychopathology* (2014), https://hewittlab.sites.olt.ubc.ca/files/2014/11/MPS.pdf.

Self-oriented perfectionism refers to "setting *unrealistic* standards for oneself and striving to attain these standards, selective attention to and overgeneralization of failure, stringent self-evaluations, and a tendency to engage in all-or-none thinking whereby only total success or total failure exist as outcomes."

Other-oriented perfectionism refers to setting "*unrealistic* standards for significant others, placing importance on other people being perfect, and stringently evaluating others' performance . . . leading to other-directed blame, lack of trust, and feelings of hostility toward others."

Socially prescribed perfectionism refers to the belief that others have *unrealistic* standards for you; they evaluate you stringently and exert pressure on you to be perfect. Because these perceived external standards are both unattainable and uncontrollable, the individual can suffer "failure experiences and emotional states, such as anger, anxiety, and depression."

The distinction among these three types of perfectionism helps us to understand the psychological dysfunctions that are associated with those who adopt them.

In our own online survey, nearly two-thirds of the respondents said they had felt pressure to be perfect as children "from parents, teachers, or other children." In adulthood, when the question included pressure from themselves, as well as others close to them, and society, those answering "yes" rose to 83%.

When asked to identify the source of the pressure to be perfect, the answers demonstrated the validity of the three-dimensional model, with just a few examples quoted here:

- "Self - lots of self-criticism, judgment, and self-punishing; Society - constant comparison to (unattainable) false perfection as an ideal."

- "It has been rough at times to accept that no one is perfect and my partner, kids, parents and friends are going to make mistakes that hurt me or let me down."

- "Originally, it was my mother and my family. There was this pressure to perform, achieve, to make [them] look good. I have internalized many of these messages and try to unlearn them but continue to see that I put this pressure on myself."

Five Perils of Perfectionism

You might be surprised to see us treating perfectionism as a negative, even a dangerous trait. Perhaps you were raised as we were, being praised for good grades or athletic achievements, criticized for points missed in either realm. The message stated or implied: perfectionism is a virtue.

But in fact, perfectionism might well be the biggest barrier to your happiness and success. Wait, what? Don't perfectionists do an uber-great job? Aren't they happy with their accomplishments?

According to the latest research, not so much. Here are five proven costs of perfectionism:

1. Perfectionism is bad for your mental health: Your average perfectionist is likely to be suffering from low self-esteem, anxiety, and depression. If you're a hard-core perfectionist, you spend a lot of time judging yourself and finding yourself in a persistent state of lack (fill in the blank with what you perceive to be missing), e.g., "I haven't achieved quite enough success yet."

But no matter how hard you try, that high bar of "perfect" is always out of reach, giving yourself further proof that you're "not good enough" in some way, shape, or form. Perfectionists tend to see the glass as half empty. If they score 95 on a test, they beat themselves up for the few answers they got wrong.

And because perfectionists can never be good enough, they fret and worry and blame themselves into a state of perpetual stress. One review of the psychology research called perfectionism "a primarily maladaptive way of being associated with *depression, suicidal ideation, anxiety, and stress.*"

These behaviors and mindsets often follow from negative messages and programming received in childhood that have been hiding out in your subconscious for most of your life.

The Pernicious Perils of Perfectionism, Timothy Pychyi, Psychology Today, Apr. 12, 2010, https://www.psychologytoday.com/us/blog/dont-delay/201004/the-pernicious-perils-perfectionism.

To questions we posed in our survey about negative consequences from perfectionism, several of our survey respondents who reported high levels of perfectionism described serious mental health impacts:

- "When I don't accomplish something, I get angry and depressed, feeling less than."

- "... anxiety, nervousness, or hypervigilance, which all contribute to an unhealthy system."

- "Pressure on myself to be perfect, which led to performance anxiety."

- Due to external pressure to be perfect in childhood, "I suffered anxiety attacks." And the same respondent said about perfectionist pressures in adulthood, "My social anxiety is terrible now."

2. Perfectionism is bad for your physical health: There is evidence that perfectionists are at a greater risk of several chronic diseases such as diabetes, Crohn's disease, ulcerative colitis, and high blood pressure. This is due in part to their high levels of chronic stress. Perfectionists often have difficulty coping with chronic illness and are pessimistic about their chances of recovery.

The Price of Perfectionism (2012), Gordon Flett, https://www.psychologicalscience.org/observer/the-price-of-perfectionism

An article on Health.com echoes these effects, citing leading experts on the impact of perfectionism. Among them, it provides several useful examples of the thinking processes a perfectionist might go through, quoting clinical psychologist and author Elizabeth Lombardo, Ph.D.

Lombardo adds eating disorders, like anorexia, and chronic, unexplained fatigue or pain syndromes, like fibromyalgia, IBS, or chronic migraines, to the list of physical ailments a perfectionist may suffer. She offers these examples of how a perfectionist's internal monologue might go:

> "They think, 'Well, I messed up and had one cookie today. I'm not perfect, so I might as well give up.' With this, there is no spectrum; it is literally all or nothing."

> "A perfectionist says, 'I don't have time to take care of myself. I must be the perfect mother and the perfect boss.' And their bodies just give out."

Oftentimes, they spend so much time trying to get things "just right" that they feel overwhelmed and burned out, which can quickly turn into physical illness and exhaustion.

Perfectionism can certainly be an unhealthy driver. And yet, we know that striving for excellence — which may *look* very similar — can lead to amazing results. Losing sight of the difference, though, can negate the achievements some try to attribute to perfectionism.

Take Tammy, for example, as a successful former military pilot and now airline pilot, her drive for perfection has put her at the top of her game in a very male-dominated field.

All of her over-striving has led to some amazing achievements that she is extremely proud of. And yet, it has also taken a toll on her, creating a perfect storm that manifested into crippling migraines which have impacted her family, her career, and her peace of mind.

In a follow-up interview with Michele, Tammy acknowledged that perfectionism can lead to burnout and explained,

"The burnout was significant, coming to a culmination last year. With the migraines getting worse and therefore having to step back from work and stepping back from flying, stepping back from my union work as well."

3. Perfectionism can harm your relationships: Perfectionism in a partner, friend, or colleague can also present challenges. They can be nitpickers, nags, and even bullies. It can feel like nothing is ever good enough for them, and your mistakes can often be seen as (or feel like) moral failures.

If you're not careful, the negative messages you're receiving from them can sink into your subconscious mind, leaving you feeling less than in a variety of ways.

Now, stop and turn it around. If you're the perfectionist, how are your words, actions, and behaviors impacting your partner, friend, or colleague? If left unchecked, perfectionism can make you less compassionate and patient and more critical and judgmental.

Tammy mentioned how perfectionism, in addition to derailing her career, had impacted her personal life:

"Probably the biggest impact, negatively, I think, is it can ruin relationships, intimate relationships, as well as family relationships, friendship relationships, *because I want things done just so...*"

And if both of you are perfectionists? Well, that can set up a vicious cycle of unreasonable expectations, leading to toxic outcomes.

4. Perfectionism lowers your creativity: If you're a perfectionist, you are more likely to stick rigidly to the rules and have to do everything the "right way." That's not

Why Perfectionism Kills Creativity and How to Overcome It, Daisy Barringer, July 13, 2016, https://www.adobe.com/express/learn/blog/whyperfectionism-is-a-creativity-killer-and-how-to-overcome-it

a recipe for creative flow or finding innovative solutions to problems.

The perfectionist mind tends to be closed to possibilities, wedded to arbitrary external standards, and risk-avoidant, a.k.a. "a fixed mindset." This can lend itself to muting one's creative ideas before they are fully formed, leaving your genius inside of you instead of sharing it with the world.

Perfectionism can create the feeling of being "stuck" when your creative juices just can't flow because of your own preconceived ideas of how things need to work or unfold to get to your intended result.

Our survey respondents put it this way:

- "I feel like this [pressure to be perfect] stifled a bit of my creativity."

- "I was 'serious,' and my fun and creative sides were stifled."

Here's an example from Michele:

As a writer and painter, I can reflect back on how my "need to get it right the first time" has stifled my own creative flow. The fear of a blank canvas (or page) is ***real*** and can leave me spinning with where to put the brush down on the canvas first.

How Perfectionism Destroys Your Productivity, Cinzia DuBois, Feb. 10, 2019), https://cinziadubois.medium.com/howperfectionism-destroys-your-productivity-how-to-overcomeit-243cfad97c9d

5. Perfectionism lowers your productivity: A perfectionist is committed to everything working out perfectly, no errors, no deviations. That might sound great for being goal-oriented. But it also makes you less likely to take action, especially the bold steps so often required to break through.

As Brené Brown explains in *Daring Greatly*,

"Perfectionism is not the key to success. In fact, research shows that perfectionism hampers achievement. Perfectionism is correlated with depression, anxiety, addiction, and life paralysis or missed opportunities. [It] keeps us outside of the arena where healthy competition and striving unfolds."

Daring Greatly: How the Courage to Be Vulnerable Transforms the Way We Live, Love, Parent, and Lead, Brené Brown (2012), pg. 129.

Perfectionism often goes hand in hand with procrastination, leading to writer's block, crippling stage fright, and other forms of performance anxiety. Unless a perfectionist can guarantee to do something one hundred percent right, they'll find it challenging to do it at all.

In later chapters, we'll talk about how to move away from toxic perfectionism to a more balanced striving for excellence.

"Perfection is merely an illusion, put forth by those trying to achieve it."

— Michele Molitor

Perfectionism is a Growing Problem

Through Michele's work in particular, we have seen a dramatic rise in the awareness of toxic perfectionism. Especially since the pandemic, which created a heightened sense of anxiety and the need to get things "right." The ways in which we worked and lived all got turned upside down for a while, leaving a societal scar that runs deep.

Our experience with clients is reflected in a recent special issue of the *Journal of Psychoeducational Assessment* reviewing 30 years of research into perfectionism. The authors warned that it shows a "rise over time in the prevalence of self-oriented, other-oriented, and socially prescribed perfectionism" and "that the prevalence of

Flett, G. and Hewitt, P, *Reflections on Three Decades of Research on Multidimensional Perfectionism: An Introduction to the Special Issue on Further Advances in the Assessment of Perfectionism (2019)*, https://journals.sagepub.com/doi/full/10.1177/0734282919881928

dysfunctional forms of perfectionism among young people has reached alarming levels."

Our online survey included age data that grouped participants into four age ranges (18-29, 30-44, 45-59, and 60+). In response to the question of whether they had ever regarded themselves as a perfectionist, 100% of those in the two younger groups answered yes. Only 53% of the 45-59 group said yes, while 68% of the 60+ group did so.

Our results appear to support the literature's findings that perfectionism is a widespread and growing problem, especially for younger people in a day and age of rampant self-comparison online with other people's "perfect" lives.

The younger groups' responses to our questions about negative impacts further support the findings of alarming dysfunctional perfectionism. One in the 18-29 group gave a terse answer regarding where and from whom she felt pressure:

> "When I come to school or how I present myself to others, family, or friends."

Another in the 30-44 group wrote:

> "Societal pressures to do it all as a mother are ridiculous!"

And a man in that group emphasized how, for him, while shying away from labeling it perfectionism, the problem is indeed growing:

> "It's not so much perfection, as the will to drive forward and achieve more. It's never enough. It's *become worse over time.*"

As you can see, perfectionism is pretty common, especially among high achievers. Yet, it doesn't mean our impulses toward excellence can't be tamed and harnessed for good purposes, instead of toxic outcomes.

Chapter 1: Journal Prompts
to help you start living Flawsomely

These are intended to get you thinking, not judging yourself. Take some quiet time to thoughtfully and honestly respond to these questions to create your own positive shifts in your perspectives around perfectionism. We invite you to use the wide margins and blank pages we've provided.

- What are the standards you set for yourself that are unrealistic or unachievable?

- When you think about being perfect, what feelings come up for you in your mind? In your heart? In your body?

- In what different ways has trying to be perfect affected your life?

Chapter 2

Science of Mind - What is at the Root of Perfectionism?

"So much of flawsomism is about regaining the joy of living, working, and playing, that we often lose during or shortly after childhood."

— Tom Collins

Perfectionism can have a variety of root causes that get embedded in your mind, creating a range of drivers and behaviors that can last a lifetime. Striving for excellence can work to your advantage, as in the case of Aly Raisman, driving her to win 6 Olympic medals (3 Gold, 2 Silver, 1 Bronze) as a world-class gymnast. Perfectionism, as we've shown, is toxic, having a detrimental impact on your mind, body, and spirit.

As you review the list below, make a mental note of which might be driving your perfectionist behaviors. Here are some of the most common drivers of perfectionism:

1. *Nature:* Research suggests that perfectionism may have a genetic component, which means that it can be inherited from one's parents. Whether this is inherited from their chromosome material or the learned patterns of perfectionistic abuse handed down from one generation to the next is worthy of further discussion.

2. *Nurture:* Excessive demands for perfectionism from parents, teachers, or other authority figures

See Michele's article, *8 Ways Toxic Perfectionism Seeps Into Your Life & Sabotages Your Happiness*, https://www.yourtango.com/self/toxic-perfectionism

E.g., *Genetic and environmental contributions to perfectionism and its common factors* (2015), Iranzo-Tatay, C., et al., https://www.sciencedirect.com/science/article/abs/pii/S0165178115306752

during childhood who were highly critical, shaming, or abusive can also contribute to the development of perfectionistic behaviors.

3. Insecure attachment: Insecure attachment styles in relationships, such as anxious or avoidant attachment styles, may also contribute to the development of perfectionism as a way to prove one's lovability in close relationships with others.

4. Fear of failure: Fear of failure or making mistakes can drive someone to strive for perfection and avoid any possibility of failure. This can be driven by outside forces such as parental controls, a boss, or from within your own internal striving.

5. Low self-esteem or feeling inadequate: People with low self-esteem and low self-worth may feel the need to be perfect to gain approval, love, or acceptance from others. They feel their value is only measured by their achievements.

6. Black and White thinking: Having a fixed mindset (vs. a growth mindset) imagining there are only two options for completion. Perfection, or anything less than that, which is unacceptable.

7. Trauma: Trauma, such as childhood abuse or neglect, can contribute to the development of perfectionism as a coping mechanism to gain control over one's environment in an attempt to feel "safe" and quiet the incessant voice of fear in your mind.

8. Cultural, educational, and social expectations: Cultural, educational, and social expectations around achievement and success can also contribute to the development of perfectionism. Social media has created a constant state of

Attached: The New Science of Adult Attachment and How It Can Help You Find and Keep Love (2012), Amir Levein,M.D. and Rachel S.F. Hellre, M.A.

compare and contrast with others' seemingly "perfect" lives, which can lead to a host of other addictions, disorders, and suicidal ideation.

Variant Strains or Perfectionism's Disguises

We've hinted at several ways perfectionism infects our thinking and hampers our ability to deliver our work or present ourselves to the world. Self-doubt, self-judgment, comparison to "ideal" others (real, fictional, or imagined), unrealistic externally imposed standards — all these are fear-based ideas rooted in an excessive need for approval.

A couple of other mutations should be highlighted because they may come with added symptoms and side effects.

Imposter syndrome has been described as a GAD, or General Anxiety Disorder. Experts are divided on whether perfectionism should be counted as one distinct type of imposter syndrome. Or if perfectionism is more of a specific reaction to imposter syndrome.

Either way, imposter syndrome remains a fear-based disorder, a feeling of not really measuring up to some standard, not truly deserving whatever praise or success has been achieved. Leaving you feeling like a fraud, an imposter in plain sight. It's feeling like you aren't good enough for the rooms you enter.

According to our research, imposter syndrome affects 79% of adults! As one woman in our survey described it:

> "I definitely had imposter syndrome, and didn't think I deserved promotions, or was worried I would not find a better job. ... I still tend to beat myself up over things I could have done better in the past."

* IMPORTANT *
If someone you know is suffering from toxic perfectionism and has suicidal ideations, please seek help by dialing or messaging 988 to reach the Suicide and Crisis hotline available 24 hours a day.

Get Michele's free ebook, *What's Causing Your Imposter Syndrome? 6 Triggers Crushing Your Confidence*, https://bit.ly/ImposterFreeEbook

Many people who identify with having Imposter Syndrome also believe that they are perfectionists — unable to push themselves to the next level because they want to be perfect.

Yet, underneath the surface layer of imposter syndrome and perfectionism is actually a more deeply rooted case of self-doubt. These beliefs create a cycle of self-doubt that perpetually feeds itself as you confirm to yourself that you are an imposter or a perfectionist; you consistently set impossibly high standards, which creates more doubt.

Imposter syndrome is often the result of toxic workplace relationships or cultures that foster a lack of dignity and respect, which can quickly diminish a person's belief in themselves, their value, and their worth. Creating a need to be "perfect" at all costs.

Dignity: It's Essential Role in Resolving Conflict (2011), pgs. 19-20, Donna Hicks Ph.D

When a person repeatedly has their dignity violated, their brain reacts in the same fight or flight manner as if they were in physical danger, triggering the release of the stress hormones cortisol and adrenaline from your adrenal glands. Over time, it is this constant barrage on the nervous system that leads to physical ailments and disease.

Another variant grew many centuries ago out of a misapplication of religious ideas about *original perfection* (e.g., Adam and Eve, before the apple) and striving to regain it.

Better by Mistake: The Unexpected Benefits of Being Wrong (2011), pgs. 28-29, Alina Tugend

In her book, *Better by Mistake*, Alina Tugend notes religious scholars who observe that strictly demanding perfection can lead people to have trouble admitting their flaws, mistakes, or failures. Such followers fear that even asking for forgiveness "destroys the original 'perfect' wholeness, which can never be restored."

While there are many kinds of experiences that may have planted the first seed of self-doubt leading to perfectionism, once you become aware of your self-doubt and perfectionism, you are on your way to freeing yourself and soaring to new levels.

Take the **Self-Doubt Quiz** to learn more about what's holding you back. https://bit.ly/SelfDoubtGotYouBlocked

"Just Say No" to Perfectionism

You might have come across claims that some form of perfectionism can be a good thing. We have, too.

Some researchers classify perfectionism as "positive vs. negative" or "adaptive vs. maladaptive" traits. They attempt to place desirable qualities like being highly motivated, detail-oriented, and striving for excellence in the "positive" perfectionist category.

Nonsense.

We've planted our flag on this one. Recall where we started: perfection exists only in the dictionary! It seems to us a pretty simple non-equation:

$$\text{Perfectionism} \neq \text{Striving for Excellence}$$

As in, if there's no such thing as perfection, then insisting on perfect looks, performance, or products is delusional.

Unhealthy.

Counterproductive.

Debilitating.

"Perfectionism is not a quest for the best. It is a pursuit of the worst in ourselves, the part that tells us that nothing we do will ever be good enough."

— Julia Cameron.
in *The Artist's Way*

Daring Greatly: How the Courage to Be Vulnerable Transforms the Way We Live, Love, Parent, and Lead (2012), pgs. 128-129, Brené Brown

Or, as Brené Brown puts it more gently:

"Perfectionism is not the same as striving for excellence. Perfectionism is not about healthy achievement and growth. Perfectionism is a defensive move. It's the belief that if we do things perfectly and look perfect, we can minimize or avoid the pain of blame, judgment, and shame. Perfectionism is a twenty-ton shield that we lug around, thinking it will protect us, when in fact it's the thing that's really preventing us from being seen."

As Michele has seen in her practice with clients, perfectionism oftentimes is a trauma response caused by feeling "not enough" in some way as a child. So you spend your entire life trying to prove your own value and worth.

We're not saying we've managed to ditch our own perfectionist tendencies completely. Indeed, writing this book for you helps us continue to internalize the message: Perfectionism will get you nowhere, literally. (Or at least take you a whole lot LONGER to get where you want to be.)

Good News!

So, what do we do instead?

That's what we'll be exploring together throughout the rest of the book. We'll also circle back to note some specific problems with perfectionism in areas like the workplace, childhood, women's issues, and aging.

The good news is that these old pathways and programming in your mind CAN be changed as you tell yourself new empowering messages that have you feeling in control.

Next, we'll take a general tour of the positive benefits from letting go of perfectionism, and adopting new mantras like these:

Quick and dirty wins the race.

Perfection is the enemy of done.

Good enough really is, most of the time.

Imperfection is welcomed and makes me unique.

I am enough and I deliver good work.

I bring my very best to all I do, and that is enough.

I am perfectly imperfect.

I am flawsome.

"Forgive.
Forgive yourself for making mistakes, and forgive others.
Nobody's perfect."

— Aly Raisman.
"The Fierce Guide to Life"

Chapter 2: Journal Prompts
to help you start living Flawsomely

These are intended to get you thinking, not judging yourself. Take some quiet time to thoughtfully and honestly respond to these questions to create your own positive shifts in your perspectives around perfectionism.

- What beliefs or experiences are driving your perfectionism?

- Is your perfectionism creating a case of "Imposter Syndrome"? If so, how else is that impacting your career?

- If you could reframe your perfectionistic thinking, what might you be saying to yourself that feels more empowering?

Flawsome-ism? More than Just the Opposite of Perfectionism

"Your wounds and imperfections are your beauty. Like Kintsugi ... breakage and mending are honest parts of a past which should not be hidden."

— Bryant McGill

"The wound is where the Light enters you."

— Rumi

As we seek to overcome our perfectionistic attitudes, fueled by the part of us that thinks or believes that we're not measuring up or just not good enough in some way, it doesn't mean that we have to swing to the other extreme of being stuck in mediocrity either.

The term "flawsome" in this book is used to capture the paradox of striving for excellence while at the same time understanding and accepting that no matter how well we do on this attempt, it won't be perfect. *Ever.*

As the supermodel Tyra Banks once said, "It's perfectly possible for flaws and awesomeness to co-exist."

We agree and posit that everything is flawed in some unique way. This is what makes everyone and everything perfectly imperfect.

It's what makes us Flawsome.

This includes every flower, every tree, and every single one of us.

So embrace the uniqueness of you instead of finding what's wrong, or what's missing, or not enough.

Out of this paradox flows another, one that we find full of beauty and hope: some of our efforts will yield excellence, others utter failure, and from both results, we learn and gain the opportunity to do better next time.

We believe there is no such thing as failure. Only learning, growing, and improving.

Once again, Aly Raisman provided her youthful yet ancient wisdom. She revealed her struggle after her first Olympics (2012), when she found herself more focused on her "failure" to win any medal in the All-Around competition than on her two golds and a bronze in the individual and team events.

By the time she was preparing for the 2016 games, she was more comfortable with the paradox of flawsome-ism, learning from mistakes, and seizing second chances. Looking back at her mistake, as well as forward to the next opportunity, she explained to ESPN:

From a 2015 ESPN.com interview, https://www.espn.com/olympics/story/_/page/bodyalyraisman/olympic-gymnast-aly-raisman-balancing-life-gymnastics-espn-magazine-body-issue

> "I should be more proud of myself, , but I'm such a perfectionist. ... I did really well. ... I almost fell and put my hand down; it was stupid, I never make that mistake on the beam. I'll have a second chance at it ... I wish I didn't have to learn that valuable lesson at the Olympics."

Fierce: How Competing for Myself Changed Everything (2018), Aly Raisman. pgs. 345-347

In her 2018 book, she listed this advice in her "Fierce Guide to Life":

> "Give it your all — and then take a breather. Resting and recharging your batteries is one of the keys to living a happy, healthy life.

"Set goals for yourself and don't be afraid to follow them as far as they'll take you. Accept the fact that if you don't accomplish your goals, that's okay. Focus on the hard work you put into it and be proud of that."

It's vitally important to take note of what you have accomplished — both big and small — and celebrate those accomplishments before raising the bar on yourself to the next level.

We found evidence in our survey of this process of becoming comfortable with the paradox as we age. One in the 60+ age group explained:

"In the last 40+ years, I've realized there's a huge difference between perfection and excellence. No one is perfect. I don't even try. I do aim for a very high level of excellence, though, and always have."

Another in that group summed up the time factor this way:

"In my 50s, I recognized that I didn't need to work as hard as I did on being perfect. (Let's hear it for maturity!)"

Perhaps the most remarkable part of Raisman's growth is that she achieved it at such a young age. By her second Olympics, her teammates took to calling her "Grandma," and she embraced the label, calling Simone Biles (only three years younger) the "Baby" of the group.

"I keep learning more and more about how imperfections add beauty and uniqueness and embracing imperfection enables creativity, productivity, and joy in life's unfolding."

— Tom Collins

Our advice: don't wait decades or for Olympic-class pressures. Embrace your imperfect excellence now!

Kintsugi and Related Philosophies

Tom's own efforts to let go of perfectionism and aspire to the practice of flawsomism have blossomed since he came across the Japanese art and philosophy of *Kintsugi*, mentioned in the Introduction.

On a physical level, kintsugi refers to the Japanese art of repairing broken pottery, then sealing the cracks with lacquer and dusting them with gold powder. This method restores the broken item's usefulness, but it also makes the broken item more beautiful and valuable.

Recently, we've been digging a bit deeper into the philosophies surrounding kintsugi and how they can apply to other activities and our lives as a whole. A couple of years ago, while reading *A Craftsman's Legacy*, by Eric Gorges, Tom stumbled across the philosophy he thinks helps explain why the Japanese developed "golden repair" in the first place: *wabi-sabi*, which celebrates imperfection.

A Craftsman's Legacy: Why Working with Our Hands Gives Us Meaning (2019), Eric Gorges

While we might quibble with the title of his chapter, "The Battle for Perfection," Gorges quickly makes clear he really means striving for excellence, noting that a battle for perfection is one "that each one of us is bound to lose." He lists wabi-sabi among several ancient practices from various cultures, some of which require *intentionally* "putting a flaw" in items from teacups to rugs to houses.

More recently, we found Candice Kumai's book, *Kintsugi Wellness*. She delves into ten related principles from Japanese culture, including wabi-sabi, that together she calls "the work" you'll need to do to practice "golden repair" on yourself.

Kintsugi Wellness: The Japanese Art of Nourishing Mind, Body, and Spirit (2018), Candice Kumai

The magic is in the way she turns kintsugi from a practical art form into a life-enhancing wellness practice.

By doing "the work" toward celebrating imperfection, while at the same time committing to continuous improvement, as we'll discuss further below, she promises that, "you'll see that the most beautiful, meaningful parts of yourself are the ones that have been broken, mended, and healed."

Furthermore, she adds:

> "Learning is the key to Kintsugi, and we never stop learning. . . . I am committed to . . . continuously improving every day."

The business-oriented among you may have picked up on her phrase, "continuously improving every day," and connected it to another Japanese practice, *kaizen*. We'll get into kaizen as a business and workplace philosophy in Chapter 5. But sure enough, kaizen is one of the ten principles she covers in the book.

We're not going to review all ten *Kintsugi Wellness* principles here. But when Kumai discussed the kaizen principle, she carefully connected it to three others: *wabi-sabi*, *ganbatte*, and *shikata ga nai*.

These four, practiced together, enable us to hold the paradox of pursuing excellence and accepting imperfection as compatible, simultaneous mindsets:

Wabi-sabi celebrates the imperfections in everything. It reminds us that life's tough stretches and dark patches enable us to learn and grow strong, cherish the good times, and appreciate the beauty in simplicity.

Ganbatte teaches we must always give our best, adding that if you always do your best, that is good enough. Don't expect perfection. As Kumai puts it, "You don't have to *be* the best; you just have to *do* your best."

These are the ten principles as she lists them (with the four we're focusing on in bold):

Wabi-sabi – **Admire imperfection**
Gaman – Live with great resilience
Eiyoshoku – Nourish your body
Ki o tsukete – Learn to take care
Ganbatte – **Always do your best**
Kaizen – **Continuously improve**
Shikata ga nai – **Accept what cannot be changed**
Yuimaru – Care for your inner circle
Kansha – Cultivate sincere gratitude
Osettai – Be of service to others, welcoming gifts

For us, it is no accident that Kumai places wabi-sabi first on her list and kaizen sixth — reflecting their relative importance in our thinking.

Kaizen urges us to continuously improve. (In the business world, this has morphed to a goal of zero defects, or perfection.) But Kumai reminds of what is inherent in the continuous improvement effort: as we strive, we have not yet reached our full potential (let alone perfection) — and never will. Improvement, not perfection, is the goal.

Shikata ga nai is about letting go and accepting what we cannot change. According to Kumai, women in Okinawa attibute their renowned longevity to embracing this principle. She says they let things roll off their backs with the philosphic:

> "This won't matter in five years, or five months, (or in some cases, even five weeks), so I'm not going to give it more than five minutes."

Boil down these four principles, and you end up with a mantra that sounds a bit like inserting the words "about myself" or "about my life" into the *Serenity Prayer*:

> "Grant me the Serenity to accept the things [about myself] I cannot change, Courage to change the things [about my life] I can, and Wisdom to know the difference."

Michele remembers clearly how her perfectionism backfired on her in a work setting:

> I did my best to practice continuous improvement every day. Yet, in my former career as a creative director in high tech, perfectionism was my badge of honor. I was always striving for perfection to stay on top of my game to go toe to toe with the bro culture, even before it had a name.
>
> And yet, despite working 80-hour weeks at the height of the dot-com boom, my perfectionism

wasn't enough to shield me from the unexpected bullying by male colleagues. It was their egotistical comments and actions, both behind my back and in front of clients that inflamed my perfectionism to new heights. Creating a massive case of imposter syndrome which eventually was my undoing.

I will never forget the day I found out I was being laid off. It was devastating. It crushed my confidence and my sense of value and worth, sending my perfectionism into overdrive. Eventually, I was able to heal the underlying trauma from my dot-com days and the corporate PTSD that went with it and reclaim my sense of self, my confidence, and the value of my gifts and talents.

What's In It for You?

To help you overcome the negative consequences of perfectionism, we suggest that imperfection deserves to become a philosophy of life in its own right:

Flawsomism.

We define Flawsomism as understanding the psychology of perfectionism and adopting the mindset of continuous improvement while embracing — indeed, celebrating — your imperfections along the way.

This is what we mean by becoming a Flawsomist, one who recognizes and embraces their flaws and loves themself nonetheless, even while they are striving for excellence.

In the coming chapters, we'll examine in more detail the many positive results you can expect from becoming a flawsomist yourself.

"Embrace your own imperfections as the distinctive attributes that make you, uniquely You."

— Michele Molitor

The benefits revealed in the next chapters should provide plenty of incentive for you to start shifting your thinking towards adopting a Flawsome mindset!

Chapter 3: Journal Prompts
to help you start living Flawsomely

These are intended to get you thinking, not judging yourself. Take some quiet time to thoughtfully and honestly respond to these questions to create your own positive shifts in your perspectives around perfectionism.

- How do YOU define success for yourself today? (Versus the definition you may have adopted from others, such as parents or partners or society.)

- What are some areas of your life where you tend to be overly critical of yourself? If you had to guess, what triggers this over-criticism?

- If you trust that there is no such thing as failure, only lessons, how can that shift your perspective on what you have already accomplished?

Chapter 4

The Power of Flawsomism

*"I've missed more than 9000 shots in my career. I've lost almost 300 games. 26 times, I've been trusted to take the game winning shot and missed. I've failed over and over and over again in my life. **And that is why I succeed.**"*

— Michael Jordan

In addition to avoiding the perils of perfectionism, it's important to recognize the benefits you gain simply by changing from a perfectionist mindset into a "flawsomist" mindset. We think you'll be pleasantly surprised.

Just like the flaws themselves, the benefits from embracing a flawsomist mindset fall into two general categories: personal and external.

Personal benefits flow from accepting those things about ourselves that can be seen as defects, inadequacies, mistakes, or failures in our actions and performance in work or life.

External benefits come to us when we extend the same acceptance to other people, to their actions, and to the world around us.

This two-pronged benefit was expressed by one of our survey participants this way:

> "I don't try to be perfect anymore. ... I don't get upset at the 'small stuff' like I used to. I give *myself and others* more grace."

(Empahsis added.)

Ask anyone what they "don't like" about themselves, and you're sure to get a list of characteristics and flaws that run the gamut from weight, height, physical imperfections, or the inability to do this or that. These perceived defects or inadequacies about ourselves, such as "I'm too short, or too loud, or too much," in some way, shape, or form, are often emotional residues from our childhood. These false truths about ourselves were left imprinted on our brains by thoughtless or deliberate comments from someone close to us.

These same misconceptions can then often overflow into our beliefs, perspectives, and ideas about others as well and their ways of being or behaving. All of which can easily create a cascade of negative dialogue within ourselves and about others. For example, this can present itself as someone who is highly critical or judgmental of others yet wholeheartedly believes that their behaviors are ideal or "right" about a particular situation, leaving them with their heels dug in and immovable.

The Magic of Becoming a Flawsomist

Let's start with a major category of imperfection in our lives: failure.

Are you ready to embrace it? As you saw at the opening of this chapter, Michael Jordan did. Like many great athletes and scholars who have embraced the wisdom that comes from failure, here are some of the personal benefits you'll gain by doing so as well:

1. Failure teaches you things success can't: We start with this because learning is at the core of our personal *ikigai*. It's a Japanese term that means "that which gives your life worth, meaning, or purpose" and is often compared to the French phrase, *raison d'être*, your reason for being.

We have both learned, on more than one occasion, that one of the best teachers in life is failure, albeit painful at times!

"We learn from failure, not from success."
— Bram Stoker

If you're alert and open to it, failure enables you to look at yourself and your surroundings in an entirely different light. Things you may not have known or noticed before will suddenly become clear to you. You'll find yourself wondering why you didn't think of that before.

Because he was aware of research confirming that failure does provide us with learning opportunities, Tom was shocked when he read the subject line of a newsletter from Angela Duckworth: "Why you don't learn from failure."

Research has shown that, rather than a detrimental force, negative feedback can be a motivating one for learning when delivered in a constructive form to help someone achieve new habits or improve existing ones.

And in the end, the writers revealed why errors and temporary "failures" do help us learn, as they shared this sage advice:

> "Do ask the young people in your life to tell you about a time they really nailed it. It will give them an opportunity to relive a win *as well as* reflect on the obstacles they faced along the way. And struggle + success is a powerful combination."

Duckworth is the author of *Grit: The Power of Passion and Perseverance* (2016), who taught several segments of the UPenn Positive Psychology Certificate program Tom completed a few years ago. She since co-founded Character Lab, an online hub with the goal of "advancing scientific insights that help kids thrive."
The newsletter came in two parts, now posted on the Character Lab website: *Oops! Why you don't learn from failure*, https://characterlab.org/character-hub/tips/oops/; and *Success Story: Describing wins helps build resilience*, https://characterlab.org/character-hub/tips/success-story-tips/

(Emphasis added.)

What are those "obstacles" and "struggles" along the way but the failures, small and large, that we learn from in order to achieve, in the end, the successes we pursue? Isn't that what *Grit* is all about?

The Emergent Approach to Strategy: Adaptive Design & Execution (2022), by Peter Compo, pg. 36 ("Probability explains why more is learned from failure than success").

Indeed, we are often more likely to learn from failure because success generally requires many things to go right, while failure often needs only one thing to go wrong. Thus when we fail, it's easier to identify what we need to work on to be more successful next time.

Successful people seemingly get to live the life they've always wanted. They worked hard to be where they're at. But before they got to that point, they almost certainly failed at many stages along their path. And you can be assured that when they did, they seized those opportunities to learn from their mistakes.

Some famous examples include:

Thomas Edison, who made over 1,000 attempts before developing a successful light bulb prototype. Edison is often quoted as saying about his projects that didn't quite work the way he expected, "I have not failed. I've just found 10,000 ways that won't work." His tenacity and genius are also responsible for the invention of the phonograph, the motion picture camera, and the alkaline battery!

Oprah Winfrey was born into poverty in rural Mississippi; she faced many hardships, including being sexually abused as a child. Oprah was fired from her job as a television co-anchor of the evening news in Baltimore because she was "unfit for TV." However, these setbacks turned into motivation, eventually getting her own talk show, laying the foundation for her to become one of the most influential women in the world.

Steve Jobs, the co-founder of Apple Inc. was actually fired from the company in 1985 after a power struggle. During his absence from

Apple, Jobs founded NeXT, a computer platform development company, and invested in Pixar, an animation studio. His ventures were successful, and in 1997, Apple acquired NeXT, bringing Jobs back to the company he co-founded. His return marked a turning point for Apple, leading to the development of products like the iPod, iPhone, and iPad.

2. Embracing failure makes you stronger, wiser, and more resilient: Each time you fail, you have the opportunity to regroup and move forward again, becoming a stronger and more resilient you.

Taking time to review, revise, and recommit to your goal is paramount to getting you from where you are to where you want to be. We get it; being in the pit of a failure can be brutal and challenging. Reviewing what worked and what didn't work is key to learning from your mistakes. These insights will help you choose to recover. From there, your path forward will be more clear. Trust your intuition, pick yourself up, dust yourself off, and set your sights back on your goal — focusing on your 'why' behind it — and keep going. This is the path of becoming Flawsome.

"You don't learn to walk by following rules. You learn by doing, and by falling over."
— Richard Branson

Simone Biles is a great example of taking a step back to become more resilient in the long run.

Her now infamous bout of "twisties" in the Tokyo 2021 Olympics caused her to prioritize her own mental and physical health and scratch in the games. While many may have categorized this as a "failure," Biles had the emotional intelligence to know when to bow out for her own safety.

Simone Biles and 'the twisties': How fear affects the mental health and physical safety of gymnasts, https://www.cnn.com/2021/07/28/us/simone-biles-olympics-gymnastics-physical-mental-health/index.html

Since then, she has made a stunning comeback, taking time away to review, revise, and recommit to her mental health, her physical health, and her continued success. Not only as the G.O.A.T. gymnast that she is, but also as a powerful voice for black women athletes around the world. This is the very definition of resilience.

Research has even suggested that resilience *depends* on our exposure to adversity, failures, and discomfort, followed by repeated experiences with overcoming them.

3. Embracing failure opens you to recognizing new opportunities: When you fail, it's often as if you hit an invisible brick wall. You can't seem to go beyond it, so what do you do?

You go exploring, of course. You ask questions. You get curious about what worked and what didn't work. If you're not afraid of failure, you can easily find new opportunities. New ways to knock down that wall or go up and over it or around it to reach your next destination along your path of learning and growth.

If need be, you can sit in your puddle of muddle, feeling sorry for your failure and your mistakes. Yet when you do, we advise you to limit your time there to a finite period. Remember from the last chapter how the women of Okinawa apply the shikata ga nai philosophy (letting go of setbacks they cannot change), "I'm not going to give this more than five minutes!" Feel what you need to feel, and then keep moving forward as you let your vision of success fuel your fire.

More from Michele:

After being laid off from my high-tech job, on the advice of my uncle, a Silicon Valley veteran,

How resilience is strengthened by exposure to stressors: the systematic self-reflection model of resilience strengthening (2019), Crane, M.F., et al., https://pubmed.ncbi.nlm.nih.gov/30067067/

I stumbled onto this new thing called "career coaching." I had no idea what it was; I just knew that I needed an outside, fresh perspective to see what I needed to see about myself and do something different. His advice proved to be golden because, in the process of being coached to figure out my next moves, I discovered my true calling and purpose as a coach.

"Your greatest source of pain is often your greatest source of passion and purpose."

— Michele Molitor

The brick wall I hit in my high-tech career led me to a career pivot that has taken me to places I had never even thought of. I never dreamed I would start my own business and have a fulfilling career for over 23 years and counting.

4. Complete failure forces you to think outside the box: If you really want to succeed at something, and you can't seem to get beyond your failure, you need to start thinking outside that box.

After all, whatever is inside your mentally-constructed box has proven that it won't help you succeed, right? By acknowledging that reality, you're forced to stop and look elsewhere and find a different path forward.

That's the beauty of embracing failure, when it does happen. Where others see only the four walls of their box, those who don't fear failure will find a way past their self-imposed walls and get moving in a new direction. Or, they'll figure out how to eliminate the box altogether to find the fresh perspectives needed to make their way forward once again. And they'll form new habits that will carry them through challenges to future successes.

Now let's look at a real-life example of facing and overcoming failure that touches all four of the perspectives we just shared. The story spans generations and involves the people behind a product that you — or your kids or grandkids — probably have played with at some point in life:

Play-Doh®.

The story behind Play-Doh shows repeated times when Cleo McVicker and later his son, Joseph, needed to find ways to go over, around, or through the walls they encountered in their business. In the 1930s, Cleo was working at a failing soap company, Kutol Products. He figured out a way to market a new form of their existing soap product, a malleable clay-like compound that could be used as a wallpaper cleaner.

That change in direction kept the company profitable for another 20 years.

But after World War II, company sales again plummeted. Homes were converting from wood and coal furnaces to gas and electric heating, eliminating the soot residue that their wallpaper cleaner targeted.

By then, Joseph had joined the company. His sister-in-law, Kay Zufall, a school teacher, suggested that the product would make a good substitute for clay in her classroom. After tinkering with colors and scents, in 1956, Joseph formed a new company, Rainbow Crafts, and launched Play-Doh, selling mostly to schools.

Still lacking a marketing budget to reach a larger audience, he got creative again. This time, he connected with Bob Keeshan (Captain Kangaroo, on the beloved kids' TV show that ran for 30 years from 1955 to 1984).

Keeshan loved the product and agreed to use it at least once per week on *The Captain Kangaroo Show*.

Sales skyrocketed, and Joseph continued to revise and recreate, adding colors and then accessories like the Play-Doh Fun Factory.

Wa-a-ay outside the Kutol soap company box!

That first step past failure, from failing soap sales to successful wallpaper cleaning compound, wasn't so huge. But it taught the fundamental lesson that failure isn't final, and going over or around the "wall" was what they needed to do.

A lesson that success can't provide.

Confidence in their resilience was gained from Cleo's response to impending failure, with that relatively small course change, soap to wall cleaner. That innovation surely helped Joseph recognize the next new opportunity and fueled his willingness to take that bigger leap into an entirely new industry.

Had the soap kept selling, would the McVickers ever have looked beyond?

Would we have Play-Doh today?

By 1964, they were shipping more than a million cans of Play-Doh per year. They sold Rainbow Crafts to General Mills in 1965, which sold the Play-Doh product line to Hasbro in 1991. It's estimated that more than 3 billion cans of Play-Doh have been sold to date. That's enough to reach the moon and back three times! More than 100 million cans of Play-Doh are sold annually, and in 1998, Play-Doh was inducted into the Toy Hall of Fame.

The History of Play-Doh: Good, Clean Fun!, https://www.museumofplay.org/blog/the-history-of-play-doh-good-clean-fun/

Embracing Your Flawsomeness

Not all imperfection involves failure. Here are some quicker takes on the array of personal advantages you can gain from embracing less drastic forms of imperfection. While some may be seen as the inverse of the "perils of perfectionism" we examined in Chapter 1, their positive sides bear notice.

1. You realize your uniqueness: Tone down the critical self-gaze, and suddenly, those little quirks stop being flaws and start being beautiful things that set you apart.

"Since you are like no other being ever created since the beginning of time, you are incomparable."

— Brenda Ueland

Your flaws make you your own unique, beautiful self. No one else has your smile or your frown of concentration. No one else can write the way you do or make your style of French toast.

2. Your self-esteem grows: Accepting that imperfection is inevitable means that you become happier with who you are and how you're doing in the moment.

It doesn't mean you don't work hard or stop having goals. It does mean you are less hung up about doing everything perfectly, right now. Which allows you to enjoy the process along the way.

You'll stop "shoulding" on yourself and let go of perfectionism. When you start embracing your authentic self, just the way you are — and just the way you aren't — your sense of self-esteem will continue to expand and grow.

3. You'll feel lighter and happier: We have seen and experienced that perfectionists carry a LOT of emotional baggage from trying to look as though their entire world is idyllic all the time. They're at a higher risk of depression and anxiety and hardly ever content with what they have. Their physical health suffers, too.

Does your life truly look or feel idyllic ALL of the time? Embrace the messy, flawed parts of your life and yourself, and you'll be happier and far less stressed. Ask your Inner Critic to stand down and put its feet up, allowing you to relax and get on with your life, unburdened by not feeling good enough.

Liberated from needing to be seen as perfect, you'll feel a lot happier and more content with who you are, what you've got, and where you're at in your life.

Michele calls her inner critic "Amy" — a nickname for her Amygdala (the part of your brain responsible for your Fight, Flight, or Freeze response). When Amy gets overly critical and kicks up the "not enough" conversation, Michele simply tells her, "Thank you for sharing, Amy, now relax! All is well."

What can you call *your* inner critic so you can direct them to new empowering habits of thought and action?

4. Your self-confidence will expand: As you own all of your unique traits, quirks, and qualities, you will feel more comfortable in your skin. This will enable you to speak your mind and share your thoughts and expertise with others more regularly. All of which helps build your self-confidence.

And Tom and Michele know that the energy of self-confidence is something that radiates outward from each of us in all directions, like a homing beacon, attracting more of the positive outcomes we seek.

The Joys of Spreading Flawsomism

As we noted above, flawsomism doesn't just benefit you. When you turn your acceptance outward and embrace the flaws in others and the world around you, everyone benefits — most importantly, the people closest to you. Here are some of the external benefits of becoming a flawsomist:

1. You spread kindness: When you're okay with your own less-than-perfect aspects, you become more accepting of other people's flaws. When you embrace imperfection, your standards become more realistic. In turn, you take a kinder view of yourself and others.

"Acts of kindness have a virtuous cycle effect that goes on after the moment has passed."

— Tom Collins

Others will notice your positive reactions and feel better about themselves. This creates a safe space for others to be themselves around you.

When your acceptance takes the form of kind action, the effect is compounded as you create a space of acceptance, belonging, and connection with another person. Thus creating a "virtuous cycle" that ripples out far beyond the moment, touching the lives of others you will never know.

The person you helped gets joy not only from the act itself but also from the implicit idea that they are worthy of being treated kindly. Thus, the joy of being flawsome spreads, one person at a time.

2. You become more compassionate and forgiving: Once you stop judging yourself for every little thing, you'll find it easier to be more compassionate and forgiving toward other people.

You'll be more patient and less irritated by quirks or habits where previously you might have reacted in a negative manner. Embracing imperfection makes you less reactive and easier to be around.

You'll also be more emotionally equipped to forgive serious mistakes or offenses against you. In this case, the benefits to the other person have the potential to create deeper learning and increased emotional intelligence, depending on the offense committed and their level of regret.

The benefits to you can be substantial as well. Studies show forgiving others provides a wide range of mental health benefits, including minimizing angry or depressive thoughts, increasing optimistic thinking, fostering life-contentment, improving physical health, and increasing productivity at work.

See Tom's blog post with a section on the reciprocal benefits of forgiveness, *HIBs? 14 Proven Ways to Increase Your Happiness* (2021), https://masterbookbuilders.com/hibs-14-proven-ways-to-increase-your-happiness/#forgive

Remember, forgiveness is an act of kindness that you give both to yourself and another person.

3. You stop comparing yourself to others: Embracing your imperfections releases you from the destructive cycle of comparing yourself with other people. Being better than the next guy suddenly stops mattering, as you learn how to be your best self each day, knowing that is enough. And letting go of your competitive stance toward those around you relieves them of a stressful interaction, too.

"Comparison is the thief of joy."

— Theodore Roosevelt

Seeing your flaws as unique elements of who you are releases you from needing external validation as well. It's wonderful to see more and more diversity in places these days — from television to advertising to social media. Embracing your authentic self, freckles, quirks, disabilities, and all is what makes each of us unique.

Let's celebrate our uniqueness instead of trying to constantly "fit in." Real validation comes from within, and what other people think or how they look doesn't matter. You CAN fit in simply by being your flawsome self.

Flawsome = being perfectly imperfect.

4. Your relationships improve: One of the perils of perfectionism that you might recall is that it can harm your relationships. Not only with yourself but with others. So, the converse holds true here.

Being a more accepting person will strengthen your relationships with family, friends, and colleagues. Accepting that imperfection and mistakes are a normal part of life means that you become less ego-driven and judgmental. Because who *really* likes to be judged?

"The imperfections – the weaknesses – the imprecisions – they are the very things which define humans as human."

— Isaac Asimov

Instead, strive to be the person who uplifts others, having them feel seen, heard, and respected — just for who they are.

5. You'll inspire others: Imperfection is the essence of being a human. It's how we learn and progress.

It connects us.

Gracefully accepting the ebbs and flows of life will make you someone other people can look up to and admire. You'll become the kind of role model we all need.

Chapter 4: Journal Prompts
to help you start living Flawsomely

These are intended to get you thinking, not judging yourself. Take some quiet time to thoughtfully and honestly respond to these questions to create your own positive shifts in your perspectives around perfectionism.

- What are some of the biggest "lessons learned" from one of your past failures?

- What's possible when you focus on progress rather than perfection?

- How would your life look and feel differently if you accepted yourself as perfectly imperfect (aka flawsome)?

Chapter 5

Wabi-Sabi in the Workplace

*"In the fixed mindset, everything is about the outcome.
If you fail — or if you're not the best — it's all been
wasted. The growth mindset allows people to value what
they're doing regardless of the outcome. They're tackling
problems, charting new courses, working on important
issues. Maybe they haven't found the cure for cancer,
but the search was deeply meaningful."*

— Carol Dweck

Back in Chapter 3, we examined the interplay
of the Japanese concept of kaizen (continuous
improvement) with wabi-sabi (celebrating
imperfection) and related personal development
philosophies. Here, we'll zero in on how these can affect
our work.

As we did with the general concepts, we'll start with
the perils of overemphasizing the pursuit of perfection in
the work we do.

The Dangers of "Continuous Improvement"

Kaizen as a business management tool was popularized
in the late 1940s and 50s through the work of W. Edwards
Deming, which began when he was consulting in Japan to
aid in its industrial recovery from World War II. Kaizen

eventually became known as The Toyota Way, though it was widely adopted throughout Japanese companies.

The notion of always seeking improvement makes sense, of course. But as we'll see, Deming himself tempered his advice with warnings that help avoid the extremes. And dangers come from both ends of the kaizen "continuous improvement" mantra. Here's how perfectionism and its imposter syndrome variant can creep in.

In the business world, large organizations somehow folded kaizen into the "Lean" (doing more with less) and "Six Sigma" (zero defects) movements. We see this corporate attitude as a key driver of toxic perfectionism in the workplace.

When the C-suite claims to be chasing the unrealistic goal of zero defects (i.e., perfect performance) and insists on doing so while removing "unnecessary, wasteful" steps in business processes (i.e., with fewer and fewer resources, including people) the workplace becomes ruthless, and the work futile.

Thus, a seemingly admirable management philosophy, with its focus on processes and systems, easily loses sight of the quality of the lives of the workers delivering the products or services.

The "doing more" part gets equated with creating more profits. The "with less" part too often morphs from the heroic corporate version of MacGyver getting the job done with materials out of the janitor closet into under-resourced teams and assignments. This sets workers up to fail or succeed at the expense of their personal lives and wellness. And the organization pays the long-term price for both.

Similarly, when we're looking at our individual work, the dangers in a continuous improvement philosophy lie in the extremes:

- "I need to improve" gets internalized as "I'm not good enough."

- "I need to continue improving" becomes the perfectionist's excuse never to launch, never to exhibit, never to click publish.

"Real artists ship."

— Steve Jobs

One indication of these toxic workplace effects came in our survey, where among those employed or self-employed, 82% said they felt pressure to be perfect. Yet in the same group, only 67% said they had ever regarded themselves as a perfectionist. This shows a significant portion of the pressure comes directly from external sources.

And we suggest that at least some of their self-directed perfectionism is internalized from the do-more-with-less, zero-defects culture permeating such workplaces.

As one participant told us:

"It boils over. My anxiety builds, and I start self-sabotaging. I am constantly being compared to others, even when I know I can perform better than them at many things. But I feel completely disregarded and overlooked at work."

Contrast these ill effects of taking Kaizen's continuous improvement concepts to their extremes with the company culture at W.L. Gore. Founder Wilbert "Bill" Gore stated,

"The objective of the enterprise is to make money and have fun doing so."

The W.L. Gore story is told in more detail in *The Tipping Point*, by Malcolm Gladwell. The focus there is on the organization's efforts to keep its teams and facilities sized and located to optimize the human connection and collaboration goals that we've noted here. Gladwell explains how "Dunbar's Number" — the concept that our brains limit the number of close relationships we can manage to somewhere around 150 — plays into W.L. Gore's systems.

For more on companies recognized for their worker-friendly cultures, see *10 companies with the best culture, according to employees*, https://www.benefitnews.com/list/comparablys-10-companies-with-the-best-culture, and *The 6 Best Company Cultures Out There Right Now*, https://www.marketveep.com/blog/the-6-best-company-cultures-out-there-right-now

In place of the usual hierarchical management structure, Gore adopted what it calls a lattice. The key feature is that every employee, or "associate," is viewed as connected to every other associate and can go to anyone they need for help in getting their job done. In addition, every associate has a "sponsor" to help them grow and develop and "find the right path to success" in the organization.

So, we're not saying you should abandon the ideal of continuous improvement! We're all about life-long learning, after all.

In fact, it's by learning a bit more about kaizen and revisiting how it fits in with those related Japanese personal and business philosophies discussed earlier that we can avoid the danger zones.

Season that Kaizen with Some Wabi-Sabi

In Chapter 3, we examined a cluster of four Japanese philosophy elements (wabi-sabi, ganbatte, kaizen, and shikata ga nai). We described that grouping as enabling us to "hold the paradox of pursuing excellence and accepting imperfection as compatible, simultaneous mindsets."

Let's take a closer look at one of those Japanese philosophies, wabi-sabi. The basic translation of wabi-sabi is celebrating imperfection. To uncover broader meanings in the term, Candice Kumai considers the two parts separately. She explains that as a term in Japanese poetry, "wabi" suggests simplicity, humbleness, and being in tune with nature, "a simple, austere beauty." The second term, "sabi" brings in concepts relating to the passage of time, aging, and the temporary nature of everything.

By blending these added nuances of simplicity, natural beauty, aging, and impermanence into the basic practice of celebrating imperfection, we can keep kaizen centered on improvement and away from the extremes of perfectionism.

As we embrace the imperfections of our own mended pieces and scars from the life lessons we've learned on our paths, we become our own art of kintsugi, making us wiser and more beautiful.

Crucial Points from Deming's List

Because the corrosive management philosophies we've described claim to follow from Deming's work and the Japanese Kaizen movement, we'll take another moment to exonerate Deming himself. Both managers and individual workers would be well served to understand the balancing tenets of his teachings that urge a mutually respectful culture of pride of workmanship, education, and worker self-improvement — without fear-based slogans, quotas and "zero defect" targets.

By 1982, when he published his book *Out of the Crisis*, Deming had refined his ideas into "14 Points for Management." Kaizen shows up in his Point 5,

> "*Improve constantly and forever* the system of production and service, to improve quality and productivity, and thus constantly decrease costs."

The extremes of perfectionism and the negative never-good-enough view of workers that emerged in the Lean, Six Sigma, and Total Quality Management movements largely hang on that ending phrase "and thus constantly decrease costs."

But Deming seemed to recognize these dangers and sought to avoid them by including the following "worker wellness" points that routinely get lost or ignored in the corporate zeal for maximizing this quarter's profits. Consider these precepts extracted from Deming's 14 points:

"6. Institute training on the job.

"7. Institute leadership. The aim of supervision should be *to help people* and machines and gadgets to do a better job. ...

"8. *Drive out fear*, so that everyone may work effectively for the company.

"10. *Eliminate* slogans, exhortations, and targets for the workforce *asking for zero defects* and new levels of productivity. ...

"11. a. Eliminate work standards (quotas) on the factory floor. Substitute leadership. [see #7] ...

"12. a. Remove barriers that rob the hourly worker of his *right to pride of workmanship*. ...

"13. Institute a vigorous program of *education and self-improvement*."

(Emphases added.)

These rules for management focusing on the training, nurturing, and well-being of workers constitute fully half of Deming's 14 Points. In them, we can hear echoes of the kaizen/ganbatte tension,

"Always do your best, but remember that your best is good enough. And keep improving."

Indeed, to our ears, Deming's #10 sounds almost mocking toward any manic quest for perfection — "zero defects" — and his emphasis on training, helping people do better, and cultivating pride of workmanship call to mind Kumai's wabi-sabi reality check:

> "Not only is perfection impossible, imperfection is beautiful in and of itself! ... Imperfection is the natural order of things — the fleeting nature of autumn, the changing color of the leaves, and, yes, the flaws in every human being."

So, if leaders need to widen their focus from increasing productivity and reducing costs to include these ways of improving the lives of the people in the organization, what lessons can we draw for ourselves, as individuals, in choosing and pursuing meaningful work?

Raisman's Rule

Let's start by fleshing out our definition of meaningful work. Based on our research and our own life experiences, we define meaningful work to include some or all of these ten elements:

E.g., *What Makes Work Meaningful?*, Lysova, E., et al., https://hbr.org/2023/07/what-makes-work-meaningful

1. Autonomy to make choices
2. Wielding some sense of control over our journey
3. Intellectually stimulating, inspiring, and engaging
4. Creativity and opportunities for expanded imagination
5. Connection between effort and reward
6. Trust and collaboration
7. Having a sense of value and worth for our contributions
8. Care and concern from and for colleagues and clients
9. Meaningful discussions and feedback loops
10. Contributing to something bigger than ourselves

Number 10 on the list is what we find to be most essential: contribution outside ourselves. This can range from supporting our families to serving customers to creating breakthroughs that benefit all humanity.

Michele has found through her experience as a transformational coach and hypnotherapist that at the heart of what makes our work meaningful is our ability to be of contribution — to contribute our talents in a purposeful way that aligns with our own emotional motivators and core values. All of which are based on our unique experiences in life that give each of us our distinctive perspectives on the world and the contributions we bring to our work.

And this distinctive contribution is vital. To feel seen, heard, and recognized for the particular skills, gifts, and talents we bring to the job at hand is what creates the intrinsic motivation that gets you out of bed each day. It is also the very foundation of our dignity and how we want to be valued and treated with respect for the contributions we're making.

For Tom, contributing value to others has always been a necessary piece, whether in a manual labor or a professional setting. All the way back to building swimming pools as a summer job through college, he can still recall how rewarding it was to see the anticipation of the family while he and his team worked and their joy when their pool was ready.

During his legal career, helping a homeowner get a zoning variance for an addition to their home meant much more than defeating a major lawsuit on behalf of an insurance company. For the last 20+ years and counting, he has gotten joy both from seeing his book design work embodied in physical and digital form and from the impact on clients when they become "the author of" the book they've dreamed about.

Now, in their distinctive ways, both Tom and Michele find deep meaning and purpose through helping others have their authentic voices be heard.

This brings us back to Aly Raisman, our poster child for commitment to cultivating and sharing her talents from an early age, fighting through perfectionism and imposter syndrome along the way. Recall how she expressed what she learned about her work:

> "Set goals for yourself, and don't be afraid to follow them as far as they'll take you. Accept the fact that if you don't accomplish your goals, that's okay. Focus on the hard work you put into it and be proud of that."

Fierce, Aly Raisman, "The Fierce Guide to Life, pg. 346.

We noted in the Introduction how she struggled with winning two gold medals at the 2012 Olympics while "only" a bronze on the beam. And she "failed" to medal in the individual All-Around. When we read the details, however, we were shocked to find out she actually tied for the bronze. The tie-breaker rule was to drop the lowest score on the four events, and when that was done, her remaining total placed her fourth.

Note that this method of tie-breaking meant that the bronze went to the one who had done much worse on her one event that was dropped. Ironically, Raisman was penalized for being more consistently excellent!

By 2016, however, she had grown into her roles as both team Captain and "Grandma Aly" to her younger teammates. She was able to revel in the outcome when she finished second to "Baby" Simone Biles in the All-Around. They shared the joy, and Biles pulled Raisman up on the top podium with her, later saying she was more pleased about Raisman's silver than her own gold, because "I've seen how hard she worked for it."

In her post-event interview, team coordinator Martha Karolyi presaged Raisman's rule:

> "In all the years ... I could not say, 'Aly, try harder' because she always tried her best. It doesn't always turn out the best, but you could not blame her because she always gave what she had."

Letting Go of Perfection in Our Work

We covered a broad range of benefits from flawsomism in Chapter 3. Now let's look at a "Top 5" list of reasons to practice it in your work:

1. Imperfect is all there is: The common wisdom that "nobody's perfect" is not just true of people and our actions. It's true of everything. We are all perfectly imperfect.

As we've noted, even the Laws of Physics can't escape uncertainty, chaos, and randomness.

Strive for excellence, not perfection. Remember, the Lexus slogan "relentless pursuit of perfection" translates to stubbornly reliving failure and disappointment, which quite frankly, is exhausting.

2. Flawsomism lets you start: Embracing your own imperfection enables you to begin. You might not ever feel "ready," or smart enough, or strong enough, or knowledgeable enough, or well-funded enough.

Nobody else does, either. As James Clear explained in his blog, it's inherent when pondering a challenging, meaningful new venture that we'll feel inadequate to begin. Start anyway.

> "If you want to summarize the habits of successful people into one phrase, it's this: successful people start before they feel ready."

Unless you embrace that imperfection in yourself – all those imagined reasons you're not quite ready – you'll never start that business, that project, that piece of art you've been envisioning.

Many years ago, while working on a big proposal for a potential client, Michele found herself suddenly distracted, fidgeting in her seat, with an urge to get up and do some laundry, have a snack, anything but sit at her desk, and complete the task at hand.

Perhaps this sensation is familiar to you as well?

She also recognized that the top of her head was tingling as if to signal her to this inflection point. Michele was able to recognize the tingling sensation, the squirming in her seat for what it was, the energy of anxiety from bumping up against the edge of her comfort zone!

It was a moment of unconscious habit being brought into the light of conscious choice. This was a choice point of sitting in the discomfort. Should she keep going, leaning into the discomfort? Or shrink back from the challenge and distract herself by numbing out with other mindless things?

You see, the proposal at hand was new and bigger than any project she had worked on in the past. It was

Successful People Start Before They Feel Ready, James Clear, https://jamesclear.com/successful-people-start-before-they-feel-ready

"Whatever you can do or dream you can, begin it. Boldness has genius, power, and magic in it! At the moment of commitment, the entire universe conspires to assist you."

— Goethe

67

uncharted territory and was pushing all of her buttons of "wanting to get it right" and "needing to make sure it was perfect."

Catching herself in this moment, she had this aha:

"Uncomfortable happens. **Keep going!**"

And from that moment on, she sat in her chair until she finished the proposal. Realizing that the squirm is just energy that wants to be released as we stretch and expand the edges of our comfort zone to a new level of growth and experience in the world.

"When you look fear in the face, it turns into the nothingness that it actually is."

— Michele Molitor

While it's comfortable to be in your genius zone — that place of flow and familiarity — it is the stretch into your not-so-comfortable zone, a.k.a. Your Growth Zone, that pushes you forward, expands your thinking and opens new doors of possibilities.

Embrace the flawsome ... and start.

3. Flawsomism enables you to finish: This one should follow naturally from #1 and #2, right? First, acknowledge imperfection in everything. Second, embrace imperfection in yourself and conditions as necessary to begin.

Now realize that embracing imperfection in your work is equally necessary to finish.

It's worth repeating that, although deeply concerned with the quality and beauty of his products, Steve Jobs famously admonished his engineers against making endless refinements to their work.

Tom often describes this as the need to "let the baby (your work) be born."

When Michele is at her easel working on a painting, it will "tell her" when it's done. If she doesn't trust her gut on when to step away from the canvas, declaring it complete, she often finds herself getting annoyed because adding the "just one more thing to make it perfect," only ends up detracting from the whole.

"Finishing projects is part of what it means to deliver high quality work. It's not high quality if your perfectionism prevents you from finishing."

— James Clear

4. Flawsomism makes you more relatable: Or perhaps less insufferable? We touched on several benefits around how we relate to others in Chapter 3. Understanding, accepting, and embracing imperfection in ourselves and our work, as well as in other people and their work, will improve our relationships in all areas of life.

Acceptance is the keyword here. When we can truly accept ourselves and all of our imperfections, we can embrace them wholeheartedly. This then gives us greater compassion to see and accept the imperfections in others, instead of judging and dismissing their efforts. Or worse, violating their dignity in the process.

In our work settings, this may best be embodied in the marketing maxim that people buy from those they "know, like, and trust."

Michele has found the best way to gain insight into understanding others is to learn about their top 5 dignity traits, a.k.a. their motivational drivers. This enables you to communicate with greater understanding instead of from assumptions on how you *think* someone should be. Thus, shifting your energy signature from one of judgement to

Curious to learn what your top 5 dignity traits are? Take the **Dignify Survey** to learn your natural communication style and what constitutes honor and respect for you: www.IAmPerfectlyFlawsome.com/resources

curiosity and acceptance, which then helps foster greater belonging and connection — which we think is flawsome!

By embracing the imperfections of others, you'll find it easier to connect with coworkers and customers as they feel "safe" to be around you in a judgment-free zone. While you may think quietly judging someone in your mind is harmless, it creates a negative energy that others consciously and unconsciously pick up on. This can become socially repelling to others in a way that they can't quite put their finger on.

Think of someone you know who is always judging your actions or behaviors. How does it feel to be around them? Probably not very comfortable. Now think of someone that you work with who is kind and compassionate. How does it feel differently to be around them?

With those sensations in mind, now think about the energy that you want to emit and the impact you want to make on others with your own energy signature.

When you balance the four kintsugi concepts we've talked about, you and those around you can live and work in that paradox of striving for excellence and doing your best, while celebrating imperfection and knowing your collective best is enough.

5. Flawsomism makes growth and improvement possible: If you imagine yourself or your work as being perfect, what then?

By embracing imperfection, you can treat yesterday's work as your starting point, giving you the freedom to be better today. To improve upon your new project and continue to learn from each piece of "art" (personally or professionally) that you complete. To transfer those lessons to your next piece that is waiting to be born.

See Michele's article, *Jedi Master Secrets - How to Be Mindful of Your Energy Signature*, https://michelemolitor.com/2017/10/09/jedi-master-secrets-how-to-be-mindful-of-your-energy-signature/

This is the definition of having a growth mindset, of continuous and never-ending improvement of ourselves, our work, and our impact on the world.

Before moving on to explore the unique impacts of perfectionism on women in Chapter 6, here are some helpful and encouraging responses that our survey yielded to the question,

"How do you cope with the pressure to be perfect in the workplace?" —

- "I communicate with colleagues and share common, relatable stories. I take breaks to get away from work during the day and on weekends. I hire business coaches to provide perspective and guidance. I share frustrations with my wife (sometimes). I work out, eat healthy, and breathe."

- "Perfection is a fallacy. Any time I've sought perfection it was a massive disappointment. I strive to do my best, but perfection is not the goal, today."

- "To cope with this self-imposed pressure/ frustration, I learned to 'Just do it!' to get started and then step back to give it a rest. I also adopted the mantra, 'Good enough, move on.'"

- "I try to allow for the imperfection and accept it. Try for good enough and understand that 'perfection' often means that we are not able to execute on a project or plan."

Flawsomism at work!

Chapter 5: Journal Prompts to help you start living Flawsomely

These are intended to get you thinking, not judging yourself. Take some quiet time to thoughtfully and honestly respond to these questions to create your own positive shifts in your perspectives around perfectionism.

- What's needed so you can embrace your imperfections and flaws with compassion, both personally and professionally?

- How will embracing your imperfections improve and/or even enhance your career while preventing burnout?

- What's possible in the workplace when you increase psychological safety by fostering a culture of "Always do your best, and keep improving."

Chapter 6

Ladies, Let's Move from Fearful to Flawsome

"It is literally impossible to be a woman.
You are so beautiful and so smart, and it kills me
that you don't think you're good enough.
Like, we have to always be extraordinary, but
somehow we're always doing it wrong."
— Gloria (America Ferrera), in *Barbie* (2023)

As we have been discussing, there are many variables that create perfectionism in a person, no matter their gender, race, or religion. However, we were curious about our hunch that perfectionism tends to lean more towards women.

How Perfectionism Impacts Women

The research has shown that there are indeed some gender-specific differences to take into account here. We're learning there's evidence for a genetic component to perfectionism, influencing both self-oriented and socially prescribed perfectionism, and that females are more likely to inherit it.

Studies suggest that women do tend to experience higher levels of socially prescribed perfectionism than men, especially in the areas of appearance, relationships,

E.g., *Variables Related to Perfectionism* (2012), Marilyn Gawlik, https://www.mckendree.edu/academics/scholars/issue18/gawlik.htm

The Female Fear of Being Flawed - Study looks at gender differences in the desire to be perfect (2022), Cision PRWeb, https://www.prweb.com/releases/the-female-fear-of-being-flawed-study-looks-at-gender-differences-in-the-desire-to-be-perfect-849337475.html

performance, and academic achievement. Three findings from a 2022 study with more than 1,400 participants drive home the disparity in impact:

- Nearly half of the women (47%) believe that failing at one task or project makes them a failure as a person (vs. 38% of the men)

- Similarly, 48% of the women said they needed to be in perfect physical shape to be considered attractive (vs. 42% of the men)

- Almost two-thirds (64%) of the women admitted they "often worry about what other people think" (vs. just over half, 51%, of the men)

Our own survey data backs up this troubling gender gap. 85% of adult women surveyed said they felt pressure to be perfect (vs. a still large majority of men at 77%). One woman's answer on the pressures of the workplace sums up several similar responses:

> "Without a doubt. If I'm not perfect, people view me as 'another woman who got the job because she's a woman.' That means I have to work twice as hard, twice as long, study more, and do more."

And the pressure starts early for women, with 71% of our surveyed women saying they'd felt such pressure since childhood. Only 54% of the men said yes about feeling childhood pressure.

"Society intentionally does that to women and girls. It starts at a very early age. We question our value, our worth. We question how we look, how we talk, where we're from. They are people with power who want us to stay small. They want us to stay doubtful. And so our cultures reinforce that."

— Michelle Obama, 2022 CNN panel discussion, https://www.youtube.com/watch?v=bzNke_GYGHg

Research suggests perhaps a third of perfectionist tendencies come from genes. We don't think you have to look far to see where a lot of the remaining two-thirds and the extra impact on women comes from.

Well-publicized studies have shown the detrimental effects of social media displaying idealized images of female bodies and fashion on girls and young women. But that imagery is far more pervasive across our culture and has been for decades. From romance and graphic novels to magazine covers in grocery stores, to movies and television, to billboards on highways and stadium-sized video screens on buildings in major cities, the idealized female invades our consciousness.

We've already discussed the pressures on women in the workplace in Chapter 5, but there's the added layer of pressure for working mothers to "do it all" — perfectly. A woman in the 30-44 age range of our survey said:

> "I feel that I have to be better because I am a woman in a male-dominated field. I also have to be better at home because no one thinks I know what I'm doing as a parent."

Another in that same age group spoke for her gender, adding:

> "It seems that women put more pressure on themselves to be the perfect mom, wife, friend, caretaker, always doing for others!"

In case you're thinking this is an American or Western culture problem, a 2023 study of Taiwanese third- and sixth-graders reported:

> "Girls scored much higher than boys for self-oriented perfectionism, contingent self-worth, concern over mistakes, self-criticism, high standards, and rigid and self-critical perfectionism."

See, *The complicated ties between teenage girls and social media – and what parents should know* (2023), Jennifer Gerson (collecting research and quoting the Surgeon General on the harmful effects of social media on adolescent girls), https://19thnews.org/2023/09/social-media-teenage-girls-mental-health-body-image/

Comparing Perfectionism, Cognitive Mindset, Constructive Thinking, and Emotional Intelligence in Gifted Students by Grade and Gender (2023), Tsai, M., https://www.mdpi.com/2076-0760/12/4/233

Perfectionism in Adolescence: Associations With Gender, Age, and Socioeconomic Status in a Norwegian Sample (2021), Sand, L., et al., https://www.frontiersin.org/journals/public-health/articles/10.3389/fpubh.2021.688811/full

The pressure of perfection: five women tell their stories (2016), Sarah Marsh, https://www.theguardian.com/commentisfree/2016/oct/14/perfect-girls-five-women-stories-mental-health

A 2021 study of more than 10,000 Norwegian teens (aged 16-19) found that "there were significantly more girls than boys among the high scorers" for both self-oriented and socially prescribed perfectionism, as well as an eating disorder inventory.

And, a 2016 survey by The Guardian gathered more than 100 responses from UK women ranging in age from 18 to 37. Summing up the damaging impact of perfectionism, they reported:

> "For a lot of young women who contacted us, body image was a huge preoccupation, and many said they felt undervalued unless they met society's expectations of beauty. The pressure to be perfect also extended to the workplace, with many respondents talking about feeling inadequate at their jobs or experiencing impostor syndrome. They also complained of feeling the pressure to have it all: juggling being a mother with career and other personal pressures."

The Guardian article reminded us that consequences for such women include "anxiety, depression, panic disorder, phobia, or obsessive-compulsive disorder."

This is largely due to centuries of societal programming of men holding positions of power and dominance around the globe.

There have been notable exceptions to this rule, with these women rulers of nations such as:

- Cleopatra VII (51-30 BC) Egypt
- Catherine the Great (1729-1796) Russia
- Indira Gandhi (1917-1984) India
- Queen Elizabeth II (1926-2022) United Kingdom

Throughout human history, women have been revered for their beauty and grace. Anything less than perfection was often cast aside or, at the very least, faced with heightened scrutiny, gender bias, and criticism that negatively impacted their positions.

A set of "Rules of behavior for Young Ladies," published in New York in 1831, included these admonitions:

- Avoid every thing masculine

- Know that a man of good sense will never marry but the pious, industrious, and frugal

- … and remember that whereas the character of a young lady is considered angelic, *any blemish* in it would withdraw the respect men have for you

18 Rules Of Behavior For Young Ladies In 1831 (2015), Linton Weeks, https://www.npr.org/sections/npr-history-dept/2015/11/20/456224571/18-rules-of-behavior-for-young-ladies-in-1831 (emphasis added)

Over the last 200 years in America, a handful of women have slowly risen to positions of power across various industries, businesses, and politics. Knowing what we know now, we can speculate that most of them struggled with perfectionism to varying degrees.

For women in the spotlight, the undue focus on and criticism of personal attributes — her hair isn't just right, she doesn't smile enough, I saw her cry once — rather than qualifications, policies, and leadership abilities, show the persistent gender biases and stereotypes that women in positions of power often confront.

"And we carry them around with us our entire lives. I don't care how far you go, whether you go to the White House, you are constantly batting away those negative messages of being not enough.

"And yes, I deal with that too."

— Michelle Obama, 2022 CNN panel discussion, https://www.youtube.com/watch?v=bzNke_GYGHg

This creates an underlying and oftentimes unconscious driving need for perfection to "win" in all aspects of the world, just to compete with the men (and women) around them. We often hear this referred to as breaking the glass ceiling, but for our purposes in this book, this references the need for women to be perfect in all ways.

While there is greater equality in today's world, the subtext of those societal pressures and expectations still remains. Sheryl Sandberg is quoted as saying:

> "Trying to do it all and expecting it all can be done exactly right is a recipe for disappointment. Perfection is the enemy. Gloria Steinem said it best: 'You can't do it all. No one can have two full-time jobs, have perfect children, cook three meals, and be multi-orgasmic 'til dawn … Superwoman is the adversary of the women's movement.' "

Gender bias continues to impact how women are perceived, treated, promoted, and paid for their expertise. As of 2022, data reveals that women working full time, year-round, are still only paid 84 cents for every dollar men make in the workplace. When you include part-time and seasonal workers, women's earnings sink to 78 cents.

5 Facts From the 2022 Wage Gap Data (2023), Isabela Salas-Betsch, https://www.americanprogress.org/article/5-facts-from-the-2022-wage-gap-data/; see also, *New Research Finds The 'Old Boys Club' At Work Is Real — And Contributing To The Gender Pay Gap* (2021), Lindsay Kohler, https://www.forbes.com/sites/lindsaykohler/2021/04/22/new-research-finds-the-old-boys-club-at-work-is-real---and-contributing-to-the-gender-pay-gap/?sh=1f4ac5a84101

This bias also shows up in both overt and covert ways. Objectification, sexist jokes or body language towards women, lack of respect, and masculine practices that intimidate or exclude women. The more subtle ways it shows up are masculine-leaning recruiting and promotion practices — where women's ideas, perspectives, and voices are overlooked when they are left out of decision-making and leadership roles. And it even shows up as stigmas associated with being a working parent and the need for parental leave.

Having grown up in the South, making her way up the "corporate ladder," Michele always had to outperform her male peers and continually prove her value and worth just to maintain her seat at the table. She says, "It was infuriating and exhausting!"

After moving to San Francisco and being immersed in the high tech culture there, she realized that this was not just in the South. The "bro culture, a.k.a. the good ole boys network," is just as pervasive in Silicon Valley as she experienced it firsthand.

This bro culture can be particularly difficult to navigate for women in many male-dominated fields, exacerbating the perceived need to be perfect to outshine and outperform their male peers just to maintain equal footing. Michele experienced this when she found herself being bullied by male colleagues in ways that felt demeaning and humiliating. Their undignified words and actions diminished her sense of value and worth, only inflaming her perfectionism and increasing her imposter syndrome.

For working mothers, the stakes are even higher as they juggle mastering their careers while also striving to be nurturing, loving mothers who are always there for their children. And, of course, household chores. Most women are still tasked with keeping a clean house and cooking a delicious dinner every night.

In fact, according to the Pew Research Center analysis, "in U.S. households consisting of married or cohabiting parents and one or more children under the age of 18, 80% of mothers say they are the household member who usually prepares the meals — the same as the share who say they are the primary grocery shopper, with 71% of moms say they primarily handle both chores."

Among U.S. couples, women do more cooking and grocery shopping than men (2019), Katherine Schaeffer, https://www.pewresearch.org/short-reads/2019/09/24/among-u-s-couples-women-do-more-cooking-and-grocery-shopping-than-men/

Learn more about her at https://podopolo.com/about/

Melinda Wittstock is a serial entrepreneur of several successful companies, with her latest being Podopolo. She shared with Michele that her first business launched when her daughter was just six weeks old! Creating a need for radical prioritizing of what's really important, she learned during that time the important lesson of "Done is better than perfect."

In the early days of her first company, Capitol News Connection, she recalled carrying her briefcase on one shoulder and her breast pump in a bag on the other. Melinda had to pump in the office bathroom of former Speaker of the House, Nancy Pelosi.

Having started her career as a newscaster with the Times of London, she knows oh too well what it was like to manage her perfectionism as the only female American reporter (and the youngest) in a British news agency.

She recalls how, later in her career, being an anchor for MSNBC and the BBC, it was expected that you had to be perfect. Perfect hair, perfect makeup, perfect clothes. Be attractive, but not too much. You can't possibly be beautiful AND smart ... so many contradictions and unconscious biases that she consistently faced.

Even in groups of women, the competition was fierce instead of supportive, she said, as she tried to do it all and be it all. Thankfully, with the passing of time, wisdom set in; Melinda shared that now she is grateful for being healthy, active, and happy with herself without the need for perfectionism anymore.

The challenges women still face today were brilliantly stated in the powerful monologue given by actress America Ferrera as her character "Gloria" in the global hit movie *Barbie* (2023):

It is literally impossible to be a woman. You are so beautiful and so smart, and it kills me that you don't think you're good enough. Like, we have to always be extraordinary, but somehow, we're always doing it wrong.

You have to be thin but not too thin. And you can never say you want to be thin. You have to say you want to be healthy, but also you have to be thin. You have to have money, but you can't ask for money because that's crass. You have to be a boss, but you can't be mean. You have to lead, but you can't squash other people's ideas. You're supposed to love being a mother but don't talk about your kids all the damn time. You have to be a career woman but also always be looking out for other people.

You have to answer for men's bad behavior, which is insane, but if you point that out, you're accused of complaining. You're supposed to stay pretty for men but not so pretty that you tempt them too much or that you threaten other women because you're supposed to be a part of the sisterhood.

But always stand out and always be grateful. But never forget that the system is rigged. So, find a way to acknowledge that but also always be grateful.

You have to never get old, never be rude, never show off, never be selfish, never fall down, never fail, never show fear, never get out of line. It's too hard! It's too contradictory, and nobody gives you a medal or says thank you! And it turns out in fact, that not only are you doing everything wrong, but also everything is your fault.

I'm just so tired of watching myself and every single other woman tie herself into knots so that people will like us. And if all of that is also true for a doll just representing women, then I don't even know.

Watch the clip:
America Ferrera's Iconic Barbie Speech | Barbie | Max (2023), https://www.youtube.com/watch?v=CBqlDWHkdHk;
Read America Ferrera's Powerful Monologue in Barbie (2023), Emily Burack, https://www.townandcountrymag.com/leisure/arts-and-culture/a44725030/america-ferrera-barbie-full-monologue-transcript/

This is not to say that men aren't faced with the challenge of balancing their careers and their family lives as responsible fathers. It's worth remembering that in the research we've highlighted, whenever the results showed a higher proportion of women or girls affected by perfectionism, say 60%, that means a smaller but still very substantial proportion of men or boys suffering as well. Yet historically, the greatest pressure to be the perfect parent "raising the kids" has fallen to women. This pressure has only intensified as women have fought to take their rightful place in the workplace.

Greta Gerwig shared that when America Ferrera delivered the monologue, everyone on the set was crying, even the men. She said,

> "The men are crying too because they have their own speech they feel they can't ever give, you know? And they have their own twin tightrope, which is also painful."

The *Variables Related to Perfectionism* study cited at the beginning of this chapter had these findings to share about men where their need for perfection takes the lead:

- 38% of men and 34% of women believe that being perfect for their romantic partner is the only way to avoid being dumped.

- 27% of men and 20% of women believe the only way to gain respect from others is to be wealthy.

- 24% of men and 21% of women refuse to talk about their faults because they're afraid that others will look down on them.

The Negative Impacts of Social Media

This perfectionism-fostering bias runs rampant through social media as well. In fact, the National Health Service in the UK did a study that found 28.2% of 16- to 24-year-olds have a mental health condition, with one in four women aged 16 to 24 experiencing anxiety, depression, panic disorder, phobia, or obsessive-compulsive disorder, specifically noting the impact of social media.

Mental illness soars among young women – England – survey (2016), Campbell, D., et al., https://www.theguardian.com/lifeandstyle/2016/sep/29/self-harm-ptsd-and-mental-illness-soaring-among-young-women-in-england-survey

The Guardian article we noted earlier in this chapter gathered personal stories about women's experiences of overwhelming pressure to be perfect both at work and at home, some pointing the finger directly at social media. For example, Miranda, 18, from Cambridge, said this:

The pressure of perfection: five women tell their stories (2016), Sarah Marsh, https://www.theguardian.com/commentisfree/2016/oct/14/perfect-girls-five-women-stories-mental-health

> "I certainly feel the pressure to be perfect, and it has got to the point where it's damaging my health. Social media is the main culprit. I had to delete my Instagram account because it would actually make me cry. I am a mature person with a firm grip on reality, but I have so many peers whose lives seem so perfect and sociable that it left me feeling worthless and lonely."

Whether they were young working moms, career women of color, or college students, they all shared similar experiences of the need to be perfect as they continually compared themselves to others — to other moms, to other colleagues, to other college students who all seemed to "have it all together." Yet what they each shared was that eventually, they learned that perfectionism is just an unattainable illusion that was making them feel terrible and even unhealthy in their bodies.

Lotta, a 22-year-old student and single mother, said:

"I am quite critical of myself as a single parent. I am conscious of trying to portray myself online and to family as the perfect mother and now I am at university I also want to be a perfect student.

"I made a conscious decision only very recently to limit time spent on social media. I did not want it to impact on how I viewed my life with my daughter and what I could and could not provide for her. The best thing I can give her is a mum who's totally happy and present in the here and now — she doesn't care that her mum isn't a size six or that the flat gets cluttered."

And Chardene, 31, from London, exemplified the added pressures on women of color:

"The pressure to be perfect feels heightened to me as a black woman because my mum always told me I would have to work harder than a white person to get ahead. It's true, but it's a self-defeating aspiration.

"Perfection, or what society deems perfect, is not attainable for everyone, but it feels even further away for a woman of color. The image of perfection is a certain physical type: a skinny woman with blond hair, etc. Those things are not even half attainable to you, and you sometimes feel you were born imperfect."

Overcoming Perfectionism — Don't Be A "Should-Head"

Perfectionism, a relentless pursuit of flawlessness and an aversion to making mistakes, affects individuals from all walks of life. But this chapter has shown why it is essential to recognize that perfectionism can manifest differently in men and women, often influenced by societal and cultural expectations.

Now let's delve into some of the thinking errors that can lead women to perfectionism and, more importantly, share 11 practical tips to help you overcome them. To embrace your Flawsome self and achieve a healthier, more balanced life.

Another textbook showed a variety of unconscious ways that our minds can get caught in a pattern of perfectionistic thinking.

Cognitive-Behavioral Treatment of Perfectionism (2014), Sarah Egan, Tracey Wade, Roz Shafran, and Martin Antony, pg. 291 (our list of thinking errors is adapted from theirs)

Ladies, which of these rings true for you? Check off all the ones that resonate with you that you might like to change on your move to becoming more flawsome.

Negative Labels Thinking –
Sounds like: *"I messed up. I'm such a loser and screw-up!"*

"Shoulding" on Yourself Thinking –
Sounds like: *"I should be doing better than I am because my peers are doing better."*

Catastrophizing Thinking –
Sounds like: *"What If I get this wrong and then I get fired, then I'll be broke and homeless!"*

Crystal Ball Thinking –
Sounds like: *"My colleagues must have thought my presentation was terrible as they were looking at their phones."*

Glass is Empty Thinking –
Sounds like: *Because I made a bad dessert, the whole meal was ruined."*

Two-Faced Thinking –
Sounds like: *"It is okay for others to make spelling mistakes, but certainly not okay for me."*

Dramatized Thinking –
Sounds like: *"Because I forgot my child at school, I am a failure as a human being."*

Emotional Thinking –
Sounds like: *"I feel super anxious; therefore, I know I am going to do poorly on my exam."*

Martyr Thinking –
Sounds like: *"If my work team does not win the bid, it is entirely my fault."*

If any of these resonated with you, you're not alone. As human beings, we tend to be much harder on ourselves and overly critical of our performance. It's when the negative dialogue we have with ourselves becomes paralyzing that it's time to seek some support.

Here are 11 concrete suggestions to help you start to reset and rewire your thinking from perfectionistic to Flawsomist:

Practical Tips for Women to Go from Fearful to Flawsome

1. Remember You Are Enough: Oftentimes, the limiting belief of not being enough is the underlying cause driving perfectionism. Recognize your strengths and your shame triggers. Self-reflection and curiosity can help dial down the inner critic as you learn to give yourself self-love and acceptance instead. As you acknowledge the presence of perfectionistic tendencies in your life and embrace your flawsomeness, you're expanding your emotional intelligence and peace of mind.

2. Practice the 80/20 Rule: Ask yourself which 20% of what you do gets you 80% of what you want? This starts to retrain your brain that the ideal of 100% perfection is not required and, with repetition, can quiet the mind and calm the body.

3. Learn to Delegate: Instead of thinking "No one else can do it as well as I can," consider all the time you'll have instead to focus on other things or relax with family and friends. And realize that the fresh perspective and actions of another person on your project can potentially teach you something new as well.

4. Get out of the Weeds: Learn to take breaks from the perfectionistic overachieving to step back and see the bigger picture of what you want to accomplish. These pauses can give you a fresh perspective on what's important vs. what is urgent so you can reprioritize your day instead of getting caught up in the "just work harder" mentality or perfectionism-driven procrastination.

5. Practice Self-Compassion: Treat yourself with kindness and understanding, especially during moments of failure or imperfection. Think about the compassion you would show a loved one in the same situation. Replace self-criticism with self-compassion as you release the negative thought loops dragging you down.

6. Stop Minimizing Yourself: Too often, women push aside compliments and recognition for their achievements. When someone offers you a compliment for who you are, what you've achieved, or how you look, say "Thank You," allowing yourself to take in their kind words and praise that you deserve as you embrace your flawsomeness.

7. Limit Social Media: Reduce exposure to social media platforms that promote constant comparison. Unfollow accounts that trigger feelings of inadequacy or shame and focus on your own journey and well-being.

8. Celebrate Yourself & Your Progress: Shift your focus from achieving the perfect end result to the progress you make along the way. Celebrate your efforts and achievements, no matter how small they may seem to be. This naturally gives your brain a mood boost of the neurotransmitter dopamine (a.k.a. one of your happy chemicals!).

9. Embrace Your Mistakes: Embrace mistakes as valued learning opportunities. Analyze what went wrong, how you can improve, and then move forward with newfound wisdom and clarity, knowing what you now know that you didn't before.

"You know, I would say define failure as not trying. Because actually going for things and falling flat on your face is fine. It's a learning experience. It makes you stronger. But if you don't try and if you don't actually follow your dreams or even admit what they are and go for it, that's something that will stay with you. So the idea is go for it."

— Amal Clooney, 2022 CNN panel discussion, https://www.youtube.com/watch?v=bzNke_GYGHg

10. Redefine Success: Re-evaluate your definition of success. Shift your perspective from seeking external validation and comparison to other people's standards to prioritizing your own personal fulfillment and overall well-being through your unique contributions to the world. Notice if you're "striving for excellence" or if your idea of success is causing toxic perfectionism instead. Be willing to adjust your expectations for greater peace of mind and confidence. Establish achievable goals that allow room for mistakes and setbacks.

11. You Are Not Alone: Reach out to a friend, coach, counselor, or hypnotherapist who can provide emotional support and guidance as you navigate the challenges of releasing the obstacles of perfectionistic thinking.

And gentlemen, if these resonated with you as well, it's a good indication that you're in touch with your feminine side!

Perfectionism can be challenging for both women and men to overcome, but it is not insurmountable. As shown in our research, women often tend to bear more of the burden of perfectionism. By implementing these practical tips for moving from fearful to flawsome, you can take meaningful steps toward breaking free from the suffocating grip of it in all areas of your life.

Remember that perfection is an unattainable illusion, but self-acceptance and personal growth are achievable goals that lead to a more satisfying, fulfilling, and flawsome life.

Chapter 6: Journal Prompts to help you start living Flawsomely

These are intended to get you thinking, not judging yourself. Take some quiet time to thoughtfully and honestly respond to these questions to create your own positive shifts in your perspectives around perfectionism.

- What's one part of you that you feel is flawed, less than perfect? How can you embrace this part of you whole-heartedly instead?

- When a perfectionistic negative thought loop starts to play on repeat in your mind, what empowering thought would you like to tell yourself instead?

- What's on your Imperfect Win list? Take time to write down in a special notebook the small, medium or large wins you've accomplished in each day. When your perfectionism starts to take over, refer to your Imperfect Win list to remind you of what's possible at less than 100%.

Intergenerational Trauma, Epigenetics, and Perfectionism

"There is little we can do to change the way we were treated when we were young, or our genes or body chemistry. In contrast, you can learn to change the way you think about things."

— David D. Burns

Perfectionism isn't new to us. Not to men or women. Research shows us how it has been handed down through the ages, one generation at a time. We're now learning that a blend of genetic and environmental factors contribute to this chain of perfectionist thinking.

Falling Into The Perfectionism Trap

You might find it surprising that a growing body of research on intergenerational trauma and epigenetics is demonstrating how these perfectionist tendencies get passed down from parent to child through both genetics and environmental factors. These studies suggest that a variety of extreme physical and psychological stresses, such as childhood abuse, family violence, food insecurity, and severe trauma caused by war, amongst other things, can be passed down from one generation to the next.

Epigenetics is the scientific study of the biological control mechanisms of DNA, the light switches that turn

E.g., *The Structure of Perfectionism: A Twin Study* (2004), Tozzi, F., et al., https://www.researchgate.net/publication/8391595_The_Structure_of_Perfectionism_A_Twin_Study; *Genetic and environmental contributions to perfectionism and its common factors* (2015), Iranzo-Tatay, C., et al., https://www.sciencedirect.com/science/article/abs/pii/S0165178115306752; *Perfectionism and Neuroticism: Evidence for a common genetic and environmental etiology* (2021), Burcas, S., et al., https://pubmed.ncbi.nlm.nih.gov/33454994/

E.g., *War's enduring legacy: How does trauma haunt future generations?* (2023), Tori DeAngelis, https://www.apa.org/topics/trauma/trauma-survivors-generations

a gene on or off, thus controlling how or why your genes are expressed in the ways that they are. There are many factors that play into the on/off switches of your genes. Trauma, malnutrition, or environmental toxins are just some of them. Conversely, exposure to positive learning opportunities can also be a factor which then develops into our habits of thinking about ourselves (good or bad) and our perceived need for perfection in a variety of different ways.

One of the first published articles to note the presence of intergenerational trauma appeared in 1966, when Canadian psychiatrist Vivian M. Rakoff, MD, and colleagues documented high rates of psychological distress among children of Holocaust survivors. Since then, researchers have been assessing anxiety, depression, and PTSD in trauma survivors and their progeny, with Holocaust survivors and their children the most widely studied, and for the longest period of time.

Addressing the question of the genetic component, another study has found that self-oriented perfectionism heritability was estimated to be 30% in girls and 23% in boys. And socially prescribed perfectionism heritability was measured at 42% in girls and 38% in boys.

Through our own research and interviewing an array of people from different backgrounds and age groups, we found our own supporting evidence of epigenetics at work.

Thomas Rosenberg is a 2nd generation holocaust survivor and shared his experience of growing up with the beliefs that his father and grandfather, who grew up in the late 1800s and early 1900s in Germany, both instilled in him. One was that in the Jewish community, "Education was one thing no one could take from you until you die."

Children and families of concentration camp survivors (1966), Rakoff, V., et al., Can Ment Health. 1967;14:24–26 (text not found online); for more recent study and references see e.g., *Transgenerational transmission of trauma and resilience: a qualitative study with Brazilian offspring of Holocaust survivors* (2012), Braga, L., et al., https://www.ncbi.nlm.nih.gov/pmc/articles/PMC3500267/

Genetic and environmental contributions to perfectionism and its common factors (2015), Iranzo-Tatay, C., et al., https://www.sciencedirect.com/science/article/abs/pii/S0165178115306752

And another,

"If you're going to do something, do it perfectly,
or don't bother starting it."

His grandfather, who fought in World War I, was highly educated, as were all the men in his family. He was led to believe if you didn't have a Ph.D., you were "just an apprentice." And there were only three professions that were "good enough:" Medicine, Law, and Banking.

But even that wasn't enough, he told Michele:

"There was a certain way that you had to think,
that you had to show up. And especially as a male,
you were expected to cultivate other skills as well.
You had to be a Renaissance man, too."

These professions require a certain kind of linear thinking, which, for Thomas, was just different from how his brain works. He sees the unique connections between things and the interplay of different systems, concepts, or problems. This led him to believe from an early age that it wasn't okay to show up as himself.

He had to be perfect to feel accepted by his own family and their impossibly high standards.

And if those high standards weren't met, the full weight of tarnishing the family honor was brought upon him. It was a heavy load that he carried for many years, going from college preparatory school to college at the University of Colorado Boulder, studying International Affairs and Asian Studies, including learning Japanese and French. He went on to achieve two master's degrees, one in environmental science and policy from Johns Hopkins University and an MBA from Thunderbird School of Global Management.

It had been less than 24 hours since receiving his first master's degree when his father and uncle didn't congratulate him on his accomplishment but asked him, almost in unison, "So when are you getting your Ph.D.?" With all of his accolades and accomplishments, the most recognition he received from his father years later was overhearing a comment made to a family friend, "Well, two master's degrees is almost like a Ph.D., so yeah, I'm proud of him."

He now considers himself a "recovering perfectionist." When Michele asked him how he would rate his current perfectionistic tendencies on a scale from 1 to 10, he still rates himself at a 6 or 7 (10 being a Super Perfectionist).

So, while he has been able to dial down his need for perfectionism in all areas of his life, it is a habit of thought that runs deep and is embedded in the very cells of his being.

Beyond DNA Determinism

Can Trauma Be Passed Down From One Generation to the Next? (2022), Karina Margit Edelyi, https://www.psycom.net/trauma/epigenetics-trauma

A recent article quoted Dr. Chris Mason, associate professor at Weill Cornell Medicine and director of the Mason Lab, on the rapid advances in epigentic research:

> "The field of epigenetics gained real traction about a decade ago, when scientists published seminal research on the Dutch Hunger Winter, an extended period of famine that took place towards the end of World War II when the Nazis blocked food supplies in October 1944, thrusting much of the Netherlands into famine. When the Dutch were liberated in May 1945, more than 20,000 had died of starvation. Pregnant women were particularly vulnerable, and the famine impacted the unborn children for the rest of their lives."

"Scientists found that those who had been in utero during the famine were a few pounds heavier than average. (The thinking goes that the mothers, because they were starving, automatically quieted a gene in their unborn children involved in burning the body's fuel.) When the children reached middle age, they had higher LDL ("bad") cholesterol and triglyceride levels. They also suffered higher rates of obesity, diabetes, cardiovascular disease, and schizophrenia. When scientists looked into why, they found that these children carried a specific chemical mark — an epigenetic signature — on one of their genes."

The writer summed up the state of current research this way:

"What would have seemed preposterous 20 years ago has become a fast-emerging field of study. Today the idea that a person's experience could alter their biology, and the behavior of their children and grandchildren, has gained serious traction. Animal and some smaller human studies have shown that exposure to stressors like immense stress or cold *can trigger metabolic changes in subsequent generations.*"

The research of psychoanalyst Galit Atlas has also shown that trauma can indeed be passed from one generation to the next, invading the psyche of a child invitro from the inside out. When a baby is forming and growing in the mother's womb, it is enveloped by the energy, hormones, and emotions of the mother.

Emotional Inheritance: A Therapist, Her Patients, and The Legacy of Trauma (2022), Galit Atlas, PhD

That embryonic fluid is full of the mother's fears, anxieties, ideas of perfectionism, and her self-doubt. Imagine the trials, traumas, and tragedies that your mother, your grandmother, and even your great-grandmother have gone through. Perhaps you know some of them, but oftentimes, we don't, as those old wounds get hidden away in the dark corners of our minds and hearts, locked away for the ages.

Examples of intergenerational trauma include the negative impacts of surviving wars, slavery, and the holocaust as the survival behaviors and triggers in a person's nervous system remain.

Regardless of your gender identity, these psychological scars are unconsciously handed down, as they leave a chemical mark on a person's DNA, which is then passed along to the next generation. This continues to happen until we become aware of the emotional patterns those scars have left on us, and we break the cycle.

Evidence of intergenerational trauma as a result of any of the major events listed above include:

- PTSD
- Domestic violence
- Low-self esteem
- Depression
- Poverty consciousness
- Codependency
- Hypervigilance
- Unhealthy attachment styles
- Difficulty trusting others
- Mental health conditions
- Substance abuse

Flipping the Gene Switches: Going From Fixed to Flawsome

In Michele's work with clients who've become caught in a cycle of emotional fear that is ingrained in their nervous system, she helps them through applied neuroscience. Her methods allow them to break free of those old patterns and build new neural pathways in their brains that then override and replace the old, well-worn grooves in their mind, body, and spirit.

Her work of over two decades as a coach and hypnotherapist was born out of her own life experience. Michele adopted perfectionistic tendencies in her work based on the imprints and environment of her own family. Her parents, both successful entrepreneurs and highly regarded pillars of the community have always operated from very high standards in all they achieved.

Michele remembers growing up, "Everything in our house was always in perfect order."

While it was never spoken of directly, and her parents were always loving and supportive of her efforts, the unspoken message was "make sure that everything is done really well, top-notch." This was further exacerbated by following in the footsteps of her older sister and brother and their successes while working in the family businesses and beyond.

This fostered a level of perfectionism in her work that then morphed into imposter syndrome when she was bullied out of her high-tech job. While it was a painful experience, it was a wake-up call for Michele and pointed her in the direction of her true calling and purpose as a coach and hypnotherapist, leading to a lifelong love of learning about what makes us tick as human beings.

Through her work, she has learned that the key to breaking intergenerational trauma is doing our own emotional work. Taking the time and effort to process our own history, pain, and patterns, so that we can release them from our system once and for all and not continue to pass them along inadvertently to those we love.

"The unexamined life repeats itself and reverberates through the generations, and doing the emotional work starts with us."
— *Galit Atlas, Ph.D*

Tom offers a specific example from his childhood that illustrates how we are not stuck with either an unalterable set of DNA instructions or the messaging conveyed by our parents. Growing up, whenever he performed chores or built something on his own, his father often focused on the imperfections and said, "You'd better get a good education because you'll never make a living with your hands."

Like most kids, Tom idolized his father and wanted to imitate his wide-ranging skills with tools, from backyard mechanics to carpentry and more. The "never good enough" messaging hurt.

But somewhere along the way, Tom's determination to make his father proud of those manual labor efforts — and the perfectionist standards that were attached — shifted. Perhaps it was when his high school "cred" came to include basic car repair for his friends. Or on that pool-building job when he advanced in the company from helper to crew-chief to opening a second installation center in Central New York and then training crews in Canada over the course of five summers.

While he could still see the occasional flaws, his work in those settings had also proved good enough.

Your Natural Instinct as Parents

As parents, our natural instinct is to protect our children. To not inflict pain on them and to prevent them from feeling our own pain. Yet, if you were raised by a strict parent or a caregiver who demanded perfection of you all the time, you will carry these habits and beliefs forward with you throughout your life. Unless you make the effort to release those old beliefs from your conscious and subconscious mind.

The challenge is that children are tuned into their parents, as their very survival depends on the adults in their lives. Children often think their parents are infallible. Dr. Atlas shares:

> "Children register not only what their parents say but also their non-verbal cues. What they don't say or what they hide. Research on parent-infant communication indicates that babies respond to their parent's implicit signals from birth and 'read' their minds."

Thus, a person's habits of perfectionism, which they learned as children, are picked up on by their own children, as the energy, atmosphere, and environment those children are being nurtured in unconsciously perpetuate the cycle of perfectionism.

In the next chapter, we'll discuss how you can work to break the cycle of perfectionism and avoid passing it on to your children.

Chapter 7: Journal Prompts to help you start living Flawsomely

These are intended to get you thinking, not judging yourself. Take some quiet time to thoughtfully and honestly respond to these questions to create your own positive shifts in your perspectives around perfectionism.

- Reflect on the lives of your parents or caregivers. What hardships, challenges, or traumas did they experience? What did their parents experience?

- What habits, characteristics, or patterns might you have unconsciously adopted early in life from your caregivers?

- Can you trace some of your own feelings of perfectionism back to your grandparents or great-grandparents? How are those patterns holding you back now from greater happiness and resilience?

Chapter 8

Kintsugi Kids

*"Every good enough mother teaches her child
that no matter how bad it seems – no matter how
many rejections or scraped knees or broken bones
there are – it is going to be okay.
Maybe not the way we wanted
or hoped it would be,
but still okay."*

— Geneen Roth

We opened this book with Tom's confession about that sign proclaiming, "Good enough . . . isn't," which hung on his office wall years ago. And worse, how that sign became one way he passed at least some of his perfectionism onto his kids.

A glimpse of the potential harm from his behavior came when his family lived through the horror of his daughter's high school classmate committing suicide. The circumstances seemed all too familiar from the many news reports of suicidal teens who seem to have so much going for them, and their despair somehow kept invisible even to those closest to them. This young man fit the profile, high achieving and popular, with no one suspecting how much he was struggling.

While Tom doesn't pretend the light of understanding went on in that dark moment or that he made immediate and dramatic changes in his own behavior, he now looks back on that event as a turning point. He talked with his family, read, and talked with other parents, teachers, and school officials. The topics of unrealistic expectations and pressures around academics, arts, sports, and college admissions were prominent.

He feels lucky and grateful that his kids did not succumb to those pressures. We've learned since then how common and toxic perfectionism can be for children and adolescents. As researchers bluntly put it:

> "Recent findings suggest that perfectionism is highly prevalent among children and adolescents, and perfectionism can be quite destructive in terms of its links with anxiety, depression, and suicide."

A proposed framework for preventing perfectionism and promoting resilience and mental health among vulnerable children and adolescents (2014), Flett, G., & Hewitt, P., https://psycnet.apa.org/record/2014-37990-001. The same authors have more recently published a textbook, *Perfectionism in Childhood and Adolescence: A Developmental Approach* (2022), in which they devote whole chapters to "Perfectionsm and Depression" and "Perfectionism and the Suicidal Adolescent."

If I'd Known Then . . .

Embracing imperfection includes acknowledging that we've always been imperfect. Tom's parenting was no exception. That silly sign and his own mindset were hardly the only examples.

But as we discussed in Chapter 3, once we've accepted our flaws, we're opening up all sorts of opportunities to learn and grow and become . . . more flawsome! So we kept learning, and when Tom first decided to write this book, he knew it had to cover what he wished he'd known about how to do better back then.

A word of warning, though. As you probably suspected, and Michele and Tom both seem to keep relearning, there is no magic formula. There is no one-size-fits-all list of tips and tactics that will save every child.

Once it became clear that perfectionism has multiple dimensions (e.g., self-directed, other-directed, socially-prescribed) and multiple harmful effects (e.g., anxiety, depression, eating disorders, suicide), researchers began advocating "the need for a complex, nuanced approach" tailored to the individual. They suggest focusing on:

> "cognitive and emotional regulation vulnerabilities of perfectionists and their ... beliefs about ability, the self, and the meaning of failure."

We spent some time with that last phrase, *the meaning of failure*, in Chapter 4, focusing on the benefits that flow from getting comfortable with failure. Being willing to risk it and encounter it, over and over. That might even provide a test for the value of the practical suggestions we'll summarize here:

Pgs. 42-48. See also, the Amal Clooney quote on pg. 88.

> Will this tactic help this particular young person better understand imperfection?

We emphasize particular young person because the key takeaway from the research is in the differences that exist among perfectionists. We are all unique — including in the ways we acquire and hold onto perfectionist traits.

The very core of flawsomism lies in accepting and then rejoicing in our differences, instead of treating them as defects or seeing someone else's differences as an ideal to be enivied and chased.

"All things are literally better, lovelier, and more beloved for their imperfections."

— John Ruskin

Since perfectionists, too, carry different mixes of the emotional and intellectual traits that make up that mindset, we'll explore a range of approaches from both science and parents.

The Science

Some of the harmful effects of perfectionism shown across numerous studies are depression, anxiety, eating disorders, and burnout. Research shows that 25-30% of teens suffer from "maladaptive perfectionism," i.e, striving for unrealistic perfection to the point of causing them pain. Sadly, these numbers have increased by 33% over the last three decades largely because of:

How Perfectionism in Children and Teens Impacts Mental Health (2022), https://www.newportacademy.com/resources/empowering-teens/perfectionism-in-children/

- Comparison promoted by social media

- More controlling parenting styles

- Tough competition to get into top colleges

Our own survey data is even more alarming: nearly two-thirds (64%) reported feeling pressure to be perfect in childhood, and more than half (53%) said it interfered with their "performance (e.g., willingness to try something new, take risks, or turn in assignments on time) or [their] relationships with others."

Signs to look for as toxic perfectionism shows up in children and teens:

- Holding themselves to unrealistically high standards

- A heightened sensitivity to flaws or mistakes

- Interpreting mistakes as complete failures

- Tendencies to have rigid all-or-nothing thinking

- Extremely critical of self or others

- Intense anxiety around possible failure

- Trouble completing assignments because they're "never good enough"

- Procrastination to avoid difficult tasks

These imperfect perceptions of themselves can lead children and teens to a place of procrastination, paralysis, not even trying, or complete burnout from overcompensation. Or, as the researchers warn, anxiety, depression, and suicide.

Unconsciously Creating Perfectionists

As parents, it's natural to want the best for your children. You pour love and attention into them with the best intentions of creating happy, healthy, and well-balanced humans that grow into well-adapted adults.

This section is based on Michele's research and work with parents, see e.g., *7 Ways Parents Unconsciously Undermine Their Own Children's Well-Being: Children aren't perfect* (2023), Michele Molitor, https://michelemolitor.com/2023/03/16/7-ways-parents-unconsciously-undermine-their-own-childrens-well-being/

However, sometimes, our well-meaning actions can lead to unintended consequences. One such consequence is creating mini-perfectionists, kids who grow up believing that anything less than perfect is a failure, which can wreak havoc on their sense of self-worth, self-esteem, and self-love. Nobody intends to raise children who become perfectionists, and yet it happens.

There are four "official" parenting types stemming from the work of developmental psychologist Diana Baumrind in the 1960s, which have since been expanded by parenting experts to include other "unofficial" styles. These include: authoritarian, permissive, attachment, free-range, and more, that can inadvertently lead to your child becoming a perfectionist.

What Are the Different Parenting Styles? (2021), Barbara Brody, https://www.webmd.com/parenting/features/parenting-styles

If you are someone who grew up with parents who were overly critical in various ways, some of these may ring true for you. Be mindful of the habits and patterns you've inherited from your caregivers, and determine which healthy habits you'd like to pass along to your children in a good way.

Here are seven ways parents unconsciously create perfectionists:

1. Overpraising — "everyone gets a trophy": Praising your child for everything they do, even for things that are not extraordinary, can be detrimental to their self-esteem. It can create a sense of pressure and expectation always to do things perfectly. Instead, focus on praising your child's effort and progress and provide constructive feedback that will help them improve all along the way.

2. Overprotecting — "momma bear": Overprotecting your child can prevent them from developing important life skills and independence. It can also make them feel incapable of dealing with challenges or failure, having them constantly seeking outside validation for their efforts. Allow your child to experience setbacks and teach them how to overcome obstacles. Encourage them to try new things, take risks, and learn from their mistakes.

3. Micromanaging — "helicopter parents": Micromanaging your child's life can create a sense of dependence and lack of autonomy. Allow your child to make their own (age-appropriate) decisions, guiding them when necessary to find effective solutions to the situation at hand. Encourage them to take responsibility for their actions and learn from their mistakes.

4. Setting unrealistic expectations — "tiger parents": Setting unrealistic expectations for your child and their success can create a sense of pressure and anxiety, which can lead to a host of issues such as eating disorders, depression, IBS (Inflammatory Bowel Syndrome), and more. It can also make them believe that anything less than perfect is unacceptable and that they're never enough. Instead, set realistic goals and expectations that are achievable and meaningful to your child and age-appropriate.

5. Criticizing mistakes — "judgmental parents": Criticizing your child's mistakes can create a fear of failure and give them a sense of inadequacy. Instead, help them understand that mistakes are a natural part of the learning process and encourage them to learn from their mistakes. Remind them that there is no such thing as failure, only opportunities for learning. Offer your kids constructive feedback that will help them improve rather than criticism that will discourage them from trying.

6. Comparing them to others — "insecure parents": Comparing your child to others (whether their siblings or those outside the family) can create a sense of inferiority and a belief that they are not good enough. It can also lead to a sense of competition that can be detrimental to their relationships with others. Social media already does this, creating false personas of "perfect" people in the world. Instead, focus on your child's unique strengths and talents and help them develop their own unique sense of identity that embraces all of who they are.

7. Being overly critical of oneself — "perfectionist parents": Being overly critical of yourself can create a negative environment that can affect your child's self-esteem. It can also make them believe that perfectionism is the only way to achieve success. Instead, model self-compassion and self-acceptance and encourage your child to do the same. Reminding them that they are perfectly imperfect just as they are.

Parenting is a lifelong, challenging task. There is no one-size-fits-all approach. And there is certainly no instruction manual. However, being aware of these seven ways we, as parents, unconsciously undermine our children's well-being, inadvertently creating a budding perfectionist, can help us make more conscious and informed parenting choices.

How do we distinguish between a healthy striving to be a high achiever versus toxic perfectionism? By focusing on building a healthy sense of self-esteem, autonomy, and resilience. Doing this helps children develop into confident and capable adults who are not afraid of the challenges and setbacks that life inevitably brings us all.

Curb Your Enthusiasm

What can you do as an adult to curb your overly enthusiastic perfectionist habits and prevent passing them along to your children?

The tips in this section are based on an article by Michele in *Brainz* magazine: *Unlocking Resilience For Busy Professional Parents – Overcome Perfectionism & Raise Happy Kids* (2023), https:// www.brainzmagazine.com/post/ unlocking-resilience-for-busy-professional-parents-overcome-perfectionism-raise-happy-kids

Here are 11 strategies to keep in mind to help foster a positive and nurturing environment for your family that builds confidence, enabling your kids to thrive.

1. Self-awareness and Acceptance: First and foremost, recognize and accept your own tendencies towards perfectionism. The first step in breaking the cycle is to be aware of it. Journaling, meditation, or therapy can help you reflect on your behavior and its origins.

2. Model healthy self-talk: Be conscious of the language you use when you talk about yourself and your accomplishments. Avoid overly critical self-talk and focus on positive aspects and the effort you put in rather than solely on outcomes.

3. Normalize Mistakes: We ALL make mistakes in life, big and small. Show your child that making mistakes is a part of learning and growing. Share stories of your own mistakes and the lessons you learned from them. Teach them that perfection isn't the goal but rather progress and effort. Adopt the motto "practice makes progress."

4. Praise Effort, Not Results: When we always focus on being the best, we can easily get caught in the vicious cycle of "striving" and never "arriving." Help yourself and your kids enjoy the process along the way of doing their best. Praise your child's hard work, determination, and effort. This reinforces the value of the process over the outcome.

5. Set Realistic Expectations: It's easy as adults to always raise the bar on yourself to get better results. This also leads to exhaustion and burnout. Imagine what that can do to the mind of your child. It can create a cycle of "Never Enough" thinking on their part that can last a lifetime if not nipped in the bud.

As a parent, set achievable and realistic expectations for both yourself and your children. Remember that it's okay not to excel in everything and that having areas of weakness is natural. Help your child focus on personal growth and individual progress.

6. Keep a Flexible Mindset: Reminding ourselves to be flexible and seek alternative options and solutions can be empowering and lower anxiety levels. Encouraging adaptability and resilience in children can help them think more intentionally. Emphasize the importance of being able to adjust to different situations and not being too rigid or set in one's ways.

This can be modeled through your own behavior, such as changing plans when something doesn't work out and not getting overly stressed about it. Encourage them to see challenges as opportunities to grow.

7. Communicate Openly: Your kids are always watching, listening, and modeling your behaviors. By cultivating a household where feelings, fears, and anxieties can be openly discussed without judgment, you are teaching your children how to be more empathetic with others. If your child expresses fears of not being good enough, be compassionate and reassure them of their worth beyond achievements.

8. Make Time for Play: As adults, we all know the value of taking time away from work to refresh and recharge our mindsets. The same holds true for your kids and their schoolwork. Ensure there's ample time for unstructured play and leisure. Not everything needs to have a goal or a purpose. This allows children to explore, be creative, and enjoy activities without the pressure of getting some expected result.

9. Limit Comparisons: Social media has created a platform for endless comparison of self to others, fueling the internal conversations of not being enough in a thousand different ways. Adults and children alike can easily fall into this comparison trap, leading to perfectionism, self-doubt, anxiety, and depression, or worse. Avoid comparing your child to siblings, peers, or even yourself when you were their age.

Each of us is on our own journey, which includes our unique strengths and weaknesses. Celebrate your children's distinctive qualities and achievements so they feel seen and heard for who they ARE, not who you expect them to be.

10. Model Self-care: As previously discussed, the science of epigenetics tells us that habits and survival behaviors can be passed along to our children. By taking care of your mental well-being and addressing your own fears and anxieties that are fueling your perfectionism, you're modeling good self-care and self-awareness for your children.

As your child sees you practicing self-care and self-love, they are more likely to do the same. Conversely, if they see you constantly stressed and striving for perfection, they might also internalize those behaviors.

11. Seek Professional Help: If your perfectionism is deeply rooted and affecting your well-being or your relationship with your child, consider seeking therapy, coaching, or hypnotherapy. A professional can offer tools and strategies to manage and reduce these tendencies. It can also be beneficial for your child to see that seeking help is a sign of strength, not weakness.

By implementing these strategies, you can, as a parent, create a nurturing environment where your children feel valued for who they are and not just for their achievements. Over time, this can help reduce the risk of your child developing debilitating perfectionist tendencies while also more effectively managing your own perfectionistic habits.

> *"Parenting has nothing to do with perfection. Perfection isn't even the goal, not for us, not for our children. Learning together to live well in an imperfect world, loving each other despite or even because of our imperfections, and growing as humans while we grow our little humans, those are the goals of gentle parenting."*
>
> — L.R. Knost, *The Gentle Parent*

How to Model Flawsomism for Your Children

Can we agree that we've all had a variety of life experiences as kids that "left a mark"?

From an event as simple as falling off your bike, getting all scraped up, or getting teased by a sibling . . .

To the complex neglect and abuse that so many children quietly suffer from in their homes because they don't know who to turn to or don't feel safe talking to the adults in the house.

No matter whether the mark was left emotionally or physically, our hearts, minds, and bodies remember those events. And these marks left on our psyche become the drivers of our behaviors to stay safe in the world.

They color how we see, act, and react to all sorts of things that happen in our lives, both personally and professionally, which can lead to a host of things, from self-doubt to perfectionism to a lack of confidence.

There are certain phrases and questions that children need to hear and experience to enhance their sense of self-esteem and self-worth. Helping them to grow up to be confident adults in today's challenging world and embrace their flawesomeness without the need to be a perfectionist.

Tapping into our collective work over the years, we've identified six areas parents should model for their kids and what they can say to help their children feel seen, heard, and understood. Thus preventing perfectionism from creeping into their subconscious and malleable minds.

1. Unconditional Love and Acceptance: Regardless of their achievements or behavior, all kids need to feel loved and accepted for who they are. They need to know that they are loved even when they fall short of expectations or make mistakes.

This can sound like:

- *"I love you unconditionally just the way you are."*

- *"It's ok to make mistakes – that's how we learn."*
- *"I'm proud of you for trying your best."*

2. Validate Their Feelings and Experiences: Kids need to know that their feelings matter and are valid. That their emotions are normal and they have a right to express their feelings. It's important that they know you're paying attention and are interested in their experiences.

This can sound like:

- *"Thank you for sharing your feelings with me."*
- *"It's ok that you're feeling [insert emotion here]."*
- *"I'm sorry you're going through that; what can I do to help?"*

3. Praise for Effort and Progress: It's important to praise and recognize kids for their efforts, not just their achievements. This helps them learn that mistakes are part of life and not everything is going to be perfect. This helps them to feel seen and valued for what they're trying to accomplish.

This can sound like:

- *"I'm proud of you for your efforts! I can see how much progress you've made."*
- *"You're doing a great job on [insert specific task here]!"*
- *"It's ok if you didn't get it right the first time. We can work on it together."* Or, *"Would you like some help with it?"*

4. Opportunities for Independence and Decision Making: Kids today have the world at their fingertips through smartphones and often can figure many things out simply by "Googling" it. Yet we need to remember to guide them and direct them by giving them age-appropriate, real-world tasks to complete on their own and opportunities for making decisions. This will help them to think critically, and seek out answers and solutions through their own lens of experience to expand their mind and feel capable and competent.

This can sound like:

- *"What do you think is the best course of action?"*
- *"Let's talk about the pros and cons of each option."*
- *"I'm here to support you no matter what decision you make."*

5. Consistent and Fair Discipline: Children need to know the rules and boundaries of what's acceptable and what's not through consistent and fair discipline. This gives them guardrails to help them learn and grow in a way that focuses on teaching, not punishment.

This can sound like:

- *"I love you and understand you're upset, but this behavior is unacceptable."*
- *"These are the rules we agreed upon together."*
- *"I'm sorry, but the consequence for breaking the rules is [insert consequence here]."*

6. Positive Role Models: In today's busy world, kids need positive role models that demonstrate healthy coping mechanisms and self-care practices. Remember, a child's brain is like a sponge and absorbs all that it sees, senses, hears, and feels in its environment. They need to see what positive conversations and interactions look like, what healthy self-care is, and be shown that it's ok to prioritize their well-being.

"Everybody is a role model, all the time, if there's another human within seeing or hearing distance. You only get to decide if what you're modeling is positive or negative."
— Tom Collins

This might sound like:

- *"I'm going to take some time to rest and recharge because taking care of ourselves is important"*

- *"I apologize for my mistake, and I'll do better next time."*
- *"I'm proud of you for being honest and showing integrity. That means a lot."*

In today's fast-paced world, it's easy to get caught up in the hustle and bustle of daily life.

Yet, it's important to slow down to meet your children where they are to help them learn and grow. Showing them that you believe in them so they can learn to believe in themselves and know that they matter.

Enabling them to feel enough just as they are and loved for the unique gifts they bring to the world. Assisting them to grow a deeply rooted sense of self-love, self-value, and self-worth each and every day.

Empowering them to become happy, healthy, and confident adults, knowing they are enough and perfectly flawsome just as they are.

Chapter 8: Journal Prompts to help you start living Flawsomely

These are intended to get you thinking, not judging yourself. Take some quiet time to thoughtfully and honestly respond to these questions to create your own positive shifts in your perspectives around perfectionism.

- Reflect on the negative words and phrases that you often heard as a child, and notice if you're passing those on to your kids.

- Write out 3 different ways to encourage your child when they are trying to make something "perfect" that honors their effort and achievement so far.

- Write a love letter to your younger self and/or to the children in your life, telling them all the words or sentiments they need to hear to feel "enough."

Chapter 9

Advanced Adulting

*"Age puzzles me. I thought it was a quiet time. My
70s were interesting and fairly serene, but my 80s are
passionate. I grow more intense as I age. To my own
surprise, I burst out with hot conviction."*

— Florida Scott-Maxwell

As with the other specific groups we've discussed in previous chapters, researchers have found that perfectionism remains harmful as we age. In a seminal study of 450 participants in later life, carried out for 6.5 years, the researchers found that "risk of death was significantly greater for high scorers in perfectionism."

More recently, leading perfectionism researchers Flett and Hewitt called for including the treatment of perfectionism as an essential part of suicide prevention. They reminded that "perfectionism is associated with mental health problems, but also with physical health issues and early mortality," citing that same older adults study.

And the earlier study found further evidence for the paradox we've urged you to embrace. They stated their finding this way:

> "Conversely, risk of death [among their later-life subjects] was significantly lower for high scorers in conscientiousness, extraversion, and optimism."

Conscientiousness readily translates to striving for excellence, and optimism inherently includes embracing today's imperfections as a way toward an even better future life. At every age.

Perfectionism and the five-factor personality traits as predictors of mortality in older adults (2009), Fry, P, et al., https://pubmed.ncbi.nlm.nih.gov/19383652/

The need to focus on perfectionism in suicide assessment, treatment and prevention (2024), Flett, G., and Hewitt, P., https://onlinelibrary.wiley.com/doi/10.1002/wps.21157

Parts of this chapter are based our previous writings, e.g., ***Earning Your Wrinkles & Grey Hair – The Challenges & Triumphs Of Overcoming Perfectionism As You Age*** (2023), Michele Molitor, https://www.brainzmagazine.com/post/earning-your-wrinkles-grey-hair-the-challenges-triumphs-of-overcoming-perfectionism-as-you-age; ***Wise up! How to grow wiser as you age*** (2022), Tom Collins, https://masterbookbuilders.com/wise-up-how-to-grow-wiser-as-you-age/

"Lots of people don't get wise with age, but you don't get wise without aging."

— Joan Erikson

On Teaching Old Dogs New Tricks (2015), Metcalfe, J., et al., https://www.ncbi.nlm.nih.gov/pmc/articles/PMC4679660/; ***Evidences for Adult Hippocampal Neurogenesis in Humans*** (2021), Moreno-Jimenez, E., et al., https://www.jneurosci.org/content/41/12/2541; ***Old Brain, New Neurons?*** (2019), Chelsea Burke, https://sitn.hms.harvard.edu/flash/2019/old-brain-new-neurons/

The wisdom that comes with age is a beautiful thing — much like the gnarled wood of ancient trees or the cracks repaired with the gold on a kintsugi bowl. Or perhaps even the wrinkles that map your experiences and the grey hairs that signify your years. Research over the past few decades has debunked the notion of aging as an inevitable state of decline. Across physical health, cognitive abilities, and emotional well-being, the science has proven we can thrive even at ages well over 50 or 60 when society would like to "put us out to pasture."

While the overall life expectancy in the U.S. has declined slightly in recent years and has lagged behind other developed countries for some time, Americans who do reach elderhood in relatively good health actually have a greater life expectancy than many peer countries. The news regularly shows us examples of men and women at advanced ages competing in sports, publishing a book, or leading an organization.

Tom completed three half-marathons in his late 60s and continues to take on home renovation projects that include the full range of construction work from demo to finishes. Michele's dad, Don Molitor, successfully did 86 push-ups on his 86th birthday just to show the rest of us how to stay healthy and fit!

Studies have confirmed that older adults maintain their ability to learn new information and skills, even outperforming younger subjects in some aspects. We grow new neurons to expand our brains' ability to learn, at least into our 90s. Think of it as adding folds and "wrinkles" inside your head as well as outside!

Attention and executive functions have been shown to improve with age across a large sample study of people ages 58-98.

A great example of this is a family friend of Michele's, author Martha Tolles. Having written 12 novels over her lifetime, at age 102, she is working on her next book! #sharpasatack

Perhaps most importantly, several aspects of our emotional well-being, including social skills, empathy, and resilience, have all been found to improve as we age. Along with those specific criteria, our overall sense of well-being improves, as the classic U-curve studies have shown.

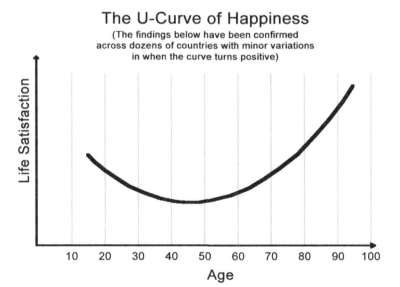

The U-Curve of Happiness
(The findings below have been confirmed across dozens of countries with minor variations in when the curve turns positive)

Evidence that ageing yields improvements as well as declines across attention and executive functions (2021), Verissimo, J., et al., https://www.nature.com/articles/s41562-021-01169-7gov/19383652/

Learning to Love Midlife: 12 Reasons Why Life Gets BETTER with AGE (2024), Chip Conley, pg. 58 ("reseachers have found this U-curve of happiness to be nearly universal across countries"); *The U-Shape of Happiness: A Response* (2021), Blanchflower, D., et al., https://pubmed.ncbi.nlm.nih.gov/34309421/ ("the finding of a U shape is, in our view, one of the most robust patterns in the data in social science"); *Why Aging and Working Makes us Happy in 4 Charts* (2014), https://www.brookings.edu/articles/why-aging-and-working-makes-us-happy-in-4-charts/

Yet, as we pass the milestone age of 50, rich with life experiences, we often find ourselves in a tug-of-war with perfectionism. How do we embrace our perfectly imperfect selves while navigating a culture obsessed with youth and flawlessness?

* Clients have given permission to share their stories while their names have been changed to honor their privacy.

Between Michele and Tom, they've had the joy of working with clients from around the globe of all ages from 7 to 75, so let's explore some client stories* of the challenges and triumphs of overcoming perfectionism as we grow older, earning every wrinkle and grey hair along the way of our advanced adulting adventures!

The Mirror Doesn't Lie, Or Does It?

Resetting and rewiring your thinking is so empowering. Meet Susan, a vibrant 59-year-old woman who used to dread her morning routine. Getting up, getting ready for work, she couldn't help but notice each line and wrinkle on her face as she looked in the mirror. To her, they seemed like a ticking time bomb, eroding her confidence.

"Gaining knowledge and developing skills in pattern recognition does not happen automatically just by getting older. Ya gotta keep doing the work."

— Tom Collins

This less-than-perfect perspective was triggering a free-fall of her self-esteem. She confided in Michele that "I am avoiding social gatherings and even virtual meetings because I'm so afraid of being judged for my aging appearance." This caused her perfectionism to go through the roof and exacerbated her overgiving and people-pleasing, so she felt "liked" and still capable of providing value to her team.

Through her work with Michele, her self-perspective started to shift dramatically. Susan started viewing each wrinkle as a badge of wisdom and experience. She no longer avoided her reflection or social situations; instead, she felt beautiful and wise as she unshackled herself from limiting self-beliefs.

This newfound self-love and acceptance not only elevated her self-esteem, it also dialed down her need for overgiving and people-pleasing, giving her more energy and enthusiasm. This, in turn, improved her professional interactions, as she carried herself with more confidence, poise, and grace, embracing all of her flawsomeness.

To provide some perspective on the beauty of aging, the actress, author, and director Justine Bateman said,

> "I don't have the time or the wherewithal to change other people, all I can do is change how I see things, and in that sense, I can say, 'Fuck it. I'm not changing my face. I think it looks great. Onward.' I want to continue to become even more confident than I am now. And I want to look like Georgia O'Keeffe when I'm really old. How am I going to get there if I do anything to my face?"

The Dilemma of Unrealistic Social Standards

"Perfection is in the eye of the beholder." This belief has been amplified 1000% through social media as we only see the "perfect" images of other people's lives. John is a handsome and successful consultant by many standards. Yet, he found himself constantly scrolling through his social media feed, comparing his 55-year-old self to pictures of his "perfect" 30-year-old self and the celebrities of his generation who seem to defy aging.

"I'm almost too embarrassed to even admit this to you," he sheepishly told Michele in their initial coaching session.

She could sense his fear of aging and losing his edge as he avoided eye contact over their Zoom call. Despite still being healthy and fit with a few minor aches and pains, his mind would go off on tangents of "What If-ing" on himself, leading him down the rabbit hole of another cycle of anxiety and depression for weeks on end. It was negatively affecting his mental health and relationships, not to mention his productivity at work.

Working with Michele, he did some rapid rewiring of his mindset and perspectives, which enabled him to appreciate the resilience and wisdom that come with age. By the completion of their work together, John reported,

> "I feel so much more at home in my current skin; my anxiety levels have significantly improved, which has rejuvenated my relationship with my partner!"

Working on his anxiety and depression, the results were felt not merely by John but by his partner, who, he had reported, suffered as much from John's issues as he did. By the end of the sessions, John started working out again and is in the best shape of his life!

The Job Market's Obsession with Youth

Robert, a 52-year-old executive, felt insecure when competing for promotions against younger professionals in their 30s and 40s. This created a damaging cascade of second-guessing himself and his abilities, negatively impacting his job performance. He shared with Michele,

> "I can't help myself. I end up doing the work of my younger teammates because they just don't get it right. It's easier and faster for me just to do it myself."

He constantly coached younger team members to get their performance up to par to maintain their high quotas. This micromanaging, driven by his need for things to be "just right," created anger and resentment in him as his teammates let him do the extra work. He knew that his work habits were unsustainable as it was taking a toll on his relationship with his wife and kids, taking away precious time with them.

By helping Robert refocus on his strengths, decades of experience, and leadership skills he had earned along the way, he finally realized that knowledge and experience were the kinds of things that can't be learned overnight. He told Michele, "I've started coaching my team more effectively instead of just doing the work for them."

This mindset shift empowered him to own his expertise, increased his self-confidence, and helped him secure a well-deserved promotion, improving his career satisfaction and financial security. It also gave him back hours of time to joyfully spend with his family, which enhanced his well-being, self-worth, and positive mental attitude.

As an article from the Harvard Business Review reminds us,

> "According to the science, for most people, raw mental horsepower declines after the age of 30, but knowledge and expertise — the main predictors of job performance — keep increasing even beyond the age of 80."

So embrace your advanced adulting wisdom and how you can apply it to your work and life.

The Case for Hiring Older Workers (2019), Bersin, J., et al., https://hbr.org/2019/09/the-case-for-hiring-older-workers

For more on the work-related advantages of elders, see Tom's blog post, *Elderships: Filling the Experience Gaps in Your Organization* (2017) (particularly the section "Busting some myths about older workers"), https://masterbookbuilders.com/elderships-filling-the-experience-gaps-in-your-organization/#bustingageistmyths

The Struggle with Imposter Syndrome

Despite a stellar career and many accolades and awards, Lisa, a 58-year-old senior director in high-tech, feared that she wasn't as competent as her peers believed. Her negative self-perception and self-doubt in her full range of abilities and skills created a constant nervous anxiety within her as she was always trying to achieve perfection in her work. The fear of being seen as a "fraud" only fueled her fears, which was affecting both her job performance and her health, including sleepless nights and stress-related illnesses, like IBS.

Lisa fully realized her self-worth and competence through her work with Michele. Her boss noticed a new level of confidence within her and recommended her for mentoring younger professionals in their global consulting firm. Adding this new responsibility to her daily workload further enhanced her self-image as the seasoned expert she actually is.

She also discovered how much she loves teaching others while learning from the different perspectives and ideas the younger team members bring to their work. She told Michele,

> "Becoming a mentor in my organization improved my professional relationships and also positively improved my mental and physical well-being! Not only do I feel more confident, but my stress levels have gone down since I'm not overworking to achieve perfection. This increased my time for self-care, and my IBS has gone away after dealing with it for years!"

The "Do-It-All" Trap

Mona is 61 and LOVES being a grandmother. She has fond memories of all the amazing things her grandmother did for her growing up, and so she was naturally trying to carry the torch forward.

The challenge showed up when her son remarried, adding two wonderful step-children to their family. Mona wanted to show those kids how loved and adored they were. Yet, her new daughter-in-law turned out to be very judgmental and derogatory about how Mona was being a grandparent.

Despite all of her efforts to be the perfect people-pleasing grandma and mother-in-law, she never felt she was getting it right, which led to overdoing, anxiety, and burnout. This took quite a toll on her health, leading to high blood pressure and frequent exhaustion.

By working closely with Michele, Mona was able to identify the root triggers of her perfectionistic need to please others and learned the power of saying, "No." This led to better boundaries, improved self-care and well-being, and a healthier dialogue with her daughter-in-law, along with the added joy of spending more time with her grandchildren.

Perfectionism in Relationships

Having grown up in a strict household with very high expectations, Phillip realized at the age of 54 that he was projecting all of those impossibly perfect standards onto his adult children. He was finally starting to see how the emotional residue he had carried forward from his upbringing had strained the relationship with his children, leaving them feeling "never enough" because there was no way they could live up to his expectations.

This disconnect left him feeling isolated, full of self-criticism, and deeply unhappy, affecting his mental well-being. Phillip came to Michele in search of a better way of communicating with his kids and with himself. By releasing his old mental programming about how perfect his kids were "supposed to be," he learned instead to appreciate them for who they are, fostering a newfound closeness with them.

This not only improved his familial relations, but he also experienced a significant boost in his well-being — even finding joy in the imperfect beauty and quirks of his unique family dynamics.

The Myth of the Golden Years

Sarah had always envisioned her 50s and 60s as the best time of her life, with more financial freedom to travel and have the experiences she had put off as she carefully planned her retirement. Yet when she got there, she found a variety of health issues plaguing her body and mind, all while she was also caring for her aging parents.

This was *not* what she was expecting, and she was determined to find a better way!

"I don't know how to do it anymore," Susan said, in a voice that kept getting smaller and smaller.

"I'm not a trained professional. I don't know what I'm doing sometimes. And what about me?" She took a deep breath before going on. "My health is being affected by this too!"

Her arthritis and psoriasis seemed to be getting worse the more stressed she became, leading to physical exhaustion and emotional drain.

Working with Michele, she was able to help reset her perspectives of what her "perfect life" was supposed to be like and instead embrace this unique time and opportunity in her life to compassionately care for her parents and herself along the way.

Her new insights led to better self-care habits, decreased stress, and an emotional resilience she had never experienced before. She was able to redefine her golden years, taking the challenges one at a time as an extension of life's ever-changing kaleidoscope with greater peace, compassion, and love.

Overcoming Perfectionism as We Age

As the saying goes, time waits for no one.

And since we haven't discovered the fountain of youth (yet), overcoming perfectionism as we age isn't about denying our flaws or wishing away our grey hairs and wrinkles. It's about embracing them as tokens of a life well-lived.

It's the wrinkles of laughter, the silver strands of wisdom, and our imperfections that make us uniquely wonderful as we move into our advanced adulting years. So, let's celebrate every chapter of our lives!

Think about how hard you've worked to earn your advanced adulting badges of honor for your enduring resilience, wisdom, and beauty – no matter how old you are! Remember, it's always your choice about how you perceive yourself, your body, your silver hair, your wrinkles, and so much more.

It's about recognizing the imperfect perspectives that can empower you and uplift your spirit rather than plunge you into despair.

Choose the mindset that works for you, not against you, because no one is perfect. Take what one of our survey participants said about himself as advice to follow:

"I think I have a better perspective now that I am older. I don't try to be perfect anymore. I have a more balanced life. ... I don't get upset at the 'Small Stuff.' I give myself and others more grace."

Chapter 9: Journal Prompts to help you start living Flawsomely

These are intended to get you thinking, not judging yourself. Take some quiet time to thoughtfully and honestly respond to these questions to create your own positive shifts in your perspectives around perfectionism.

- Write down what you most appreciate about your older, wiser self. Imagine 30+ years from now what your older, wiser self would share with you about your journey to becoming flawsome. Share what you write down with someone close to you.

- What steps can you take to embrace the flaws of your current age or situation with greater compassion and self-love? What would that look like or feel like to do so?

- Write down 3 areas that can improve as you shift your mindset and embrace the imperfections in your life.

Chapter 10

Thoughts on AI and Perfectionism

"Artificial intelligence must not be allowed to replace the imperfection of human empathy."
— Prof. Arshin Adib-Moghaddam

I t's official. AI is here to stay.

Like it or not, Artificial Intelligence has arrived and has very quickly become embedded in many aspects of our day-to-day lives. From Siri to Alexa and Google, and an array of different industries: healthcare, agriculture, cybersecurity, marketing, finance, transportation, and customer service, just to name a few.

While no experts, Tom and Michele both use common AI tools like ChatGPT and have wondered, could it be a key to embracing our imperfections, turning them into our superpower instead of constantly seeking to achieve perfection in the eyes of the world?

The rise of AI has become an undeniable reality of our time. Built to enhance our efficiency and effectiveness across all aspects of work and life, AI offers a myriad of solutions for improving productivity and our quality of life.

Examples of how it's currently being used include helping companies access additional insights faster, enhancing diagnostic accuracy, fending off malware attacks, autonomous vehicles, finding new links between

For a series of essays about the impact and future of AI across a wide range of fields, see *AI Anthology* (2023), introduced by Eric Horvitz, https://unlocked.microsoft.com/ai-anthology/

genetic codes, customer engagement and personalization, mental health support, and so much more. The healthcare company Kintsugi Health takes the art of golden repair even further with its mission to "strengthen mental wellness infrastructures," utilizing AI models as a tool "to help prevent people from falling through the cracks so more people can embrace their flaws and find beauty in their growth." We love this!

Kintsugi Mindful Wellness, Inc., https://www.kintsugihealth.com/about

It has already changed how we work and how we will in the future. It is simultaneously eliminating some jobs and creating new ones. Bringing with it a whole host of new concerns, innovations, and discoveries.

Mind the Risks

"Complex automation systems that rely on artificial intelligence solve 'most problems with ease, until they encounter a difficult, unusual case, and then do not.' When they do not, they may not know that they have failed."

— Matthew Crawford, quoting AI experts in *Why We Drive* (2020), pg. 99

However, like any powerful tool, it comes with its drawbacks when misused. The duality of AI's potential has been vividly demonstrated as more advanced AI programs have come online in the last few years. These tools have not only streamlined our work processes but have also, unfortunately, been used unethically and even negatively by some bad actors.

U.S. Senate testimony of Jennifer DeStefano, 6/13/2023, https://www.judiciary.senate.gov/imo/media/doc/2023-06-13%20PM%20-%20Testimony%20-%20DeStefano.pdf

A chilling example is a recent case where a mother testified before Congress about her 15-year-old daughter's voice being duplicated and manipulated to stage a ransom threat. Unaware of the scheme, the parents believed their daughter was in danger, while in reality, she was enjoying a skiing trip with friends.

Or Tom's favorite example of a lawyer who, in May 2023, used AI to write a brief and submitted it to the court, only for the judge to determine that several of

130

the cases cited in the brief "appear to be bogus judicial decisions with bogus quotes and bogus internal citations."

The judge demanded an explanation and the lawyer claimed he had not used AI for legal research before and "was unaware of the possibility that its content could be false." The court fined him $5,000.

Judge sanctions lawyers for brief written by A.I. with fake citations (2023), Dan Mangan, https://www.cnbc.com/2023/06/22/judge-sanctions-lawyers-whose-ai-written-filing-contained-fake-citations.html

Apparently other lawyers remained "unaware" of that possibility and outcome, since in January 2024, a Federal appeals court publicly chastised an attorney for a brief that "presents a false statement of law" by citing a case "which proved not to exist."

The lawyer explained that she "encountered difficulty in locating a relevant case" and so turned to ChatGPT which had "previously provided reliable information." The court referred her to its Grievance Panel for discipline.

2nd Circ. Rebukes Atty For Fake Citation In Latest AI Blunder, Jake Maher, https://www.law360.com/articles/1791788

For a broader look at the dangers of using AI in your work, see Tom's blog post, *Taming the AI Beast: How to make ChatGPT serve, not enslave you* (2023), https://masterbookbuilders.com/taming-the-ai-beast-how-to-make-chatgpt-serve-not-enslave-you/

Is AI Itself a Symptom of Human Perfectionism?

Some argue that artificial intelligence is actually a symptom of human perfectionism, i.e., the need to perfect every human cognitive function. Indeed, the author of the quote we opened this chapter with, Prof. Arshin Adib-Moghaddam, stated:

> "The ultimate aim of AI, even narrow AI which handles very specific tasks, is to outdo and perfect every human cognitive function. ... Unless we jettison this perfectionist attitude towards life that positions productivity and 'material growth' above sustainability and individual happiness, AI research could be another chain in the history of self-defeating human inventions."

Artificial intelligence must not be allowed to replace the imperfection of human empathy (2021), Arshin Adib-Moghaddam, https://theconversation.com/artificial-intelligence-must-not-be-allowed-to-replace-the-imperfection-of-human-empathy-151636

While we understand the argument, it could apply to all human tool-making. We prefer to posit that AI is another tool for extending human creativity. Helping us expand the boundaries of what's possible and seeing more deeply into issues, more completely than we can see with our naked eye and mind, if you will.

The challenge is when we allow technology to replace our humanity. When the need for hyper-efficiency and perfection to lower costs replaces the need for human connection, touch, kindness, and the imperfection of human empathy.

While the debate will continue about how best to use and regulate these powerful tools, the positive implications of AI cannot be overlooked. From business to education to science to medicine, powerful AI tools are helping us expand our thinking like never before in human history.

On the Rise or More Apparent?

Throughout her career as a coach and mental health professional, Michele has constantly endeavored to expand her knowledge, always seeking to learn and stay up-to-date on the latest tools and resources to best serve her clients.

However, her enthusiasm has not been without its challenges and setbacks. One recurring friend and foe of both Michele and Tom has been managing our own bouts of perfectionism and imposter syndrome.

As we discussed in chapter two, imposter syndrome and perfectionism are on the rise. Or perhaps it's just more apparent now that we know what to look for. The job search site Indeed reports that 70% of people have grappled with imposter syndrome at some point in their careers. It is characterized by an internal struggle or nagging feeling that others see you as smarter, more effective, and more capable than you believe yourself to be.

3 Ways to Overcome Impostor Syndrome in the Workplace (2019), Emily Fu, https://www.indeed.com/lead/impostor-syndrome

Caused by underlying issues of self-doubt, low self-worth, self-esteem, or self-confidence, Imposter Syndrome can severely impact productivity, resulting in toxic perfectionism that leads to:

- Increased procrastination
- Extended work hours
- Higher staff turnover
- Decreased productivity
- Reluctance in applying for internal promotions
- Rising stress and related health issues
- Even depression, anxiety, and other mental health challenges, if left unchecked

How Can AI Help Alleviate These Symptoms?

Through her more than two decades of study and research, Michele has discovered that the core drivers of self-doubt, low self-worth, and lack of confidence typically stem from deeply seated subconscious beliefs about ourselves. These limiting mindsets and mental saboteurs distract us, fostering negative thoughts such as "I'm not enough" or "Who am I to do XYZ...?" that can lead to excessive perfectionism, procrastination, and second-guessing our every step.

More and more AI tools are coming online every day, offering ways to swiftly bypass these mental obstacles. For example, when you find yourself stuck, use AI tools to generate outlines for your writing, or image ideas for your design work to jump-start your thinking. Such tools can get you back to a place of *flow*, the state of total immersion in an activity that opens up channels to greater levels of creative thinking and intuition.

This theta brain wave state (3.5 to 8 Hz) is the state of being fully in the now moment, where the ego falls away and enables us to tap into deeper levels of expansive creative thinking to apply to the challenges at hand. Theta and alpha brain wave states are also associated with increased calm and a decrease in depressive and anxious thoughts.

And while there are a variety of apps these days that utilize technology to help quiet those inner critics, Michele always recommends guided meditations and hypnosis recordings as a way to help you sink into that relaxed, deeper state of mind and flow state. Empowering you to get back on track with greater clarity and productivity.

Michele has created a special *I Am Perfectly Flawsome Guided Meditation* for our readers. You can find it in the bonus resources section of the website: www.IAmPerfectlyFlawsome.com/resources

As an analogy, consider Michele's approach to painting. To overcome the intimidation of a blank canvas, she begins by covering it entirely in gold acrylic paint. This simple strategy bypasses her critical judging mind and initial fears of "What should I paint and where do I start!?" and redirects her thoughts to "How can I incorporate this gold texture into the vision in my mind's eye?"

"Something imperfect that exists is better than something perfect that doesn't!."
— Neil Hughes

Similarly, AI tools like Chat GPT can help eliminate the intimidating 'blank canvas' of a task, enabling our subconscious to relax and work with us rather than against us. Thus, they empower our creative genius to expand further so that we can achieve a state of productive flow more quickly.

Friend, Coach, or ChatGPT?

The next time you find yourself in the grip of imposter syndrome or spinning in perfectionistic circles that are stirring up your procrastination or self-doubt, consider reaching for an AI tool. These days, there's most likely an App for that! Whatever you're working on, there are a plethora of AI tools to help you get over the proverbial hump. It might be just what you need to break free from your self-imposed constraints, assisting you to remove the blinders of self-doubt and boosting your confidence.

Remember, a healthy degree of self-reflection versus toxic perfectionism can serve as a beneficial motivator, prompting you to challenge norms, seek innovative solutions, and strive to better your work. Whether you need assistance in drafting an article, visualizing a project, or outlining a successful business strategy, AI can be a powerful ally, guiding you back to your zone of genius. Enabling you to move forward more creatively as you make your way down the path of flawsomism.

It's when these feelings and perspectives of imposter syndrome and the need to be perfect become debilitating or chronic that asking for support is key.

Whether you reach for an AI tool, or call a friend or a coach, we all can benefit from a little support now and then. Giving you a fresh perspective can assist you in moving beyond your self-perceived limitations so you can share your ideas and expertise in ways you hadn't yet imagined.

And in the spirit of human-machine collaboration, we'll add this bit of advice from one of Tom's recent blog posts. The quote is from Lori Mazor's article, but written (apparently) by Claude, the AI tool she was using:

> "So, dear readers, I urge you to be cautious in this brave new world of AI authorship. Don't be fooled by the shiny allure of machine-generated content. Embrace the imperfections, the quirks, and the idiosyncrasies that make human writing so compelling."

Even the AI itself knows that embracing imperfection makes us — and our work — better!

Remember, every tool is only as good as the hands that wield it. In the right hands, AI can help us embrace our imperfections for greater success and peace of mind, as we learn to navigate these rapidly changing landscapes.

When we embrace our mistakes and missteps, not as failures but as creative iterations in an ongoing process, we can grow, innovate, and thrive.

Enabling us to fully embrace our Flawsomeness.

Chapter 10: Journal Prompts to help you start living Flawsomely

These are intended to get you thinking, not judging yourself. Take some quiet time to thoughtfully and honestly respond to these questions to create your own positive shifts in your perspectives around perfectionism.

- How can you creatively use AI to help you overcome your project-related perfectionism and bring more of your natural genius to the task at hand?

- How can AI become part of your toolset, allowing you to maintain a striving for excellence mentality, rather than an over-achievers need for perfection?

- How will you live your life differently when you accept yourself as you are, perfectly flawsome, while still striving for excellence in a healthy way?

Conclusion: The Way of the Flawsomist

"Holding the paradox of celebrating imperfection and striving for excellence as co-existing mindsets. That is the heart — or the way — of the flawsomist."

— Tom Collins & Michele Molitor

We've covered a lot of ground together. We've reviewed the serious harm inflicted on ourselves and others by perfectionist attitudes. We've offered you a variety of ideas for overcoming perfectionism, both in general and for specific groups and settings.

We'd like to close with a question that we think will help you nurture that "embrace and celebrate imperfection" (wabi-sabi) side of the paradox:

What things in life are better because they're imperfect?

"If you look through squinted eyes, you can see it."

The gifts of imperfection are all around us.

It's challenging to ignore the illusions of perfection. We see it in the media, on the billboards, in our social feeds.

It seems that we seek to constantly achieve it, perhaps to overcome our own self-doubt or imposter syndrome.

Gifts of Imperfection (2021), Michele Molitor, https://michelemolitor.com/2021/11/20/gifts-of-imperfection/

One of the gifts of imperfection is truly embracing that perfection is in the eye of the beholder. What we might think is exquisite beauty and perfection, like the sunlight lighting up the bright fuchsia feathers of the hummingbird's throat sitting in a nearby tree, someone else might think, "What's the big deal? It's just a bird."

Or the wonky-shaped tomato from Michele's vegetable garden. Or perhaps the lush green fields across the East Bay hills, where, upon closer inspection, you can see the rocks, the cracks in the earth, and yet a bounty of flowers have bloomed despite the odds. Mother Nature herself never asks for perfection. She knows that those imperfections are what make us each unique and lovely.

Throughout this book, we've demonstrated that we are far better served by looking for the beauty that lies in the imperfections of life — the imperfections within each person you meet — their golden repair work.

Especially within ourselves.

This perspective gives us such freedom from constantly trying to one-up another, to be better than, instead of just embracing who we are ... fully, completely, authentically, perfectly flawsome.

It is in this imperfection that we are free to show up more wholly and without hesitation.

Imagine for Just a Moment ...

How would you move through the world differently if you knew no one was judging you? If it didn't matter if you weren't at your best today? If your hair wasn't done just right and your makeup just so? (Michele grew up in the south ... it IS a thing ...).

Imagine if you could just relax in your skin fully and ...

Just.

Be.

You.

Without apology.

What would your life be like in this place?

How might it look, feel, and flow differently?

Would you make choices and decisions in the same way?

How much time would you win back from the internal critics of toxic perfectionism? And how would you use that time, effort, and energy differently?

Michele reached out to her Rewire For Success community to get their take on this perfectly imperfect conundrum. She simply asked them the same question:

"What things in life are better because they're imperfect?"

Visit Michele's group on Facebook, https://www.facebook.com/group/ RewireForSuccessWithMichele

Here are just some of the amazing gifts of imperfection they shared with us, imperfect gifts to be found all around us and within us, if we're looking.

Michele's long-time friend Marvin Schlaak, who has a perfectly imperfect and inquisitive mind, was the one who had posed the question to her to begin with, so let's start with a few of his thoughts:

- "When someone is imperfect, they become relatable. Often, we think that our 'perfectionism' draws others to us. We crave connection. But that 'perfectionism' is so unrelatable to the very people we want to connect with that it actually pushes them away from us unconsciously."

- "Accepting my imperfectness allows (and encourages) me to accept the flaws in others. Without that approach, I will end up having not-so-subtle judgmental looks and words that seep out of me, no matter how carefully I try to mask them."

- "A toddler's mixed-up words — you know what they mean, but often they say it in a way that brings new, fresh meaning to your understanding and a lifetime of smiles and warmth as we recount them to each other."

- "That quirkiness in our partner that makes them unique to us as if they are the only one in the world. It drives me bonkers when they xyz, but they wouldn't be themselves without that behavior."

- "Wrinkles around my eyes — they tell a story of a life in ways that words often cannot: the laughter, the struggles against the flow and even the failures."

- "A quickly written text to tell someone you are thinking of them rather than waiting for the perfect moment to draft a letter. That perfect moment rarely arrives; thus nothing gets said."

- "Slightly burned (Marshmallows, hotdogs, toast) come with more love methinks."

- "Off-key birthday songs. Who doesn't like the childishness of belting out with laughter the birthday song to your friend of many years? It floods us with the warmth and laughter of the best of childhood years."

- "Old books that have been well used over the decades. Especially if it is a well-worn Bible with notes from your mom in the margins."

- "A handmade (most anything from cake to craft) thing including a handwritten note (as opposed to the same thing said in an email)."

The Gifts of Imperfection Range Far and Wide, Large and Small

Here are some favorites from Michele's and Tom's own perspectives:

- The one white whisker on my all-black cat

- The flecks of paint that inadvertently went where they weren't supposed to and made the finished painting that much better

- The peace of mind that comes from being able to laugh at yourself and all those silly mistakes we've made in life and the wisdom to know that those mistakes have made us a better, stronger, more resilient person

- Being able to recognize the imperfections of our parents, their wounds, and their flaws which inadvertently directly shaped our lives, and love them despite their imperfections instead of holding them to a higher standard of parental perfection

- The freedom and time savings that come from knowing that 90% of perfection (versus 100%) is "pretty dang good" in most cases

- The knowing that our imperfections are what make us so very unique as individuals and set us apart from the rest of the world

- The simple shift in your perspective about that perceived "flaw" (in humans or otherwise) can turn it into a powerful positive attribute — "one person's trash is another person's treasure"

What we have learned as we wrote this book: There are a myriad of ways that imperfections are far better than perfection any day, in ways that bring us joy and a smile to our face.

Even our editor, Yvonne DiVita, shared that when coaching her book clients, she tells them,

> "Don't edit yourself! Write as much as you need to. Let it just flow. I want to find the nuggets in your original stream of consciousness. That's where the book will come together."

As you can see, the subtle gifts of imperfection can improve your life immensely.

Everyday is a New Day to Begin!

So here we are at the end of our journey together toward becoming Flawsome. Yet it's really just another beginning!

We wholeheartedly believe that you'll find releasing the need for perfection is very freeing! Letting go of the need for things to be "just right" and "perfect," gives you more energy, space, and time in your life. Time to be with the people you love, and to give your time, talents, and attention to the other important aspects of your life that matter most to you.

As you release the tension in your body and nervous system that has trapped the patterns of perfectionism in place, you'll find yourself more at ease and relaxed too. Thus allowing more well-being and life balance to flow through your days. (Did we mention life balance is one of the many benefits you'll appreciate along this winding road of becoming a Flawsomist?!)

Remember that perfection is an unattainable illusion, but self-acceptance and personal growth are achievable goals that lead to a more satisfying and fulfilling life with every step along your path.

We encourage you to continue to reflect on your own perfectionistic habits of mind and begin to modify them to healthier habits of striving for excellence. As you do, we know you'll find greater peace of mind and satisfaction in your day-to-day life.

So to help strengthen the flawsomist habits and pathways in your mind, heart, and spirit, we'll leave you with one final question for you to ponder each day:

How will embracing the imperfections you see today,
free you to be better tomorrow?

Embracing that paradox is the way of the flawsomist.

Before going back to your day . . .

. . . if you haven't already done so, visit this webpage for free bonus material to help you on your journey to flawsome:

- I Am Perfectly Flawsome Guided Meditation

- Complete Book Club Readers Guide

- Reference List with live links to online research

- Bonus eBooks (*Imposter Syndrome*, by Michele; *Pivot*, by Tom)

- Self-Doubt Quiz

- Special Discount Code to assess your Top 5 Dignity Traits

www.IAmPerfectlyFlawsome.com/resources

Type in the URL or scan the QR Code —>

Appendix

Kintsugi and Related Concepts

We suspect that you may be as curious to learn more about the Japanese art and philosophies around the practice of kintsugi as we were. Although it's one of our inspirations for the book, we're not masters of the art, nor experts in the cultural tradition behind it. We did gather a good number of resources in our research — more than we had room for in the text — so we decided to provide you with some additional entry points to explore.

In the following pages, we delve a bit deeper into kintsugi and the four related terms we touched on in the Introduction, pgs. 5-6, and Chapter 3, pgs. 36-38: wabi-sabi, shikata ga nai, ganbatte, and kaizen.

The sharp-eyed among you may notice that we've changed the order slightly. In the text, we ordered them from the list in Candice Kumai's book, *Kintsugi Wellness*. Here, we want you to take note of how these terms nest within the paradox of embracing imperfection while striving for excellence.

So, after revisiting kintsugi, we're placing wabi-sabi and shikata ga nai next, as both relate to celebrating, accepting, and embracing imperfection and the world as it is. Then, we cover kaizen and ganbatte, which relate to the contrasting mindset of striving for excellence.

Note: We've also left you lots of extra space in this Appendix for jotting down your own ideas and learnings from these Japanese concepts.

Kintsugi Wellness: The Japanese Art of Nourishing Mind, Body, and Spirit, Candice Kumai (2018)

Kintsugi

"Kintsugi has a beauty within the imperfection.
This developed from a concept called wabi sabi which is
treasured in the tea ceremony."

— Nakamura Kunio

The quote above is from the Japanese government's PR website, which tells us that **kintsugi** translates literally as "gold seams." It's described there as a traditional method for repairing "the broken or chipped parts of broken vessels." The alternate term for the art **kintsukoroi** translates as "golden repair."

The website also notes about the treasured bowls used in the tea ceremony, "sometimes a perfect piece of pottery is even purposefully broken and repaired."

Nakamura, a Tokyo book cafe owner who offers kintsugi workshops, waxes poetic about the meanings that can be gleaned from the visible kintsugi mends:

> "The cracks in the pottery form a dramatic landscape. When the gold color is added along the joins of the broken parts, the lines look like lightning brightening the darkness, a golden-colored river, or a branch reaching into the firmament. New scenes are thus born in the pottery."

When viewed as a philosophy of life, of mending our mistakes and healing our broken spirits, of creating "new scenes" in our lives, we think these other expressions of the meaning of kinstugi we've come across will resonate:

"precious scars"   "beauty in the broken"   "golden joinery"
"beauty of broken pieces"   "beautifying the cracks"

Kintsugi: The Healing Power of Pottery Repair (2020), https://www.gov-online.go.jp/eng/publicity/book/hlj/html/202008/202008_07_en.html

Wabi-Sabi

"Wabi-Sabi is a philosophy and aesthetic, which centers around an appreciation of imperfection, impermanence, and incompleteness."

— Matt Johnson, PhD

The quote above is from a neuroscientist attempting to teach us about the value of accepting ourselves and the world with all the imperfections we find.

He adds that a most succinct definition of wabi-sabi might be "the beauty of imperfection."

Noting the connection to kintsugi, he explains:

"This technique accentuates these so-called defects, making them the most stunning and visually salient aspect of the pottery. The approach celebrates each artifact by emphasizing and **appreciating its imperfection.**"

Urging us to apply wabi-sabi to our lives, he writes that "an acceptance, and even a celebration, of imperfection can liberate one from the self-imposed strain [of perfectionism]."

What Wabi-Sabi Teaches Us About The Psychology of Imperfection, (undated), Matt Johnson, https://www.neuroscienceof.com/human-nature-blog/wabi-sabi-philosophy-imperfection

Shikata ga nai

"Shikata Ga Naï means letting go. It's about accepting what you cannot change and doing your best to let it roll off your back."

— Arno Slabbinck

When we discussed these Japanese approaches to life in Chapter 3, we took note of a saying used especially among women in Okinawa to remind themselves of the wisdom of shikata ga nai. The author of the quote above did the same, so we think it bears repeating once more here:

"This won't matter in five years, or five months, (or in some cases, even five weeks), so I'm not going to give it more than five minutes."

He adds, "And then wash your hands of it."

We also agree with his two caveats: One, that shikata gai nai is not always easy to apply in real life, when bad things happen. He urges, as we have throughout, not to go it alone, but connect with friends, family, or a coach when needed. And two, shikata ga nai "is an ongoing process, something that you will need to work on continuously."

When you connect this ability to let go of things we perceive as "bad" with the wabi-sabi acceptance and celebration of imperfection, you've got the "flawed" part of flawsome covered!

Shikata Ga Naï: The Japanese Art Of Letting Go, (2019), Arno Slabbinck, https://medium.com/swlh/shikata-ga-nai-the-japanese-art-of-letting-go-776db8eda8ef

Kaizen

"Hint: kaizen is more than improving processes!
It's about improving ourselves."

— Katie Andereson

Because kaizen is so firmly linked to business and The Toyota Way in our culture, we spent a good bit of space in Chapter 5 showing the dangers of too much focus on the common translation as meaning "continuous improvement" in our work.

As we did, the author of the quote above explains that kaizen has a much deeper meaning in Japan that moves the focus back to the individual. She breaks the kai + zen down into the simpler phrase, "good change." Digging deeper, she finds elements of discipline and sacrifice to produce the good change.

Going beyond the business setting, she writes:

"Kaizen is about having the self-discipline to improve yourself for the better in service of the collective good. And through that we improve processes, help others improve, and improve the world!"

This deeper meaning for kaizen helps us see how the practice of flawsomism is not a surrender to mediocrity, but a balanced way of approaching our work and our personal lives.

The Real Meaning of Kaizen (2021), Katie Anderson, https://kbjanderson.com/the-real-meaning-of-kaizen/

157

Ganbatte

"Almost any scenario that is short of being perfect is faced head on by the Japanese community with a 'ganbatte' spirit."

— YABAI Writers

When we discussed ganbatte in Chapter 3, we placed emphasis on Candice Kumai's advice that it's not about being the best, but about doing your best. The writers quoted above show their agreement by focusing solely on the doing.

They emphasize that it is used as an encouragement, not a command (which would use the term *ganbare*). And they provide a list of related phrases, like "I will do my best" (*ganbarimasu*) and "I did my best" (*ganbatta*).

They expand on the quote above with the following:

"Although the expression may be commonly said and used, it serves as an effective form of encouragement, especially in times of great hardship. The expression reminds each individual that the true obstacle lies in how he trusts his own abilities."

When you combine this understanding of ganbatte with the deeper meaning of kaizen, you have the other side of the flawsomism paradox, striving for excellence, without worrying about any illusion of perfection.

"Ganbatte" - More than Just a Popular Japanese Expression (2017), YABAI Writers, http://yabai.com/p/2495

FYI, "yabai" can mean very bad, or very good, like the American slang uses of "bad" or "wicked."

A Note On Our Usage of
Japanese Hiragana Characters

When displaying Japanese writing, we've used the Japanese script characters called *hiragana* for simplicity and consistency. Modern Japanese writing uses the hiragana characters in combination with *kanji*, a more ornate script derived from Chinese ideograms, and *katakana*, a modified version of hiragana.

To justify our choice to stick with just one form of script, here's how the YABAI article quoted on the previous page described the options:

> "'Ganbatte' can be written in three different ways using kanji, hiragana, or katakana – the three writing systems of the Japanese language. Kanji serves as the major alphabet and consists of more than eight thousand Chinese ideograms, while hiragana and katakana serve as syllabic alphabets, each made out of 47 characters that represent different sounds.

> "A single kanji character can have multiple meanings and pronunciations. As such, hiragana is sometimes used with kanji to indicate the correct idea."

Rather than attempt to navigate the 8,000+ symbols of kanji and their combinations with the other two, we opted for the simplest, hiragana.

"Hiragana"

Acknowledgements

We must start with our joint and unending gratitude to Yvonne DiVita, our developmental editor, for keeping this project on course and driving us to finish. The imperfections remain ours, but she has helped us apply all the kintsugi concepts to this work. We think it's more beautiful for the "golden repairs" that she prompted.

As many who attempt giving thanks know, it's impossible to list all those who've contributed to our thinking and writing (many without knowing us personally). The dozens of authors we've noted in our sidebar references are a good example. And hundreds more authors, conference speakers, and idea-rich social media postings and comments we've read and listened to over the years.

Deepest gratitude to our community at BOSS Academy, founded by our friend and colleague Paul Kirch. If not for the amazing group of experts who attend our weekly gatherings, we would not have met and this book may never have come to life in the beautiful way it has.

We'd like to thank all of those who contributed their personal stories and insights to the survey we conducted and to those we interviewed in particular for the book (You know who you are!). Your stories have brought much more color and light to the research and ideas presented here.

We sincerely appreciate all the beta readers who took time to read and review the book, sharing thoughtful feedback and insightful comments that have helped us put the finishing touches on our new book baby.

Thank you to our family, friends, and teachers over the years who helped us culminate in this moment of clarity and understanding to bring this book to life. Their influence and support created our combined history and the lessons learned are woven throughout the pages of our book — with the intention of making the path a little easier for those who read it.

And one last note of gratitude to those readers who've taken the time to post a review on Amazon. As of publication, we're still working on the companion *I Am Perfectly Flawsome Journal* and the audiobook edition. And we have further plans for more resources on the topics covered in this book.

Those Amazon reviews and feedback both inspire us and remind us that our work can always be improved in the next piece. If you haven't already done so, please take a moment to add your voice to the conversation.

Tom Collins "retired" for the first time in 2001 after a 25-year career as an appellate lawyer. He'd discovered a passion for document design, while using the desktop computers that he'd kept upgrading in power and publishing capabilities in his home office. He'd become known for including images from trial evidence to illustrate his points in his appeal briefs. His first solo business sought to marshal those communication tools for his former legal colleagues.

From there, his story can't be told alone. Enter, Yvonne DiVita, two years later. The "Tom and Yvonne" husband and wife show began when the two business consultants met at a networking event. They discovered an equal passion for books, writing, reading, and helping other people flourish.

Tom "retired" again to join her company, Windsor Media Enterprises, and they formed a print-on-demand publishing division, aka WME Books. Yvonne, with her lifelong passion for books and degree in Creative Writing, became the developmental editor, book coach, and salesperson. Tom was the designer for the books, inside and out, along with managing the production end.

At the same time they were growing their publishing business, blogging became a "thing." All WME Books authors were encouraged to blog as a way to grow their audiences, and new lines of business emerged, WME Blogs and the Business Blogging Bootcamp.

In 2009, a new "big idea" popped up while talking with a few other professionals: Influencer Marketing – with pet bloggers. BlogPaws was born and grew in influence over 10 years. During that time, WME was closed and their focus was given to BlogPaws. A couple of years later, the influencer company was acquired by a much larger company, which, in turn, was acquired by PetSmart. Tom "retired" again, and then Yvonne did, too.

Just before starting BlogPaws, the two entrepreneurs had moved from NY to CO. While in CO, they moved homes three times. The third of those moves was to a house that was framed but not finished, giving them the chance to add their touches, and make it their own. After moving in, Tom finished the 1500 square foot walkout basement to add his office and more living space.

Though the two loved CO, family back home called. In 2018 they packed up and moved back to upstate NY. Today, their home is another work-in-progress.

Their experiences and shared passions led them back to books. Tom wrote and published *Read 'Em & Reap: 6 Science-Backed Ways Reading Puts You on the Road to Achieving More and Living Longer* in 2019.

And in 2020, they combined their talents for *The How to Write a Book Book: Your Step-by-Step Plans for Bringing Big Ideas to Life One Page at a Time*. The "Book Book," as they call it, is a testament to their continued love of books and writing, and their vagabond nature of moving and remodeling homes. Its tagline: How writing a book is like building a house.

Now unretired again, via their **Master Book Builders** practice, they apply their knowledge of the ever-changing Indie Publishing landscape to helping authors reach their dreams of becoming "the author of" that book inside.

Tom's curiosity frequently takes him on research and writing journeys into the science behind topics like reading, happiness, and healthy aging — here, the benefits of embracing imperfection. I.e., he's a practicing flawsomist.

You can find them both online most days. www.MasterBookBuilders.com

Or connect with Tom on LinkedIn:
https://www.linkedin.com/in/tomcollins-bookartisan/

If you write and they don't reply, they are likely out walking in the hilly neighborhood around their home.

Michele Molitor is a force for positive change in today's challenging mental health landscape. As a master coach, hypnotherapist, speaker, and author, she has dedicated her career to helping others activate positive change in their lives, both personally and professionally.

As CEO of Nectar Consulting, Inc., Michele's expertise focuses on empowering professionals to overcome anxiety, self-doubt, and the stress that often saturates modern work environments. Her approach is practical: to bring dignity into our communications that foster emotional well-being through genuine acceptance, belonging, and meaningful connection – with ourselves and others.

Clients affectionately dubbed her "The Mind Detective," not just for her intuitive insights but for her unique Rapid Rewiring™ approach that effectively combines the science of positive psychology and neuroscience with the healing powers of somatic and mindfulness practices. The results? Tangible improvements that make a real, lasting difference in people's lives.

Michele's expertise is backed by decades of training and credentials. She's a Certified Professional Co-Active Coach (CPCC) through the Co-Active Training Institute and a Professional Certified Coach (PCC) through the International Coach Federation. She is also a Certified Clinical Hypnotherapist with specializations in Rapid Transformational Therapy® and HeartHealing® and a Usui Holy Fire Reiki Master. Michele also holds a Bachelor of Science in Advertising and Psychology from the University of Florida, a degree in Graphic Design from the Art Institute, as well as studies in French linguistics at La Sorbonne, Paris France. She is also a Dignify® Certified Partner.

Beyond her practice, Michele is a sought-after speaker and writer. Her discussions on overcoming imposter syndrome, tackling perfectionism, and preventing burnout are deeply relatable topics today. She's not just talking at you; she's talking with you, bringing dignity back into how we communicate with each other. Her practical wisdom is also captured in this, her latest co-authored book.

Michele's insights have graced multiple media outlets and conferences, offering actionable advice for personal and professional growth. You can find more of her published writing at Brainz Magazine, YourTango, Medium, Substack, MSN, Flipboard, CNN, SelfGrowth, Lifehack, and The Mogul Mom. She has spoken at various leadership conferences nationwide, such as the IEEE Leadership Conference, SHRM Leadership Development Forum, NCCEP, and SSATB.

Through her work, Nectar Consulting Inc. upholds the values of a Certified B Corporation, proving you can do well by truly doing good.

Find out more at:
https://michelemolitor.com/

Connect with Michele on LinkedIn:
https://www.linkedin.com/in/michelemolitor/

Book Club Reader's Guide

Given the depth and complexity of the topics discussed in the book, we recommend discussing one to two chapters at a time with your group.

Introduction: Starting the Journey

- Before you dive in, consider what perfectionism means to you.
- Does it evoke a sense of aspiration, or carry a weight of pressure?
- Discuss your initial thoughts on embracing imperfections and how you hope this book might shift your perspective.

Chapter 1: Perfectionism and Its Variants

Discussion Points:

- Share the standards you set for yourself that feel unrealistic. Why do you hold onto them?
- Discuss the emotions that surface when striving for perfection. How do they manifest in your life?

Journal Reflections:

- Consider how striving for perfection has influenced different aspects of your life. Reflect on both the positive and negative outcomes.

Chapter 2: Science of Mind - The Roots of Perfectionism

Discussion Points:

- Explore the underlying beliefs that fuel your perfectionism. Are they based on personal experiences or societal expectations?
- Delve into how perfectionism may be creating a sense of imposter syndrome in your professional life.

Journal Reflections:

- Imagine reframing your perfectionist thoughts into empowering statements. What would these new messages to yourself be?

Chapter 3: Flawsome-ism? Beyond Perfectionism

Discussion Points:

- Discuss your current definition of success. How does it differ from the definitions you've adopted from others?
- Identify areas in your life where you are overly critical. What triggers this?

Journal Reflections:

- Reflect on the concept that "there is no such thing as failure, only lessons." How does this perspective change your view on past experiences?

Chapter 4: The Power of Flawsomism

Discussion Points:

- Share a significant lesson learned from a past failure. How did it contribute to your growth?

- Envision a life where progress is the focus, not perfection. What does that life look like?

Journal Reflections:

- How would fully accepting yourself as 'flawsome' transform your current life?

Chapter 5: Wabi-Sabi in the Workplace

Discussion Points:

- Contemplate the need for imperfection and compassion in the workplace. How can this shift affect your career and prevent burnout?

- Consider the impact of a psychologically safe workplace that values continuous improvement without the pressure of perfection.

Journal Reflections:

- What's needed to embrace your flaws and imperfections with greater compassion in all realms of your life?

Chapter 6: Ladies, Let's Move from Fearful to Flawsome

Discussion Points:

- Identify a perceived flaw you have. How can you accept it as part of your whole self?

- Discuss the power of replacing perfectionistic thoughts with empowering affirmations.

Journal Reflections:

- What's on your "Imperfect Win" list? Reflect on your daily achievements and how they counterbalance perfectionistic tendencies.

Chapter 7: Intergenerational Trauma and Epigenetics

Discussion Points:

- Reflect on the hardships that your family lineage faced and consider how the experiences of your ancestors may have shaped family behaviors and expectations.

- Identify characteristics you've unconsciously adopted from your caregivers that contribute to perfectionism.

Journal Reflections:

- Reflect on how releasing these inherited patterns can improve your happiness and even the lives of your children?

- Explore how historical patterns of perfectionism within your family may be influencing your life now.

Chapter 8: Kintsugi Kids

Discussion Points:

- Reflect on the positive and negative messages that you received as a child and notice how you might be perpetuating these messages with your own children.

- Brainstorm positive ways to encourage kids in your life that reinforces appreciating and honoring their efforts and achievements versus perfect results.

Journal Reflections:

- Write a compassionate letter to your younger self or the children in your life, that reinforces that they are 'enough'.

Chapter 9: Advanced Adulting

Discussion Points:

- Share the qualities you appreciate about your older, wiser self. What wisdom would your future self say to you about embracing your imperfections?

- Discuss ways to accept the flaws of your life with more compassion, self-acceptance and self-love.

Journal Reflections:

- Consider the imperfections in your current life stage and how you can transform your perspective to embrace them.

Chapter 10: Thoughts on AI and Perfectionism

Discussion Points:

- Explore creative ways AI can help you move past perfectionism in your projects, enabling you to step more into a place of creative flow.

- Discuss how AI can be a tool for striving for excellence without succumbing to perfectionism.

Journal Reflections:

- Reflect on how accepting yourself as 'perfectly flawsome' can alter your life's course while still striving for excellence in a healthy fashion that embraces life-balance.

Conclusion: Embracing the Way of the Flawsomist

- As you close the book, ponder your overall journey.
- Reflect on your ah-ha moments that came from shifting your perspectives through reading the book and discussing the nuances of the information provided throughout its pages.
- Listen to the guided meditation (that can be downloaded from the website) together as a group and discuss what comes up for you and what you're taking away from this experience.

Life And Habit

by

Samuel Butler

CHAPTER I—ON CERTAIN ACQUIRED HABITS

It will be our business in the following chapters to consider whether the unconsciousness, or quasi-unconsciousness, with which we perform certain acquired actions, would seem to throw any light upon Embryology and inherited instincts, and otherwise to follow the train of thought which the class of actions above-mentioned would suggest; more especially in so far as they appear to bear upon the origin of species and the continuation of life by successive generations, whether in the animal or vegetable kingdoms.

In the outset, however, I would wish most distinctly to disclaim for these pages the smallest pretension to scientific value, originality, or even to accuracy of more than a very rough and ready kind—for unless a matter be true enough to stand a good deal of misrepresentation, its truth is not of a very robust order, and the blame will rather lie with its own delicacy if it be crushed, than with the carelessness of the crusher. I have no wish to instruct, and not much to be instructed; my aim is simply to entertain and interest the numerous class of people who, like myself, know nothing of science, but who enjoy speculating and reflecting (not too deeply) upon the phenomena around them. I have therefore allowed myself a loose rein, to run on with whatever came uppermost, without regard to whether it was new or old; feeling sure that if true, it must be very old or it never could have occurred to one so little versed in science as myself; and knowing that it is sometimes pleasanter to meet the old under slightly changed conditions, than to go through the formalities and uncertainties of making new acquaintance. At the same time, I should say that whatever I have knowingly taken from any one else, I have always acknowledged.

It is plain, therefore, that my book cannot be intended for the perusal of scientific people; it is intended for the general public only, with whom I believe myself to be in harmony, as knowing neither much more nor much less than they do.

Taking then, the art of playing the piano as an example of the kind of action we are in search of, we observe that a practised player will perform very difficult pieces apparently without effort, often, indeed, while thinking and talking of something quite other than his music; yet he will play accurately and, possibly, with much expression. If he has been playing a fugue, say in four parts, he will have kept each part well distinct, in such a manner as to prove that his mind was not prevented, by its other occupations, from consciously or unconsciously following four distinct trains of musical thought at the same time, nor from making his fingers act in exactly the required manner as regards each note of each part.

It commonly happens that in the course of four or five minutes a player may have struck four or five thousand notes. If we take into consideration the rests, dotted notes, accidentals, variations of time, &c., we shall find his attention must have been exercised on many more occasions than when he was actually striking notes: so that it may not be too much to say that the attention of a first-rate player may have been exercised—to an infinitesimally small extent—but still truly exercised—on as many as ten thousand occasions within the space of five minutes, for no note can be struck nor point attended to without a certain amount of attention, no matter how rapidly or unconsciously given.

Moreover, each act of attention has been followed by an act of volition, and each act of volition by a muscular action, which is composed of many minor actions; some so small that we can no more follow them than the player himself can perceive them; nevertheless, it may have been perfectly plain that the player was not attending to what he was doing, but was listening to conversation on some other subject, not to say joining in it himself. If he has been playing the violin, he may have done all the above, and may also have been walking about. Herr Joachim would unquestionably be able to do all that has here been described.

So complete would the player's unconsciousness of the attention he is giving, and the brain power he is exerting appear to be, that we shall find it difficult to awaken his attention to any particular part of his performance without putting him out. Indeed we cannot do so. We shall observe that he finds it hardly less difficult to compass a voluntary consciousness of what he has once learnt so thoroughly that it has passed, so to speak, into the domain of unconsciousness, than he found it to learn the note or passage in the first instance. The effort after a second consciousness of detail baffles him—compels him to turn to his music or play slowly. In fact it seems as though he knew the piece too well to be able to know that he knows it, and is only conscious of knowing those passages which he does not know so thoroughly.

At the end of his performance, his memory would appear to be no less annihilated than was his consciousness of attention and volition. For of the thousands of acts requiring the exercise of both the one and the other, which he has done during the five minutes, we will say, of his performance, he will remember hardly one when it is over. If he calls to mind anything beyond the main fact that he has played such and such a piece, it will probably be some passage which he has found more difficult than the others, and with the like of which he has not been so long familiar. All the rest he will forget as completely as the breath which he has drawn while playing.

He finds it difficult to remember even the difficulties he experienced in learning to play. A few may have so impressed him that they remain with him, but the greater part will have escaped him as completely as the remembrance of what he ate, or how he put on his clothes, this day ten years ago; nevertheless, it is plain he remembers more than he remembers remembering, for he avoids mistakes which he made at one time, and his performance proves that all the notes are in his memory, though if called upon to play such and such a bar at random from the middle of the piece, and neither more nor less, he will probably say that he cannot remember it unless he begins from the beginning of the phrase which leads to it. Very commonly he will be obliged to begin from the beginning of the movement itself, and be unable to start at any other point unless he have the music before him; and if disturbed, as we have seen above, he will have to start *de novo* from an accustomed starting-point.

Yet nothing can be more obvious than that there must have been a time when what is now so easy as to be done without conscious effort of the brain was only done by means of brain work which was very keenly perceived, even to fatigue and positive distress. Even now, if the player is playing something the like of which he has not met before, we observe he pauses and becomes immediately conscious of attention.

We draw the inference, therefore, as regards pianoforte or violin playing, that the more the familiarity or knowledge of the art, the less is there consciousness of such knowledge; even so far as that there should seem to be almost as much difficulty in awakening consciousness which has become, so to speak, latent,—a consciousness of that which is known too well to admit of recognised self-analysis while the knowledge is being exercised—as in creating a consciousness of that which is not yet well enough known to be properly designated as known at all. On the other hand, we observe that the less the familiarly or knowledge, the greater the consciousness of whatever knowledge there is.

Considering other like instances of the habitual exercise of intelligence and volition, which, from long familiarity with the method of procedure, escape the notice of the person exercising them, we naturally think of writing. The formation of each letter requires attention and volition, yet in a few minutes a practised writer will form several hundred letters, and be able to think and talk of something else all the time he is doing so. It will not probably remember the formation of a single character in any page that he has written; nor will he be able to give more than the substance of his writing if asked to do so. He knows how to form each letter so well, and he knows so well each word that he is about to write, that he has ceased to be conscious of his knowledge or to notice his acts of volition, each one of which is, nevertheless, followed by a corresponding muscular action. Yet the uniformity of our handwriting, and the manner in which we almost invariably adhere to one method of forming the same character, would seem to suggest that during the momentary formation of each letter our memories must revert (with an intensity too rapid for our perception) to many if not to all the occasions on which we have ever written the same letter previously — the memory of these occasions dwelling in our minds as what has been called a residuum—an unconsciously struck balance or average of them all —a fused mass of individual reminiscences of which no trace can be found in our consciousness, and of which the only effect would seem to lie in the gradual changes of handwriting which are perceptible in most people till they have reached middle-age, and sometimes even later. So far are we from consciously remembering any one of the occasions on which we have written such and such a letter, that we are not even conscious of exercising our memory at all, any more than we are in health conscious of the action of our heart. But, if we are writing in some unfamiliar way, as when printing our letters instead of writing them in our usual running hand, our memory is so far awakened that we become conscious of every character we form; sometimes it is even perceptible as memory to ourselves, as when we try to remember how to print some letter, for example a g, and cannot call to mind on which side of the upper half of the letter we ought to put the link which connects it with the lower, and are successful in remembering; but if we become very conscious of remembering, it shows that we are on the brink of only trying to remember,—that is to say, of not remembering at all.

As a general rule, we remember for a time the substance of what we have written, for the subject is generally new to us; but if we are writing what we have often written before, we lose consciousness of this too, as fully as we do of the characters necessary to convey the substance to another person, and we shall find ourselves writing on as it were mechanically while thinking and talking of something else. So a paid copyist, to whom the subject of what he is writing is of no importance, does not even notice it. He deals only with familiar words and familiar characters without caring to go behind them, and thereupon writes on in a quasi-unconscious manner; but if he comes to a word or to characters with which he is but little acquainted, he becomes immediately awakened to the consciousness of either remembering or trying to remember. His consciousness of his own knowledge or memory would seem to belong to a period, so to speak, of twilight between the thick darkness of ignorance and the brilliancy of perfect knowledge; as colour which vanishes with extremes of light or of shade. Perfect ignorance and perfect knowledge are alike unselfconscious.

The above holds good even more noticeably in respect of reading. How many thousands of individual letters do our eyes run over every morning in the "Times" newspaper, how few of them do we notice, or remember having noticed? Yet there was a time when we had such difficulty in reading even the simplest words, that we had to take great pains to impress them upon our memory so as to know them when we came to then again. Now, not even a single word of all we have seen will remain with us, unless it is a new one, or an old one used in an unfamiliar sense, in which case we notice, and may very likely remember it. Our memory retains the substance only, the substance only being unfamiliar. Nevertheless, although we do not perceive more than the general result of our perception, there can be no doubt of our having perceived every letter in every word that we have read at all, for if we come upon a word misspelt our attention is at once aroused; unless, indeed, we have actually corrected the misspelling, as well as noticed it, unconsciously, through exceeding familiarity with the way in which it ought to be spelt. Not only do we perceive the letters we have seen without noticing that we have perceived them, but we find it almost impossible to notice that we notice them when we have once learnt to read fluently. To try to do so puts us out, and prevents our being able to read. We may even go so far as to say that if a man can attend to the individual characters, it is a sign that he cannot yet read fluently. If we know how to read well, we are as unconscious of the means and processes whereby we attain the desired result as we are about the growth of our hair or the circulation of our blood. So that here again it would seem that we only know what we know still to some extent imperfectly, and that what we know thoroughly escapes our conscious perception though none the less actually perceived. Our perception in fact passes into a latent stage, as also our memory and volition.

Walking is another example of the rapid exercise of volition with but little perception of each individual act of exercise. We notice any obstacle in our path, but it is plain we do not notice that we perceive much that we have nevertheless been perceiving; for if a man goes down a lane by night he will stumble over many things which he would have avoided by day, although he would not have noticed them. Yet time was when walking was to each one of us a new and arduous task - as arduous as we should now find it to wheel a wheelbarrow on a tight-rope; whereas, at present, though we can think of our steps to a certain extent without checking our power to walk, we certainly cannot consider our muscular action in detail without having to come to a dead stop.

Talking—especially in one's mother tongue—may serve as a last example. We find it impossible to follow the muscular action of the mouth and tongue in framing every letter or syllable we utter. We have probably spoken for years and years before we became aware that the letter h is a labial sound, and until we have to utter a word which is difficult from its unfamiliarity we speak "trippingly on the tongue" with no attention except to the substance of what we wish to say. Yet talking was not always the easy matter to us which it is at present— as we perceive more readily when we are learning a new language which it may take us months to master. Nevertheless, when we have once mastered it we speak it without further consciousness of knowledge or memory, as regards the more common words, and without even noticing our consciousness. Here, as in the other instances already given, as long as we did not know perfectly, we were conscious of our acts of perception, volition, and reflection, but when our knowledge has become perfect we no longer notice our consciousness, nor our volition; nor can we awaken a second artificial consciousness without some effort, and disturbance of the process of which we are endeavouring to become conscious. We are no longer, so to speak, under the law, but under grace.

An ascending scale may be perceived in the above instances.

In playing, we have an action acquired long after birth, difficult of acquisition, and never thoroughly familiarised to the power of absolutely unconscious performance, except in the case of those who have either an exceptional genius for music, or who have devoted the greater part of their time to practising. Except in the case of these persons it is generally found easy to become more or less conscious of any passage without disturbing the performance, and our action remains so completely within our control that we can stop playing at any moment we please.

In writing, we have an action generally acquired earlier, done for the most part with great unconsciousness of detail, fairly well within our control to stop at any moment; though not so completely as would be imagined by those who have not made the experiment of trying to stop in the middle of a given character when writing at fit speed. Also, we can notice our formation of any individual character without our writing being materially hindered.

Reading is usually acquired earlier still. We read with more unconsciousness of attention than we write. We find it more difficult to become conscious of any character without discomfiture, and we cannot arrest ourselves in the middle of a word, for example, and hardly before the end of a sentence; nevertheless it is on the whole well within our control.

Walking is so early an acquisition that we cannot remember having acquired it. In running fast over average ground we find it very difficult to become conscious of each individual step, and should possibly find it more difficult still, if the inequalities and roughness of uncultured land had not perhaps caused the development of a power to create a second consciousness of our steps without hindrance to our running or walking. Pursuit and flight, whether in the chase or in war, must for many generations have played a much more prominent part in the lives of our ancestors than they do in our own. If the ground over which they had to travel had been generally as free from obstruction as our modern cultivated lands, it is possible that we might not find it as easy to notice our several steps as we do at present. Even as it is, if while we are running we would consider the action of our muscles, we come to a dead stop, and should probably fall if we tried to observe too suddenly; for we must stop to do this, and running, when we have once committed ourselves to it beyond a certain point, is not controllable to a step or two without loss of equilibrium.

We learn to talk, much about the same time that we learn to walk, but talking requires less muscular effort than walking, and makes generally less demand upon our powers. A man may talk a long while before he has done the equivalent of a five-mile walk; it is natural, therefore, that we should have had more practice in talking than in walking, and hence that we should find it harder to pay attention to our words than to our steps. Certainly it is very hard to become conscious of every syllable or indeed of every word we say; the attempt to do so will often bring us to a check at once; nevertheless we can generally stop talking if we wish to do so, unless the crying of infants be considered as a kind of *quasi*-speech: this comes earlier, and is often quite uncontrollable, or more truly perhaps is done with such complete control over the muscles by the will, and with such absolute certainty of his own purpose on the part of the wilier, that there is no longer any more doubt, uncertainty, or suspense, and hence no power of perceiving any of the processes whereby the result is attained—as a wheel which may look fast fixed because it is so fast revolving. {2}

We may observe therefore in this ascending scale, imperfect as it is, that the older the habit the longer the practice, the longer the practice, the more knowledge—or, the less uncertainty; the less uncertainty the less power of conscious self-analysis and control.

It will occur to the reader that in all the instances given above, different individuals attain the unconscious stage of perfect knowledge with very different degrees of facility. Some have to attain it with a great sum; others are free born. Some learn to play, to read, write, and talk, with hardly an effort—some show such an instinctive aptitude for arithmetic that, like Zerah Colburn, at eight years old, they achieve results without instruction, which in the case of most people would require a long education. The account of Zerah Colburn, as quoted from Mr. Baily in Dr. Carpenter's "Mental Physiology," may perhaps be given here.

"He raised any number consisting of *one* figure progressively to the tenth power, giving the results (by actual multiplication and not by memory) *faster than they could be set down in figures* by the person appointed to record them. He raised the number 8 progressively to the *sixteenth* power, and in naming the last result, which consisted of 15 figures, he was right in every one. Some numbers consisting of *two* figures he raised as high as the eighth power, though he found a difficulty in proceeding when the products became very large.

"On being asked the *square root* of 106,929, he answered 327 before the original number could be written down. He was then required to find the cube root of 268,336,125, and with equal facility and promptness he replied 645.

"He was asked how many minutes there are in 48 years, and before the question could be taken down he replied 25,228,800, and immediately afterwards he gave the correct number of seconds.

"On being requested to give the factors which would produce the number 247,483, he immediately named 941 and 263, which are the only two numbers from the multiplication of which it would result. On 171,395 being proposed, he named $5 \times 34,279$, $7 \times 24,485$, 59×2905, 83×2065, 35×4897, 295×581, and 413×415.

"He was then asked to give the factors of 36,083, but he immediately replied that it had none, which was really the case, this being a prime number. Other numbers being proposed to him indiscriminately, he always succeeded in giving the correct factors except in the case of prime numbers, which he generally discovered almost as soon as they were proposed to him. The number 4,294,967,297, which is $2^{32} + 1$, having been given him, he discovered, as Euler had previously done, that it was not the prime number which Fermat had supposed it to be, but that it is the product of the factors $6,700,417 \times 641$. The solution of this problem was only given after the lapse of some weeks, but the method he took to obtain it clearly showed that he had not derived his information from any extraneous source.

"When he was asked to multiply together numbers both consisting of more than these figures, he seemed to decompose one or both of them into its factors, and to work with them separately. Thus, on being asked to give the square of 4395, he multiplied 293 by itself, and then twice multiplied the product by 15. And on being asked to tell the square of 999,999 he obtained the correct result, 999,998,000,001, by twice multiplying the square of 37,037 by 27. He then of his own accord multiplied that product by 49, and said that the result (viz., 48,999,902,000,049) was equal to the square of 6,999,993. He afterwards multiplied this product by 49, and observed that the result (viz., 2,400,995,198,002,401) was equal to the square of 48,999,951. He was again asked to multiply the product by 25, and in naming the result (viz., 60,024,879,950,060,025) he said it was equal to the square of 244,999,755.

"On being interrogated as to the manner in which he obtained these results, the boy constantly said he did not know *how* the answers came into his mind. In the act of multiplying two numbers together, and in the raising of powers, it was evident (alike from the facts just stated and from the motion of his lips) that *some* operation was going forward in his mind; yet that operation could not (from the readiness with which his answers were furnished) have been at all allied to the usual modes of procedure, of which, indeed, he was entirely ignorant, not being able to perform on paper a simple sum in multiplication or division. But in the extraction of roots, and in the discovery of the factors of large numbers, it did not appear that any operation *could* take place, since he gave answers *immediately* , or in a very few seconds, which, according to the ordinary methods, would have required very difficult and laborious calculations, and prime numbers cannot be recognised as such by any known rule."

I should hope that many of the above figures are wrong. I have verified them carefully with Dr. Carpenter's quotation, but further than this I cannot and will not go. Also I am happy to find that in the end the boy overcame the mathematics, and turned out a useful but by no means particularly calculating member of society.

The case, however, is typical of others in which persons have been found able to do without apparent effort what in the great majority of cases requires a long apprenticeship. It is needless to multiply instances; the point that concerns us is, that knowledge under such circumstances being very intense, and the ease with which the result is produced extreme, it eludes the conscious apprehension of the performer himself, who only becomes conscious when a difficulty arises which taxes even his abnormal power. Such a case, therefore, confirms rather than militates against our opinion that consciousness of knowledge vanishes on the knowledge becoming perfect—the only difference between those possessed of any such remarkable special power and the general run of people being, that the first are born with such an unusual aptitude for their particular specialty that they are able to dispense with all or nearly all the preliminary exercise of their faculty, while the latter must exercise it for a considerable time before they can get it to work smoothly and easily; but in either case when once the knowledge is intense it is unconscious.

Nor again would such an instance as that of Zerah Colburn warrant us in believing that this white heat, as it were, of unconscious knowledge can be attained by any one without his ever having been originally cold. Young Colburn, for example, could not extract roots when he was an embryo of three weeks' standing. It is true we can seldom follow the process, but we know there must have been a time in every case when even the desire for information or action had not been kindled; the forgetfulness of effort on the part of those with exceptional genius for a special subject is due to the smallness of the effort necessary, so that it makes no impression upon the individual himself, rather than to the absence of any effort at all. {3}

It would, therefore, appear as though perfect knowledge and perfect ignorance were extremes which meet and become indistinguishable from one another; so also perfect volition and perfect absence of volition, perfect memory and utter forgetfulness; for we are unconscious of knowing, willing, or remembering, either from not yet having known or willed, or from knowing and willing so well and so intensely as to be no longer conscious of either. Conscious knowledge and volition are of attention; attention is of suspense; suspense is of doubt; doubt is of uncertainty; uncertainty is of ignorance; so that the mere fact of conscious knowing or willing implies the presence of more or less novelty and doubt.

It would also appear as a general principle on a superficial view of the foregoing instances (and the reader may readily supply himself with others which are perhaps more to the purpose), that unconscious knowledge and unconscious volition are never acquired otherwise than as the result of experience, familiarity, or habit; so that whenever we observe a person able to do any complicated action unconsciously, we may assume both that he must have done it very often before he could acquire so great proficiency, and also that there must have been a time when he did not know how to do it at all.

We may assume that there was a time when he was yet so nearly on the point of neither knowing nor willing perfectly, that he was quite alive to whatever knowledge or volition he could exert; going further back, we shall find him still more keenly alive to a less perfect knowledge; earlier still, we find him well aware that he does not know nor will correctly, but trying hard to do both the one and the other; and so on, back and back, till both difficulty and consciousness become little more than a sound of going in the brain, a flitting to and fro of something barely recognisable as the desire to will or know at all— much less as the desire to know or will definitely this or that. Finally, they retreat beyond our ken into the repose—the inorganic kingdom—of as yet unawakened interest.

In either case,—the repose of perfect ignorance or of perfect knowledge —disturbance is troublesome. When first starting on an Atlantic steamer, our rest is hindered by the screw; after a short time, it is hindered if the screw stops. A uniform impression is practically no impression. One cannot either learn or unlearn without pains or pain.

CHAPTER II—CONSCIOUS AND UNCONSCIOUS KNOWERS—THE LAW AND GRACE

In this chapter we shall show that the law, which we have observed to hold as to the vanishing tendency of knowledge upon becoming perfect, holds good not only concerning acquired actions or habits of body, but concerning opinions, modes of thought, and mental habits generally, which are no more recognised as soon as firmly fixed, than are the steps with which we go about our daily avocations. I am aware that I may appear in the latter part of the chapter to have wandered somewhat beyond the limits of my subject, but, on the whole, decide upon leaving what I have written, inasmuch as it serves to show how far-reaching is the principle on which I am insisting. Having said so much, I shall during the remainder of the book keep more closely to the point.

Certain it is that we know best what we are least conscious of knowing, or at any rate least able to prove, as, for example, our own existence, or that there is a country England. If any one asks us for proof on matters of this sort, we have none ready, and are justly annoyed at being called to consider what we regard as settled questions. Again, there is hardly anything which so much affects our actions as the centre of the earth (unless, perhaps, it be that still hotter and more unprofitable spot the centre of the universe), for we are incessantly trying to get as near it as circumstances will allow, or to avoid getting nearer than is for the time being convenient. Walking, running, standing, sitting, lying, waking, or sleeping, from birth till death it is a paramount object with us; even after death— if it be not fanciful to say so—it is one of the few things of which what is left of us can still feel the influence; yet what can engross less of our attention than this dark and distant spot so many thousands of miles away?

The air we breathe, so long as it is neither too hot nor cold, nor rough, nor full of smoke—that is to say, so long as it is in that state within which we are best acquainted—seldom enters into our thoughts; yet there is hardly anything with which we are more incessantly occupied night and day.

Indeed, it is not too much to say that we have no really profound knowledge upon any subject—no knowledge on the strength of which we are ready to act at all moments unhesitatingly without either preparation or after-thought—till we have left off feeling conscious of the possession of such knowledge, and of the grounds on which it rests. A lesson thoroughly learned must be like the air which feels so light, though pressing so heavily against us, because every pore of our skin is saturated, so to speak, with it on all sides equally. This perfection of knowledge sometimes extends to positive disbelief in the thing known, so that the most thorough knower shall believe himself altogether ignorant. No thief, for example, is such an utter thief— so *good* a thief—as the kleptomaniac. Until he has become a kleptomaniac, and can steal a horse as it were by a reflex action, he is still but half a thief, with many unthievish notions still clinging to him. Yet the kleptomaniac is probably unaware that he can steal at all, much less that he can steal so well. He would be shocked if he were to know the truth. So again, no man is a great hypocrite until he has left off knowing that he is a hypocrite. The great hypocrites of the world are almost invariably under the impression that they are among the very few really honest people to be found and, as we must all have observed, it is rare to find any one strongly under this impression without ourselves having good reason to differ from him.

Our own existence is another case in point. When we have once become articulately conscious of existing, it is an easy matter to begin doubting whether we exist at all. As long as man was too unreflecting a creature to articulate in words his consciousness of his own existence, he knew very well that he existed, but he did not know that he knew it. With introspection, and the perception recognised, for better or worse, that he was a fact, came also the perception that he had no solid ground for believing that he was a fact at all. That nice, sensible, unintrospective people who were too busy trying to exist pleasantly to trouble their heads as to whether they existed or no—that this best part of mankind should have gratefully caught at such a straw as "*cogito ergo sum,*" is intelligible enough. They felt the futility of the whole question, and were thankful to one who seemed to clench the matter with a cant catchword, especially with a catchword in a foreign language; but how one, who was so far gone as to recognise that he could not prove his own existence, should be able to comfort himself with such a begging of the question, would seem unintelligible except upon the ground of sheer exhaustion.

At the risk of appearing to wander too far from the matter in hand, a few further examples may perhaps be given of that irony of nature, by which it comes about that we so often most know and are, what we least think ourselves to know and be—and on the other hand hold most strongly what we are least capable of demonstrating.

Take the existence of a Personal God,—one of the most profoundly-received and widely-spread ideas that have ever prevailed among mankind. Has there ever been a *demonstration* of the existence of such a God as has satisfied any considerable section of thinkers for long together? Hardly has what has been conceived to be a demonstration made its appearance and received a certain acceptance as though it were actual proof, when it has been impugned with sufficient success to show that, however true the fact itself, the demonstration is naught. I do not say that this is an argument against the personality of God; the drift, indeed, of the present reasoning would be towards an opposite conclusion, inasmuch as it insists upon the fact that what is most true and best known is often least susceptible of demonstration owing to the very perfectness with which it is known; nevertheless, the fact remains that many men in many ages and countries - the subtlest thinkers over the whole world for some fifteen hundred years— have hunted for a demonstration of God's personal existence; yet though so many have sought,—so many, and so able, and for so long a time—none have found. There is no demonstration which can be pointed to with any unanimity as settling the matter beyond power of reasonable cavil. On the contrary, it may be observed that from the attempt to prove the existence of a personal God to the denial of that existence altogether, the path is easy. As in the case of our own existence, it will be found that they alone are perfect believers in a personal Deity and in the Christian religion who have not yet begun to feel that either stands in need of demonstration. We observe that most people, whether Christians, or Jews, or Mohammedans, are unable to give their reasons for the faith that is in them with any readiness or completeness; and this is sure proof that they really hold it so utterly as to have no further sense that it either can be demonstrated or ought to be so, but feel towards it as towards the air which they breathe but do not notice. On the other hand, a living prelate was reported in the

"Times" to have said in one of his latest charges: "My belief is that a widely extended good practice must be founded upon Christian doctrine." The fact of the Archbishop's recognising this as among the number of his beliefs is conclusive evidence with those who have devoted attention to the laws of thought, that his mind is not yet clear as to whether or no there is any connection at all between Christian doctrine and widely extended good practice. {4}

Again, it has been often and very truly said that it is not the conscious and self-styled sceptic, as Shelley for example, who is the true unbeliever. Such a man as Shelley will, as indeed his life abundantly proves, have more in common than not with the true unselfconscious believer. Gallio again, whose indifference to religious animosities has won him the cheapest immortality which, so far as I can remember, was ever yet won, was probably if the truth were known, a person of the sincerest piety. It is the unconscious unbeliever who is the true infidel, however greatly he would be surprised to know the truth. Mr. Spurgeon was reported as having recently asked the Almighty to "change our rulers *as soon as possible* ." There lurks a more profound distrust of God's power in these words than in almost any open denial of His existence.

So it rather shocks us to find Mr. Darwin writing ("Plants and Animals under Domestication," vol. ii., p. 275): "No doubt, in every case there must have been some exciting cause." And again, six or seven pages later: "No doubt, each slight variation must have its efficient cause." The repetition within so short a space of this expression of confidence in the impossibility of causeless effects would suggest that Mr. Darwin's mind at the time of writing was, unconsciously to himself, in a state of more or less uneasiness as to whether effects could not occasionally come about of themselves, and without cause of any sort,—that he may have been standing, in fact, for a short time upon the brink of a denial of the indestructibility of force and matter.

In like manner, the most perfect humour and irony is generally quite unconscious. Examples of both are frequently given by men whom the world considers as deficient in humour; it is more probably true that these persons are unconscious of their own delightful power through the very mastery and perfection with which they hold it. There is a play, for instance, of genuine fun in some of the more serious scientific and theological journals which for some time past we have looked for in vain in " —- ."

The following extract, from a journal which I will not advertise, may serve as an example:

"Lycurgus, when they had abandoned to his revenge him who had put out his eyes, took him home, and the punishment he inflicted upon him was sedulous instructions to virtue." Yet this truly comic paper does not probably know that it is comic, any more than the kleptomaniac knows that he steals, or than John Milton knew he was a humorist when he wrote a hymn upon the circumcision, and spent his honeymoon in composing a treatise on divorce. No more again did Goethe know how exquisitely humorous he was when he wrote, in his Wilhelm Meister, that a beautiful tear glistened in Theresa's right eye, and then went on to explain that it glistened in her right eye and not in her left, because she had had a wart on her left which had been removed—and successfully. Goethe probably wrote this without a chuckle; he believed what a good many people who have never read Wilhelm Meister believe still, namely, that it was a work full of pathos, of fine and tender feeling; yet a less consummate humorist must have felt that there was scarcely a paragraph in it from first to last the chief merit of which did not lie in its absurdity.

Another example may be taken from Bacon of the manner in which sayings which drop from men unconsciously, give the key of their inner thoughts to another person, though they themselves know not that they have such thoughts at all; much less that these thoughts are their only true convictions. In his Essay on Friendship the great philosopher writes: "Reading good books on morality is a little flat and dead." Innocent, not to say pathetic, as this passage may sound it is pregnant with painful inferences concerning Bacon's moral character. For if he knew that he found reading good books of morality a little flat and dead, it follows he must have tried to read them; nor is he saved by the fact that he found them a little flat and dead; for though this does indeed show that he had begun to be so familiar with a few first principles as to find it more or less exhausting to have his attention directed to them further—yet his words prove that they were not so incorporate with him that he should feel the loathing for further discourse upon the matter which honest people commonly feel now. It will be remembered that he took bribes when he came to be Lord Chancellor.

It is on the same principle that we find it so distasteful to hear one praise another for earnestness. For such praise raises a suspicion in our minds (*pace* the late Dr. Arnold and his following) that the praiser's attention must have been arrested by sincerity, as by something more or less unfamiliar to himself. So universally is this recognised that the world has for some time been discarded entirely by all reputable people. Truly, if there is one who cannot find himself in the same room with the life and letters of an earnest person without being made instantly unwell, the same is a just man and perfect in all his ways.

But enough has perhaps been said. As the fish in the sea, or the bird in the air, so unreasoningly and inarticulately safe must a man feel before he can be said to know. It is only those who are ignorant and uncultivated who can know anything at all in a proper sense of the words. Cultivation will breed in any man a certainty of the uncertainty even of his most assured convictions. It is perhaps fortunate for our comfort that we can none of us be cultivated upon very many subjects, so that considerable scope for assurance will still remain to us; but however this may be, we certainly observe it as a fact that the greatest men are they who are most uncertain in spite of certainty, and at the same time most certain in spite of uncertainty, and who are thus best able to feel that there is nothing in such complete harmony with itself as a flat contradiction in terms. For nature hates that any principle should breed, so to speak, hermaphroditically, but will give to each an help meet for it which shall cross it and be the undoing of it; as in the case of descent with modification, of which the essence would appear to be that every offspring should resemble its parents, and yet, at the same time, that no offspring should resemble its parents. But for the slightly irritating stimulant of this perpetual crossing, we should pass our lives unconsciously as though in slumber.

Until we have got to understand that though black is not white, yet it may be whiter than white itself (and any painter will readily paint that which shall show obviously as black, yet it shall be whiter than that which shall show no less obviously as white), we may be good logicians, but we are still poor reasoners. Knowledge is in an inchoate state as long as it is capable of logical treatment; it must be transmuted into that sense or instinct which rises altogether above the sphere in which words can have being at all, otherwise it is not yet vital. For sense is to knowledge what conscience is to reasoning about right and wrong; the reasoning must be so rapid as to defy conscious reference to first principles, and even at times to be apparently subversive of them altogether, or the action will halt. It must, in fact, become automatic before we are safe with it. While we are fumbling for the grounds of our conviction, our conviction is prone to fall, as Peter for lack of faith sinking into the waves of Galilee; so that the very power to prove at all is an *à priori* argument against the truth—or at any rate the practical importance to the vast majority of mankind—of all that is supported by demonstration. For the power to prove implies a sense of the need of proof, and things which the majority of mankind find practically important are in ninety-nine cases out of a hundred above proof. The need of proof becomes as obsolete in the case of assumed knowledge, as the practice of fortifying towns in the middle of an old and long settled country. Who builds defences for that which is impregnable or little likely to be assailed? The answer is ready, that unless the defences had been built in former times it would be impossible to do without them now; but this does not touch the argument, which is not that demonstration is unwise, but that as long as a demonstration is still felt necessary, and therefore kept ready to hand, the subject of such demonstration is not yet securely known. *Qui s'excuse, s'accuse*; and unless a matter can hold its own without the brag and self-assertion of continual demonstration, it is still more or less of a parvenu, which we shall not lose much by neglecting till it has less occasion to blow its own trumpet. The only alternative is that it is an error in process of detection, for if evidence concerning any opinion has long been denied superfluous, and ever after this comes to be again felt necessary, we know that the opinion is doomed.

If there is any truth in the above, it should follow that our conception of the words "science" and "scientific" should undergo some modification. Not that we should speak slightingly of science, but that we should recognise more than we do, that there are two distinct classes of scientific people corresponding not inaptly with the two main parties unto which the political world is divided. The one class is deeply versed in those sciences which have already become the common property of mankind; enjoying, enforcing, perpetuating, and engraving still more deeply unto the mind of man acquisitions already approved by common experience, but somewhat careless about extension of empire, or at any rate disinclined, for the most part, to active effort on their own part for the sake of such extension— neither progressive, in fact, nor aggressive—but quiet, peaceable people, who wish to live and let live, as their fathers before them; while the other class is chiefly intent upon pushing forward the boundaries of science, and is comparatively indifferent to what is known already save in so far as necessary for purposes of extension. These last are called pioneers of science, and to them alone is the title "scientific" commonly accorded; but pioneers, unimportant to an army as they are, are still not the army itself; which can get on better without the pioneers than the pioneers without the army. Surely the class which knows thoroughly well what it knows, and which adjudicates upon the value of the discoveries made by the pioneers—surely this class has as good a right or better to be called scientific than the pioneers themselves.

These two classes above described blend into one another with every shade of gradation. Some are admirably proficient in the well-known sciences—that is to say, they have good health, good looks, good temper, common sense, and energy, and they hold all these good things in such perfection as to lie altogether without introspection—to be not under the law, but so utterly and entirely under grace that every one who sees them likes them. But such may, and perhaps more commonly will, have very little inclination to extend the boundaries of human knowledge; their aim is in another direction altogether. Of the pioneers, on the other hand, some are agreeable people, well versed in the older sciences, though still more eminent as pioneers, while others, whose services in this last capacity have been of inestimable value, are noticeably ignorant of the sciences which have already become current with the larger part of mankind—in other words, they are ugly, rude, and disagreeable people, very progressive, it may be, but very aggressive to boot.

The main difference between these two classes lies in the fact that the knowledge of the one, so far as it is new, is known consciously, while that of the other is unconscious, consisting of sense and instinct rather than of recognised knowledge. So long as a man has these, and of the same kind as the more powerful body of his fellow-countrymen, he is a true man of science, though he can hardly read or write. As my great namesake said so well, "He knows what's what, and that's as high as metaphysic wit can fly." As usual, these true and thorough knowers do not know that they are scientific, and can seldom give a reason for the faith that is in them. They believe themselves to be ignorant, uncultured men, nor can even the professors whom they sometimes outwit in their own professorial domain perceive that they have been outwitted by men of superior scientific attainments to their own. The following passage from Dr. Carpenter's "Mesmerism, Spiritualism," &c., may serve as an illustration:-

"It is well known that persons who are conversant with the geological structure of a district are often able to indicate with considerable certainty in what spot and at what depth water will be found; and men *of less scientific knowledge, but of considerable practical experience*"—(so that in Dr. Carpenter's mind there seems to be some sort of contrast or difference in kind between the knowledge which is derived from observation of facts and scientific knowledge)—"frequently arrive at a true conclusion upon this point without being able to assign reasons for their opinions.

"Exactly the same may be said in regard to the mineral structure of a mining district; the course of a metallic vein being often correctly indicated by the shrewd guess of an *observant* workman, when *the scientific reasoning* of the mining engineer altogether fails."

Precisely. Here we have exactly the kind of thing we are in search of: the man who has observed and observed till the facts are so thoroughly in his head that through familiarity he has lost sight both of them and of the processes whereby he deduced his conclusions from them—is apparently not considered scientific, though he knows how to solve the problem before him; the mining engineer, on the other hand, who reasons scientifically—that is to say, with a knowledge of his own knowledge—is found not to know, and to fail in discovering the mineral.

"It is an experience we are continually encountering in other walks of life," continues Dr. Carpenter, "that particular persons are guided - some apparently by an original and others by *an acquired intuition* —to conclusions for which they can give no adequate reason, but which subsequent events prove to have been correct." And this, I take it, implies what I have been above insisting on, namely, that on becoming intense, knowledge seems also to become unaware of the grounds on which it rests, or that it has or requires grounds at all, or indeed even exists. The only issue between myself and Dr. Carpenter would appear to be, that Dr. Carpenter, himself an acknowledged leader in the scientific world, restricts the term "scientific" to the people who know that they know, but are beaten by those who are not so conscious of their own knowledge; while I say that the term "scientific" should be applied (only that they would not like it) to the nice sensible people who know what's what rather than to the discovering class.

And this is easily understood when we remember that the pioneer cannot hope to acquire any of the new sciences in a single lifetime so perfectly as to become unaware of his own knowledge. As a general rule, we observe him to be still in a state of active consciousness concerning whatever particular science he is extending, and as long as he is in this state he cannot know utterly. It is, as I have already so often insisted on, those who do not know that they know so much who have the firmest grip of their knowledge: the best class, for example, of our English youth, who live much in the open air, and, as Lord Beaconsfield finely said, never read. These are the people who know best those things which are best worth knowing—that is to say, they are the most truly scientific. Unfortunately, the apparatus necessary for this kind of science is so costly as to be within the reach of few, involving, as it does, an experience in the use of it for some preceding generations. Even those who are born with the means within their reach must take no less pains, and exercise no less self-control, before they can attain the perfect unconscious use of them, than would go to the making of a James Watt or a Stephenson; it is vain, therefore, to hope that this best kind of science can ever be put within the reach of the many; nevertheless it may be safely said that all the other and more generally recognised kinds of science are valueless except in so far as they tend to minister to this the highest kind. They have no *raison d'être* except so far as they tend to do away with the necessity for work, and to diffuse good health, and that good sense which is above self-consciousness. They are to be encouraged because they have rendered the most fortunate kind of modern European possible, and because they tend to make possible a still more fortunate kind than any now existing. But the man who devotes himself to science cannot—with the rarest, if any, exceptions—belong to this most fortunate class himself. He occupies a lower place, both scientifically and morally, for it is not possible but that his drudgery should somewhat soil him both in mind and health of body, or, if this be denied, surely it must let him and hinder him in running the race for unconsciousness. We do not feel that it increases the glory of a king or great nobleman that he should excel in what is commonly called science. Certainly he should not go further than Prince Rupert's drops. Nor should he excel in music, art, literature, or theology—all which things are more or less parts of science. He should be above them all, save in so far as he can without effort reap renown from the labours of others. It is a *lâche* in him that he should write music or books, or paint pictures at all; but if he must do so, his work should be at best contemptible. Much as we must condemn Marcus Aurelius, we condemn James I. ever more severely.

It is a pity there should exist so general a confusion of thought upon this subject, for it may be asserted without fear of contradiction that there is hardly any form of immorality now rife which produces more disastrous effects upon those who give themselves up to it, and upon society in general, than the so-called science of those who know that they know too well to be able to know truly. With very clever people—the people who know that they know—it is much as with the members of the early Corinthian Church, to whom St. Paul wrote, that if they looked their numbers over, they would not find many wise, nor powerful, nor well-born people among them. Dog-fanciers tell us that performing dogs never carry their tails; such dogs have eaten of the tree of knowledge, and are convinced of sin accordingly—they know that they know things, in respect of which, therefore, they are no longer under grace, but under the law, and they have yet so much grace left as to be ashamed. So with the human clever dog; he may speak with the tongues of men and angels, but so long as he knows that he knows, his tail will droop. More especially does this hold in the case of those who are born to wealth and of old family. We must all feel that a rich young nobleman with a taste for science and principles is rarely a pleasant object. We do not even like the rich young man in the Bible who wanted to inherit eternal life, unless, indeed, he merely wanted to know whether there was not some way by which he could avoid dying, and even so he is hardly worth considering. Principles are like logic, which never yet made a good reasoner of a bad one, but might still be occasionally useful if they did not invariably contradict each other whenever there is any temptation to appeal to them. They are like fire, good servants but bad masters. As many people or more have been wrecked on principle as from want of principle. They are, as their name implies, of an elementary character, suitable for beginners only, and he who has so little mastered them as to have occasion to refer to them consciously, is out of place in the society of well-educated people. The truly scientific invariably hate him, and, for the most part, the more profoundly in proportion to the unconsciousness with which they do so.

If the reader hesitates, let him go down into the streets and look in the shop-windows at the photographs of eminent men, whether literary, artistic, or scientific, and note the work which the consciousness of knowledge has wrought on nine out of every ten of them; then let him go to the masterpieces of Greek and Italian art, the truest preachers of the truest gospel of grace; let him look at the Venus of Milo, the Discobolus, the St. George of Donatello. If it had pleased these people to wish to study, there was no lack of brains to do it with; but imagine "what a deal of scorn" would "look beautiful" upon the Venus of Milo's face if it were suggested to her that she should learn to read. Which, think you, knows most, the Theseus, or any modern professor taken at random? True, the advancement of learning must have had a great share in the advancement of beauty, inasmuch as beauty is but knowledge perfected and incarnate—but with the pioneers it is *sic vos non vobis*; the grace is not for them, but for those who come after. Science is like offences. It must needs come, but woe unto that man through whom it comes; for there cannot be much beauty where there is consciousness of knowledge, and while knowledge is still new it must in the nature of things involve much consciousness.

It is not knowledge, then, that is incompatible with beauty; there cannot be too much knowledge, but it must have passed through many people who it is to be feared must be more or less disagreeable, before beauty or grace will have anything to say to it; it must be so incarnate in a man's whole being that he shall not be aware of it, or it will fit him constrainedly as one under the law, and not as one under grace.

And grace is best, for where grace is, love is not distant. Grace! the old Pagan ideal whose charm even unlovely Paul could not understand, but, as the legend tells us, his soul fainted within him, his heart misgave him, and, standing alone on the seashore at dusk, he "troubled deaf heaven with his bootless cries," his thin voice pleading for grace after the flesh.

The waves came in one after another, the sea-gulls cried together after their kind, the wind rustled among the dried canes upon the sandbanks, and there came a voice from heaven saying, "Let My grace be sufficient for thee." Whereon, failing of the thing itself, he stole the word and strove to crush its meaning to the measure of his own limitations. But the true grace, with her groves and high places, and troups of young men and maidens crowned with flowers, and singing of love and youth and wine—the true grace he drove out into the wilderness—high up, it may be, into Piora, and into such-like places. Happy they who harboured her in her ill report.

It is common to hear men wonder what new faith will be adopted by mankind if disbelief in the Christian religion should become general. They seem to expect that some new theological or quasi-theological system will arise, which, *mutatis mutandis,* shall be Christianity over again. It is a frequent reproach against those who maintain that the supernatural element of Christianity is without foundation, that they bring forward no such system of their own. They pull down but cannot build. We sometimes hear even those who have come to the same conclusions as the destroyers say, that having nothing new to set up, they will not attack the old. But how can people set up a new superstition, knowing it to be a superstition? Without faith in their own platform, a faith as intense as that manifested by the early Christians, how can they preach? A new superstition will come, but it is in the very essence of things that its apostles should have no suspicion of its real nature; that they should no more recognise the common element between the new and the old than the early Christians recognised it between their faith and Paganism. If they did, they would be paralysed. Others say that the new fabric may be seen rising on every side, and that the coming religion is science. Certainly its apostles preach it without misgiving, but it is not on that account less possible that it may prove only to be the coming superstition— like Christianity, true to its true votaries, and, like Christianity, false to those who follow it introspectively.

It may well be we shall find we have escaped from one set of taskmasters to fall into the hands of others far more ruthless. The tyranny of the Church is light in comparison with that which future generations may have to undergo at the hands of the doctrinaires. The Church did uphold a grace of some sort as the *summum bonum,* in comparison with which all so-called earthly knowledge—knowledge, that is to say, which had not passed through so many people as to have become living and incarnate—was unimportant. Do what we may, we are still drawn to the unspoken teaching of her less introspective ages with a force which no falsehood could command. Her buildings, her music, her architecture, touch us as none other on the whole can do; when she speaks there are many of us who think that she denies the deeper truths of her own profounder mind, and unfortunately her tendency is now towards more rather than less introspection. The more she gives way to this—the more she becomes conscious of knowing—the less she will know. But still her ideal is in grace.

The so-called man of science, on the other hand, seems now generally inclined to make light of all knowledge, save of the pioneer character. His ideal is in self-conscious knowledge. Let us have no more Lo, here, with the professor; he very rarely knows what he says he knows; no sooner has he misled the world for a sufficient time with a great flourish of trumpets than he is toppled over by one more plausible than himself. He is but medicine-man, augur, priest, in its latest development; useful it may be, but requiring to be well watched by those who value freedom. Wait till he has become more powerful, and note the vagaries which his conceit of knowledge will indulge in. The Church did not persecute while she was still weak. Of course every system has had, and will have, its heroes, but, as we all very well know, the heroism of the hero is but remotely due to system; it is due not to arguments, nor reasoning, nor to any consciously recognised perceptions, but to those deeper sciences which lie far beyond the reach of self-analysis, and for the sturdy of which there is but one schooling—to have had good forefathers for many generations.

Above all things, let no unwary reader do me the injustice of believing in *me*. In that I write at all I am among the dammed. If he must believe in anything, let him believe in the music of Handel, the painting of Giovanni Bellini, and in the thirteenth chapter of St. Paul's First Epistle to the Corinthians.

But to return. Whenever we find people knowing that they know this or that, we have the same story over and over again. They do not yet know it perfectly.

We come, therefore, to the conclusion that our knowledge and reasoning thereupon, only become perfect, assured, unhesitating, when they have become automatic, and are thus exercised without further conscious effort of the mind, much in the same way as we cannot walk nor read nor write perfectly till we can do so automatically.

CHAPTER III—APPLICATION OF FOREGOING CHAPTERS TO CERTAIN HABITS ACQUIRED AFTER BIRTH WHICH ARE COMMONLY CONSIDERED INSTINCTIVE.

What is true of knowing is also true of willing. The more intensely we will, the less is our will deliberate and capable of being recognised as will at all. So that it is common to hear men declare under certain circumstances that they had no will, but were forced into their own action under stress of passion or temptation. But in the more ordinary actions of life, we observe, as in walking or breathing, that we do not will anything utterly and without remnant of hesitation, till we have lost sight of the fact that we are exercising our will.

The question, therefore, is forced upon us, how far this principle extends, and whether there may not be unheeded examples of its operation which, if we consider them, will land us in rather unexpected conclusions. If it be granted that consciousness of knowledge and of volition vanishes when the knowledge and the volition have become intense and perfect, may it not be possible that many actions which we do without knowing how we do them, and without any conscious exercise of the will—actions which we certainly could not do if we tried to do them, nor refrain from doing if for any reason we wished to do so—are done so easily and so unconsciously owing to excess of knowledge or experience rather than deficiency, we having done them too often, knowing how to do them too well, and having too little hesitation as to the method of procedure, to be capable of following our own action without the utter derangement of such action altogether; or, in other cases, because we have so long settled the question, that we have stowed away the whole apparatus with which we work in corners of our system which we cannot now conveniently reach?

It may be interesting to see whether we can find any class or classes of actions which would seem to link actions which for some time after birth we could not do at all, and in which our proficiency has reached the stage of unconscious performance obviously through repeated effort and failure, and through this only, with actions which we could do as soon as we were born, and concerning which it would at first sight appear absurd to say that they can have been acquired by any process in the least analogous to that which we commonly call experience, inasmuch as the creature itself which does them has only just begun to exist, and cannot, therefore, in the very nature of things, have had experience.

Can we see that actions, for the acquisition of which experience is such an obvious necessity, that whenever we see the acquisition we assume the experience, gradate away imperceptibly into actions which would seem, according to all reasonable analogy, to presuppose experience, of which, however, the time and place seem obscure, if not impossible?

Eating and drinking would appear to be such actions. The new-born child cannot eat, and cannot drink, but he can swallow as soon as he is born; and swallowing would appear (as we may remark in passing) to have been an earlier faculty of animal life than that of eating with teeth. The ease and unconsciousness with which we eat and drink is clearly attributable to practice; but a very little practice seems to go a long way—a suspiciously small amount of practice—as though somewhere or at some other time there must have been more practice than we can account for. We can very readily stop eating or drinking, and can follow our own action without difficulty in either process; but, as regards swallowing, which is the earlier habit, we have less power of self-analysis and control: when we have once committed ourselves beyond a certain point to swallowing, we must finish doing so,—that is to say, our control over the operation ceases. Also, a still smaller experience seems necessary for the acquisition of the power to swallow than appeared necessary in the case of eating; and if we get into a difficulty we choke, and are more at a loss how to become introspective than we are about eating and drinking.

Why should a baby be able to swallow—which one would have said was the more complicated process of the two—with so much less practice than it takes him to learn to eat? How comes it that he exhibits in the case of the more difficult operation all the phenomena which ordinarily accompany a more complete mastery and longer practice? Analogy would certainly seem to point in the direction of thinking that the necessary experience cannot have been wanting, and that, too, not in such a quibbling sort as when people talk about inherited habit or the experience of the race, which, without explanation, is to plain-speaking persons very much the same, in regard to the individual, as no experience at all, but *bonâ fide* in the child's own person.

Breathing, again, is an action acquired after birth, generally with some little hesitation and difficulty, but still acquired in a time seldom longer, as I am informed, than ten minutes or a quarter of an hour. For an ant which has to be acquired at all, there would seem here, as in the case of eating, to be a disproportion between, on the one hand, the intricacy of the process performed, and on the other, the shortness of the time taken to acquire the practice, and the ease and unconsciousness with which its exercise is continued from the moment of acquisition.

We observe that in later life much less difficult and intricate operations than breathing acquire much longer practice before they can be mastered to the extent of unconscious performance. We observe also that the phenomena attendant on the learning by an infant to breathe are extremely like those attendant upon the repetition of some performance by one who has done it very often before, but who requires just a little prompting to set him off, on getting which, the whole familiar routine presents itself before him, and he repeats his task by rote. Surely then we are justified in suspecting that there must have been more *bonâ fide* personal recollection and experience, with more effort and failure on the part of the infant itself than meet the eye.

It should be noticed, also, that our control over breathing is very limited. We can hold our breath a little, or breathe a little faster for a short time, but we cannot do this for long, and after having gone without air for a certain time we must breath.

Seeing and hearing require some practice before their free use is mastered, but not very much. They are so far within our control that we can see more by looking harder, and hear more by listening attentively—but they are beyond our control in so far as that we must see and hear the greater part of what presents itself to us as near, and at the same time unfamiliar, unless we turn away or shut our eyes, or stop our ears by a mechanical process; and when we do this it is a sign that we have already involuntarily seen or heard more than we wished. The familiar, whether sight or sound, very commonly escapes us.

Take again the processes of digestion, the action of the heart, and the oxygenisation of the blood—processes of extreme intricacy, done almost entirely unconsciously, and quite beyond the control of our volition.

Is it possible that our unconsciousness concerning our own performance of all these processes arises from over-experience?

Is there anything in digestion, or the oxygenisation of the blood, different in kind to the rapid unconscious action of a man playing a difficult piece of music on the piano? There may be in degree, but as a man who sits down to play what he well knows, plays on, when once started, almost, as we say, mechanically, so, having eaten his dinner, he digests it as a matter of course, unless it has been in some way unfamiliar to him, or he to it, owing to some derangement or occurrence with which he is unfamiliar, and under which therefore he is at a loss now to comport himself, as a player would be at a loss how to play with gloves on, or with gout in his fingers, or if set to play music upside down.

Can we show that all the acquired actions of childhood and after-life, which we now do unconsciously, or without conscious exercise of the will, are familiar acts—acts which we have already done a very great number of times?

Can we also show that there are no acquired actions which we can perform in this automatic manner, which were not at one time difficult, requiring attention, and liable to repeated failure, our volition failing to command obedience from the members which should carry its purposes into execution?

If so, analogy will point in the direction of thinking that other acts which we do even more unconsciously may only escape our power of self-examination and control because they are even more familiar— because we have done them oftener; and we may imagine that if there were a microscope which could show us the minutest atoms of consciousness and volition, we should find that even the apparently most automatic actions were yet done in due course, upon a balance of considerations, and under the deliberate exercise of the will.

We should also incline to think that even such an action as the oxygenisation of its blood by an infant of ten minutes' old, can only be done so well and so unconsciously, after repeated failures on the part of the infant itself.

True, as has been already implied, we do not immediately see when the baby could have made the necessary mistakes and acquired that infinite practice without which it could never go through such complex processes satisfactorily; we have therefore invented the words "hereditary instinct," and consider them as accounting for the phenomenon; but a very little reflection will show that though these words may be a very good way of stating the difficulty, they do little or nothing towards removing it.

Why should hereditary instinct enable a creature to dispense with the experience which we see to be necessary in all other cases before difficult operations can be performed successfully?

What is this talk that is made about the experience *of the race* , as though the experience of one man could profit another who knows nothing about him? If a man eats his dinner, it nourishes *him* and not his neighbour; if he learns a different art, it is *he* that can do it and not his neighbour. Yet, practically, we see that the vicarious experience, which seems so contrary to our common observation, does nevertheless appear to hold good in the case of creatures and their descendants. Is there, then, any way of bringing these apparently conflicting phenomena under the operation of one law? Is there any way of showing that this experience of the race, of which so much is said without the least attempt to show in what way it may or does become the experience of the individual, is in sober seriousness the experience of one single being only, repeating in a great many different ways certain performances with which he has become exceedingly familiar?

It would seem that we must either suppose the conditions of experience to differ during the earlier stages of life from those which we observe them to become during the heyday of any existence—and this would appear very gratuitous, tolerable only as a suggestion because the beginnings of life are so obscure, that in such twilight we may do pretty much whatever we please without danger of confutation—or that we must suppose the continuity of life and sameness between living beings, whether plants or animals, and their descendants, to be far closer than we have hitherto believed; so that the experience of one person is not enjoyed by his successor, so much as that the successor is *bonâ fide* but a part of the life of his progenitor, imbued with all his memories, profiting by all his experiences—which are, in fact, his own—and only unconscious of the extent of his own memories and experiences owing to their vastness and already infinite repetitions.

Certainly it presents itself to us at once as a singular coincidence -

I. That we are *most conscious of, and have most control over*, such habits as speech, the upright position, the arts and sciences, which are acquisitions peculiar to the human race, always acquired after birth, and not common to ourselves and any ancestor who had not become entirely human.

II. That we are *less conscious of, and have less control over*, eating and drinking, swallowing, breathing, seeing and hearing, which were acquisitions of our prehuman ancestry, and for which we had provided ourselves with all the necessary apparatus before we saw light, but which are still, geologically speaking, recent, or comparatively recent.

III. That we are *most unconscious of, and have least control over*, our digestion and circulation, which belonged even to our invertebrate ancestry, and which are habits, geologically speaking, of extreme antiquity.

There is something too like method in this for it to be taken as the result of mere chance—chance again being but another illustration of Nature's love of a contradiction in terms; for everything is chance, and nothing is chance. And you may take it that all is chance or nothing chance, according as you please, but you must not have half chance and half not chance.

Does it not seem as though the older and more confirmed the habit, the more unquestioning the act of volition, till, in the case of the oldest habits, the practice of succeeding existences has so formulated the procedure, that, on being once committed to such and such a line beyond a certain point, the subsequent course is so clear as to be open to no further doubt, to admit of no alternative, till the very power of questioning is gone, and even the consciousness of volition? And this too upon matters which, in earlier stages of a man's existence, admitted of passionate argument and anxious deliberation whether to resolve them thus or thus, with heroic hazard and experiment, which on the losing side proved to be vice, and on the winning virtue. For there was passionate argument once what shape a man's teeth should be, nor can the colour of his hair be considered as ever yet settled, or likely to be settled for a very long time.

It is one against legion when a creature tries to differ from his own past selves. He must yield or die if he wants to differ widely, so as to lack natural instincts, such as hunger or thirst, or not to gratify them. It is more righteous in a man that he should "eat strange food," and that his cheek should "so much as lank not," than that he should starve if the strange food be at his command. His past selves are living in him at this moment with the accumulated life of centuries. "Do this, this, this, which we too have done, and found our profit in it," cry the souls of his forefathers within him. Faint are the far ones, coming and going as the sound of bells wafted on to a high mountain; loud and clear are the near ones, urgent as an alarm of fire. "Withhold," cry some. "Go on boldly," cry others. "Me, me, me, revert hitherward, my descendant," shouts one as it were from some high vantage-ground over the heads of the clamorous multitude. "Nay, but me, me, me," echoes another; and our former selves fight within us and wrangle for our possession. Have we not here what is commonly called an *internal tumult*, when dead pleasures and pains tug within us hither and thither? Then may the battle be decided by what people are pleased to call our own experience. Our own indeed! What is our own save by mere courtesy of speech? A matter of fashion. Sanction sanctifieth and fashion fashioneth. And so with death—the most inexorable of all conventions.

However this may be, we may assume it as an axiom with regard to actions acquired after birth, that we never do them automatically save as the result of long practice, and after having thus acquired perfect mastery over the action in question.

But given the practice or experience, and the intricacy of the process to be performed appears to matter very little. There is hardly anything conceivable as being done by man, which a certain amount of familiarity will not enable him to do, as it were mechanically and without conscious effort. "The most complex and difficult movements," writes Mr Darwin, "can in time be performed without the least effort or consciousness." All the main business of life is done thus unconsciously or semi-unconsciously. For what is the main business of life? We work that we may eat and digest, rather than eat and digest that we may work; this, at any rate, is the normal state of things: the more important business then is that which is carried on unconsciously. So again the action of the brain, which goes on prior to our realising the idea in which it results, is not perceived by the individual. So also all the deeper springs of action and conviction. The residuum with which we fret and worry ourselves is a mere matter of detail, as the higgling and haggling of the market, which is not over the bulk of the price, but over the last halfpenny.

Shall we say, then, that a baby of a day old sucks (which involves the whole principle of the pump, and hence a profound practical knowledge of the laws of pneumatics and hydrostatics), digests, oxygenises its blood (millions of years before Sir Humphry Davy discovered oxygen), sees and hears—all most difficult and complicated operations, involving a knowledge of the facts concerning optics and acoustics, compared with which the discoveries of Newton sink into utter insignificance? Shall we say that a baby can do all these things at once, doing them so well and so regularly, without being even able to direct its attention to them, and without mistake, and at the same time not know how to do them, and never have done them before?

Such an assertion would be a contradiction to the whole experience of mankind. Surely the *onus probandi* must rest with him who makes it.

A man may make a lucky hit now and again by what is called a fluke, but even this must be only a little in advance of his other performances of the same kind. He may multiply seven by eight by a fluke after a little study of the multiplication table, but he will not be able to extract the cube root of 4913 by a fluke, without long training in arithmetic, any more than an agricultural labourer would be able to operate successfully for cataract. If, then, a grown man cannot perform so simple an operation as that we will say, for cataract, unless he have been long trained in other similar operations, and until he has done what comes to the same thing many times over, with what show of reason can we maintain that one who is so far less capable than a grown man, can perform such vastly more difficult operations, without knowing how to do them, and without ever having done them before? There is no sign of "fluke" about the circulation of a baby's blood. There may perhaps be some little hesitation about its earliest breathing, but this, as a general rule, soon passes over, both breathing and circulation, within an hour after birth, being as regular and easy as at any time during life. Is it reasonable, then, to say that the baby does these things without knowing how to do them, and without ever having done them before, and continues to do them by a series of lifelong flukes?

It would be well if those who feel inclined to hazard such an assertion would find some other instances of intricate processes gone through by people who know nothing about them, and never had any practice therein. What *is* to know how to do a thing? Surely to do it. What is proof that we know how to do a thing? Surely the fact that we can do it. A man shows that he knows how to throw the boomerang by throwing the boomerang. No amount of talking or writing can get over this; *ipso facto*, that a baby breathes and makes its blood circulate, it knows how to do so and the fact that it does not know its own knowledge is only proof of the perfection of that knowledge, and of the vast number of past occasions on which it must have been exercised already. As we have said already, it is less obvious when the baby could have gained its experience, so as to be able so readily to remember exactly what to do; but it is more easy to suppose that the necessary occasions cannot have been wanting, than that the power which we observe should have been obtained without practice and memory.

If we saw any self-consciousness on the baby's part about its breathing or circulation, we might suspect that it had had less experience, or profited less by its experience, than its neighbours— exactly in the same manner as we suspect a deficiency of any quality which we see a man inclined to parade. We all become introspective when we find that we do not know our business, and whenever we are introspective we may generally suspect that we are on the verge of unproficiency. Unfortunately, in the case of sickly children, we observe that they sometimes do become conscious of their breathing and circulation, just as in later life we become conscious that we have a liver or a digestion. In that case there is always something wrong. The baby that becomes aware of its breathing does not know how to breathe, and will suffer for his ignorance and incapacity, exactly in the same way as he will suffer in later life for ignorance and incapacity in any other respect in which his peers are commonly knowing and capable. In the case of inability to breath, the punishment is corporal, breathing being a matter of fashion, so old and long settled that nature can admit of no departure from the established custom, and the procedure in case of failure is as much formulated as the fashion itself in the case of the circulation, the whole performance has become one so utterly of rote, that the mere discovery that we could do it at all was considered one of the highest flights of human genius.

It has been said a day will come when the Polar ice shall have accumulated, till it forms vast continents many thousands of feet above the level of the sea, all of solid ice. The weight of this mass will, it is believed, cause the world to topple over on its axis, so that the earth will be upset as an ant-heap overturned by a ploughshare. In that day time icebergs will come crunching against our proudest cities, razing them from off the face of the earth as though they were made of rotten blotting-paper. There is no respect now of Handel nor of Shakespeare; the works of Rembrandt and Bellini fossilise at the bottom of the sea. Grace, beauty, and wit, all that is precious in music, literature, and art—all gone. In the morning there was Europe. In the evening there are no more populous cities nor busy hum of men, but a sea of jagged ice, a lurid sunset, and the doom of many ages. Then shall a scared remnant escape in places, and settle upon the changed continent when the waters have subsided—a simple people, busy hunting shellfish on the drying ocean beds, and with little time for introspection yet they can read and write and sum, for by that time these accomplishments will have become universal, and will be acquired as easily as we now learn to talk; but they do so as a matter of course, and without self-consciousness. Also they make the simpler kinds of machinery too easily to be able to follow their own operations - the manner of their own apprenticeship being to them as a buried city. May we not imagine that, after the lapse of another ten thousand years or so, some one of them may again become cursed with lust of introspection, and a second Harvey may astonish the world by discovering that it can read and write, and that steam-engines do not grow, but are made? It may be safely prophesied that he will die a martyr, and be honoured in the fourth generation.

CHAPTER IV—APPLICATION OF THE FOREGOING PRINCIPLES TO ACTIONS AND HABITS ACQUIRED BEFORE BIRTH

But if we once admit the principle that consciousness and volition have a tendency to vanish as soon as practice has rendered any habit exceedingly familiar, so that the mere presence of an elaborate but unconscious performance shall carry with it a presumption of infinite practice, we shall find it impossible to draw the line at those actions which we see acquired after birth, no matter at how early a period. The whole history and development of the embryo in all its stages forces itself on our consideration. Birth has been made too much of. It is a salient feature in the history of the individual, but not more salient than a hundred others, and far less so than the commencement of his existence as a single cell uniting in itself elements derived from both parents, or perhaps than any point in his whole existence as an embryo. For many years after we are born we are still very incomplete. We cease to oxygenise our blood vicariously as soon as we are born, but we still derive our sustenance from our mothers. Birth is but the beginning of doubt, the first hankering after scepticism, the dreaming of a dawn of trouble, the end of certainty and of settled convictions. Not but what before birth there have been unsettled convictions (more's the pity) with not a few, and after birth we have still so made up our minds upon many points as to have no further need of reflection concerning them; nevertheless, in the main, birth is the end of that time when we really knew our business, and the beginning of the days wherein we know not what we would do, or do. It is therefore the beginning of consciousness, and infancy is as the dosing of one who turns in his bed on waking, and takes another short sleep before he rises. When we were yet unborn, our thoughts kept the roadway decently enough; then were we blessed; we thought as every man thinks, and held the same opinions as our fathers and mothers had done upon nearly every subject. Life was not an art—and a very difficult art—much too difficult to be acquired in a lifetime; it was a science of which we were consummate masters.

In this sense, then, birth may indeed be looked upon as the most salient feature in a man's life; but this is not at all the sense in which it is commonly so regarded. It is commonly considered as the point at which we begin to live. More truly it is the point at which we leave off knowing how to live.

A chicken, for example, is never so full of consciousness, activity, reasoning faculty, and volition, as when it is an embryo in the eggshell, making bones, and flesh, and feathers, and eyes, and claws, with nothing but a little warmth and white of egg to make them from. This is indeed to make bricks with but a small modicum of straw. There is no man in the whole world who knows consciously and articulately as much as a half-hatched hen's egg knows unconsciously. Surely the egg in its own way must know quite as much as the chicken does. We say of the chicken that it knows how to run about as soon as it is hatched. So it does; but had it no knowledge before it was hatched? What made it lay the foundations of those limbs which should enable it to run about? What made it grow a horny tip to its bill before it was hatched, so that it might peck all round the larger end of the eggshell and make a hole for itself to get out at? Having once got outside the eggshell, the chicken throws away this horny tip; but is it reasonable to suppose that it would have grown it at all unless it had known that it would want something with which to break the eggshell? And again, is it in the least agreeable to our experience that such elaborate machinery should be made without endeavour, failure, perseverance, intelligent contrivance, experience, and practice?

In the presence of such considerations, it seems impossible to refrain from thinking that there must be a closer continuity of identity, life, and memory, between successive generations than we generally imagine. To shear the thread of life, and hence of memory, between one generation and its successor, is so to speak, a brutal measure, an act of intellectual butchery, and like all such strong high-handed measures, a sign of weakness in him who is capable of it till all other remedies have been exhausted. It is mere horse science, akin to the theories of the convulsionists in the geological kingdom, and of the believers in the supernatural origin of the species of plants and animals. Yet it is to be feared that we have not a few among us who would feel shocked rather at the attempt towards a milder treatment of the facts before them, than at a continuance of the present crass tyranny with which we try to crush them inside our preconceived opinions. It is quite common to hear men of education maintain that not even when it was on the point of being hatched, had the chicken sense enough to know that it wanted to get outside the eggshell. It did indeed peck all round the end of the shell, which, if it wanted to get out, would certainly be the easiest way of effecting its purpose; but it did not, they say, peck because it was aware of this, but "promiscuously." Curious, such a uniformity of promiscuous action among so many eggs for so many generations. If we see a man knock a hole in a wall on finding that he cannot get out of a place by any other means, and if we see him knock this hole in a very workmanlike way, with an implement with which he has been at great pains to make for a long the past, but which he throws away as soon as he has no longer use for it, thus showing that he had made it expressly for the purpose of escape, do we say that this person made the implement and broke the wall of his prison promiscuously? No jury would acquit a burglar on these grounds. Then why, without much more evidence to the contrary than we have, or can hope to have, should we not suppose that with chickens, as with men, signs of contrivance are indeed signs of contrivance, however quick, subtle, and untraceable, the contrivance may be? Again, I have heard people argue that though the chicken, when nearly hatched, had such a glimmering of sense that it pecked the shell because it wanted to get out, yet that it is not conceivable that, so long before it was hatched, it should have had the sense to grow the horny tip to its bill for use when wanted. This, at any rate, they say, it must have grown, as the persons previously referred to would maintain, promiscuously.

Now no one indeed supposes that the chicken does what it does, with the same self-consciousness with which a tailor makes a suit of clothes. Not any one who has thought upon the subject is likely to do it so great an injustice. The probability is that it knows what it is about to an extent greater than any tailor ever did or will, for, to say the least of it, many thousands of years to come. It works with such absolute certainty and so vast an experience, that it is utterly incapable of following the operations of its own mind—as accountants have been known to add up long columns of pounds, shillings, and pence, running the three fingers of one hand, a finger for each column, up the page, and putting the result down correctly at the bottom, apparently without an effort. In the case of the accountant, we say that the processes which his mind goes through are so rapid and subtle as to elude his own power of observation as well as ours. We do not deny that his mind goes though processes of some kind; we very readily admit that it must do so, and say that these processes are so rapid and subtle, owing, as a general rule, to long experience in addition. Why then should we find it so difficult to conceive that this principle, which we observe to play so large a part in mental physiology, wherever we can observe mental physiology at all, may have a share also in the performance of intricate operations otherwise inexplicable, though the creature performing them is not man, or man only in embryo?

Again, after the chicken is hatched, it grows more feathers and bones and blood, but we still say that it knows nothing about all this. What then do we say it *does* know? One is almost ashamed to confess that we only credit it with knowing what it appears to know by processes which we find it exceedingly easy to follow, or perhaps rather, which we find it absolutely impossible to avoid following, as recognising too great a family likeness between them, and those which are most easily followed in our own minds, to be able to sit down in comfort under a denial of the resemblance. Thus, for example, if we see a chicken running away from a fox, we do admit that the chicken knows the fox would kill it if it caught it.

On the other hand, if we allow that the half-hatched chicken grew the horny tip to be ready for use, with an intensity of unconscious contrivance which can be only attributed to experience, we are driven to admit that from the first moment the men began to sit upon it—and earlier too than this—the egg was always full of consciousness and volition, and that during its embryological condition the unhatched chicken is doing exactly what it continues doing from the moment it is hatched till it dies; that is to say, attempting to better itself, doing (as Aristotle says all creatures do all things upon all occasions) what it considers most for its advantage under the existing circumstances. What it may think most advantageous will depend, while it is in the eggshell, upon exactly the same causes as will influence its opinions in later life—to wit, upon its habits, its past circumstances and ways of thinking; for there is nothing, as Shakespeare tells us, good or ill, but thinking makes it so.

The egg thinks feathers much more to its advantage than hair or fur, and much more easily made. If it could speak, it would probably tell us that we could make them ourselves very easily after a few lessons, if we took the trouble to try, but that hair was another matter, which it really could not see how any protoplasm could be got to make. Indeed, during the more intense and active part of our existence, in the earliest stages, that is to say, of our embryological life, we could probably have turned our protoplasm into feathers instead of hair if we had cared about doing so. If the chicken can make feathers, there seems no sufficient reason for thinking that we cannot do so, beyond the fact that we prefer hair, and have preferred it for so many ages that we have lost the art along with the desire of making feathers, if indeed any of our ancestors ever possessed it. The stuff with which we make hair is practically the same as that with which chickens make feathers. It is nothing but protoplasm, and protoplasm is like certain prophecies, out of which anything can be made by the creature which wants to make it. Everything depends upon whether a creature knows its own mind sufficiently well, and has enough faith in its own powers of achievement. When these two requisites are wanting, the strongest giant cannot lift a two-ounce weight; when they are given, a bullock can take an eyelash out of its eye with its hind-foot, or a minute jelly speck can build itself a house out of various materials which it will select according to its purpose with the nicest care, though it have neither brain to think with, nor eyes to see with, nor hands nor feet to work with, nor is it anything but a minute speck of jelly—faith and protoplasm only.

That this is indeed so, the following passage from Dr. Carpenter's "Mental Physiology" may serve to show:-

"The simplest type of an animal consists of a minute mass of 'protoplasm,' or living jelly, which is not yet *differentiated* into 'organs;' every part having the same endowments, and taking an equal share in every action which the creature performs. One of these 'jelly specks,' the amba, moves itself about by changing the form of its body, extemporising a foot (or pseudopodium), first in one direction, and then in another; and then, when it has met with a nutritive particle, extemporises a stomach for its reception, by wrapping its soft body around it. Another, instead of going about in search of food, remains in one place, but projects its protoplasmic substance into long pseudopodia, which entrap and draw in very minute particles, or absorb nutrient material from the liquid through which they extend themselves, and are continually becoming fused (as it were) into the central body, which is itself continually giving off new pseudopodia. Now we can scarcely conceive that a creature of such simplicity should possess any distinct *consciousness* of its needs" (why not?), "or that its actions should be directed by any *intention* of its own; and yet the writer has lately found results of the most singular elaborateness to be wrought out by the instrumentality of these minute jelly specks, which build up tests or casings of the most regular geometrical symmetry of form, and of the most artificial construction."

On this Dr. Carpenter remarks:- "Suppose a human mason to be put down by the side of a pile of stones of various shapes and sizes, and to be told to build a dome of these, smooth on both surfaces, without using more than the least possible quantity of a very tenacious, but very costly, cement, in holding the stones together. If he accomplished this well, he would receive credit for great intelligence and skill. Yet this is exactly what these little 'jelly specks' do on a most minute scale; the 'tests' they construct, when highly magnified, bearing comparison with the most skilful masonry of man. From *the same sandy bottom* one species picks up the *coarser* quartz grains, cements them together with *phosphate of iron* secreted from its own substance" (should not this rather be, "which it has contrived in some way or other to manufacture"?) and thus constructs a flask-shaped 'test,' having a short neck and a large single orifice. Another picks up the *finest* grains, and puts them together, with the same cement, into perfectly spherical 'tests' of the most extraordinary finish, perforated with numerous small pores disposed at pretty regular intervals. Another selects the *minutest* sand grains and the terminal portions of sponge spicules, and works them up together—apparently with no cement at all, by the mere laying of the spicules—into perfect white spheres, like homopathic globules, each having a single-fissured orifice. And another, which makes a straight, many-chambered 'test,' that resembles in form the chambered shell of an orthoceratite—the conical mouth of each chamber projecting into the cavity of the next—while forming the walls of its chambers of ordinary sand grains rather loosely held together, shapes the conical mouth of the successive chambers by firmly cementing together grains of ferruginous quartz, which it must have picked out from the general mass."

"To give these actions," continues Dr. Carpenter, "the vague designation of 'instinctive' does not in the least help us to account for them, since what we want is to discover the *mechanism* by which they are worked out; and it is most difficult to conceive how so artificial a selection can be made by a creature so simple" (Mental Physiology, 4th ed. pp. 41-43)

This is what protoplasm can do when it has the talisman of faith— of faith which worketh all wonders, either in the heavens above, or in the earth beneath, or in the waters under the earth. Truly if a man have faith, even as a grain of mustard seed, though he may not be able to remove mountains, he will at any rate be able to do what is no less difficult—make a mustard plant.

Yet this is but a barren kind of comfort, for we have not, and in the nature of things cannot have, sufficient faith in the unfamiliar, inasmuch as the very essence of faith involves the notion of familiarity, which can grow but slowly, from experience to confidence, and can make no sudden leap at any time. Such faith cannot be founded upon reason,—that is to say, upon a recognised perception on the part of the person holding it that he is holding it, and of the reasons for his doing so—or it will shift as other reasons come to disturb it. A house built upon reason is a house built upon the sand. It must be built upon the current cant and practice of one's peers, for this is the rock which, though not immovable, is still most hard to move.

But however this may be, we observe broadly that the intensity of the will to make this or that, and of the confidence that one can make it, depends upon the length of time during which the maker's forefathers have wanted the same thing before it; the older the custom the more inveterate the habit, and, with the exception, perhaps, that the reproductive system is generally the crowning act of development— an exception which I will hereafter explain—the earlier its manifestation, until, for some reason or another, we relinquish it and take to another, which we must, as a general rule, again adhere to for a vast number of generations, before it will permanently supplant the older habit. In our own case, the habit of breathing like a fish through gills may serve as an example. We have now left off this habit, yet we did it formerly for so many generations that we still do it a little; it still crosses our embryological existence like a faint memory or dream, for not easily is an inveterate habit broken. On the other hand—again speaking broadly—the more recent the habit the later the fashion of its organ, as with the teeth, speech, and the higher intellectual powers, which are too new for development before we are actually born.

But to return for a short time to Dr. Carpenter. Dr. Carpenter evidently feels, what must indeed be felt by every candid mind, that there is no sufficient reason for supposing that these little specks of jelly, without brain or eyes, or stomach, or hands, or feet, but the very lowest known form of animal life, are not imbued with a consciousness of their needs, and the reasoning faculties which shall enable them to gratify those needs in a manner, all things considered, equalling the highest flights of the ingenuity of the highest animal— man. This is no exaggeration. It is true, that in an earlier part of the passage, Dr. Carpenter has said that we can scarcely conceive so simple a creature to "possess any distinct *consciousness* of its needs, or that its actions should be directed by any intention of its own;" but, on the other hand, a little lower down he says, that if a workman did what comes to the same thing as what the amba does, he "would receive credit for great intelligence and skill." Now if an amba can do that, for which a workman would receive credit as for a highly skilful and intelligent performance, the amba should receive no less credit than the workman; he should also be no less credited with skill and intelligence, which words unquestionably involve a distinct consciousness of needs and an action directed by an intention of its own. So that Dr. Carpenter seems rather to blow hot and cold with one breath. Nevertheless there can be no doubt to which side the minds of the great majority of mankind will incline upon the evidence before them; they will say that the creature is highly reasonable and intelligent, though they would readily admit that long practice and familiarity may have exhausted its powers of attention to all the stages of its own performance, just as a practised workman in building a wall certainly does not consciously follow all the processes which he goes through.

As an example, however, of the extreme dislike which philosophers of a certain school have for making the admissions which seem somewhat grudgingly conceded by Dr. Carpenter, we may take the paragraph which immediately follows the ones which we have just quoted. Dr. Carpenter there writes:-

"The writer has often amused himself and others, when by the seaside, with getting a *terebella* (a marine worm that cases its body in a sandy tube) out of its house, and then, putting it into a saucer of water with a supply of sand and comminuted shell, watching its appropriation of these materials in constructing a new tube. The extended tentacles soon spread themselves over the bottom of the saucer and lay hold of whatever comes in their way, 'all being fish that comes to their net,' and in half an hour or thereabouts the new house is finished, though on a very rude and artificial type. Now here the organisation is far higher; the instrumentality obviously serves the needs of the animal and suffices for them; and we characterise the action, on account of its uniformity and apparent *un* intelligence, as instinctive."

No comment will, one would think, be necessary to make the reader feel that the difference between the terebella and the amba is one of degree rather than kind, and that if the action of the second is as conscious and reasonable as that, we will say, of a bird making her nest, the action of the first should be so also. It is only a question of being a little less skilful, or more so, but skill and intelligence would seem present in both cases. Moreover, it is more clever of the terebella to have made itself the limbs with which it can work, than of the amba to be able to work without the limbs; and perhaps it is more sensible also to want a less elaborate dwelling, provided it is sufficient for practical purposes. But whether the terebella be less intelligent than the amba or not, it does quite enough to establish its claim to intelligence of a higher order; and one does not see ground for the satisfaction which Dr. Carpenter appears to find at having, as it were, taken the taste of the amba's performance out of our mouth, by setting us about the less elaborate performance of the terebella, which he thinks we can call unintelligent and instinctive.

I may be mistaken in the impression I have derived from the paragraphs I have quoted. I commonly say they give me the impression that I have tried to convey to the reader, *i.e.*, that the writer's assent to anything like intelligence, or consciousness of needs, an animal low down in the scale of life, is grudging, and that he is more comfortable when he has got hold of onto to which he can point and say that mere, at any rate, is an unintelligent and merely instinctive creature. I have only called attention to the passage as an example of the intellectual bias of a large number of exceedingly able and thoughtful persons, among whom, so far as I am able to form an opinion at all, few have greater claims to our respectful attention than Dr. Carpenter himself.

For the embryo of a chicken, then, we damn exactly the same kind of reasoning power and contrivance which we damn for the amba, or for our own intelligent performances in later life. We do not claim for it much, if any, perception of its own forethought, for we know very well that it is among the most prominent features of intellectual activity that, after a number of repetitions, it ceases to be perceived, and that it does not, in ordinary cases, cease to be perceived till after a very great number of repetitions. The fact that the embryo chicken makes itself always as nearly as may be in the same way, would lead us to suppose that it would be unconscious of much of its own action, *provided it were always the same chicken which made itself over and over again*. So far we can see, it always *is* unconscious of the greater part of its own wonderful performance. Surely then we have a presumption that *it is the same chicken which makes itself over and over again*; for such unconsciousness is not won, so far as our experience goes, by any other means than by frequent repetition of the same act on the part of one and the same individual. How this can be we shall perceive in subsequent chapters. In the meantime, we may say that all knowledge and volition would seem to be merely parts of the knowledge and volition of the primordial cell (whatever this may be), which slumbers but never dies—which has grown, and multiplied, and differentiated itself into the compound life of the womb, and which never becomes conscious of knowing what it has once learnt effectually, till it is for some reason on the point of, or in danger of, forgetting it.

The action, therefore, of an embryo making its way up in the world from a simple cell to a baby, developing for itself eyes, ears, hands, and feet while yet unborn, proves to be exactly of one and the same kind as that of a man of fifty who goes into the City and tells his broker to buy him so many Great Northern A shares—that is to say, an effort of the will exercised in due course on a balance of considerations as to the immediate expediency, and guided by past experience; while children who do not reach birth are but prenatal spendthrifts, ne'er-do-weels, inconsiderate innovators, the unfortunate in business, either through their own fault or that of others, or through inevitable mischances, beings who are culled out before birth instead of after; so that even the lowest idiot, the most contemptible in health or beauty, may yet reflect with pride that they were *born* . Certainly we observe that those who have had good fortune (mother and sole cause of virtue, and sole virtue in itself), and have profited by their experience, and known their business best before birth, so that they made themselves both to be and to look well, do commonly on an average prove to know it best in after-life: they grow their clothes best who have grown their limbs best. It is rare that those who have not remembered how to finish their own bodies fairly well should finish anything well in later life. But how small is the addition to their unconscious attainments which even the Titans of human intellect have consciously accomplished, in comparison with the problems solved by the meanest baby living, nay, even by one whose birth is untimely! In other words, how vast is that back knowledge over which we have gone fast asleep, through the prosiness of perpetual repetition; and how little in comparison, is that whose novelty keeps it still within the scope of our conscious perception! What is the discovery of the laws of gravitation as compared with the knowledge which sleeps in every hen's egg upon a kitchen shelf?

It is all a matter of habit and fashion. Thus we see kings and councillors of the earth admired for facing death before what they are pleased to call dishonour. If, on being required to go without anything they have been accustomed to, or to change their habits, or do what is unusual in the case of other kings under like circumstances, then, if they but fold their cloak decently around them, and die upon the spot of shame at having had it even required of them to do thus or thus, then are they kings indeed, of old race, that know their business from generation to generation. Or if, we will say, a prince, on having his dinner brought to him ill-cooked, were to feel the indignity so keenly as that he should turn his face to the wall, and breathe out his wounded soul in one sigh, do we not admire him as a *real* prince," who knows the business of princes so well that he can conceive of nothing foreign to it in connection with himself, the bare effort to realise a state of things other than what princes have been accustomed to being immediately fatal to him? Yet is there no less than this in the demise of every half-hatched hen's egg, shaken rudely by a schoolboy, or neglected by a truant mother; for surely the prince would not die if he knew how to do otherwise, and the hen's egg only dies of being required to do something to which it is not accustomed.

But the further consideration of this and other like reflections would too long detain us. Suffice it that we have established the position that all living creatures which show any signs of intelligence, must certainly each one have already gone through the embryonic stages an infinite number of times, or they could no more have achieved the intricate process of self-development unconsciously, than they could play the piano unconsciously without any previous knowledge of the instrument. It remains, therefore, to show the when and where of their having done so, and this leads us naturally to the subject of the following chapter—Personal Identity.

CHAPTER V—PERSONAL IDENTITY

"Strange difficulties have been raised by some," says Bishop Butler, "concerning personal identity, or the sameness of living agents as implied in the notion of our existing now and hereafter, or indeed in any two consecutive moments." But in truth it is not easy to see the strangeness of the difficulty, if the words either "personal" or "identity" are used in any strictness.

Personality is one of those ideas with which we are so familiar that we have lost sight of the foundations upon which it rests. We regard our personality as a simple definite whole; as a plain, palpable, individual thing, which can be seen going about the streets or sitting indoors at home, which lasts us our lifetime, and about the confines of which no doubt can exist in the minds of reasonable people. But in truth this "we," which looks so simple and definite, is a nebulous and indefinable aggregation of many component parts which war not a little among themselves, our perception of our existence at all being perhaps due to this very clash of warfare, as our sense of sound and light is due to the jarring of vibrations. Moreover, as the component parts of our identity change from moment to moment, our personality becomes a thing dependent upon the present, which has no logical existence, but lives only upon the sufferance of times past and future, slipping out of our hands into the domain of one or other of these two claimants the moment we try to apprehend it. And not only is our personality as fleeting as the present moment, but the parts which compose it blend some of them so imperceptibly into, and are so inextricably linked on to, outside things which clearly form no part of our personality, that when we try to bring ourselves to book, and determine wherein we consist, or to draw a line as to where we begin or end, we find ourselves completely baffled. There is nothing but fusion and confusion.

Putting theology on one side, and dealing only with the common daily experience of mankind, our body is certainly part of our personality. With the destruction of our bodies, our personality, as far as we can follow it, comes to a full stop; and with every modification of them it is correspondingly modified. But what are the limits of our bodies? They are composed of parts, some of them so unessential as to be hardly included in personality at all, and to be separable from ourselves without perceptible effect, as the hair, nails, and daily waste of tissue. Again, other parts are very important, as our hands, feet, arms, legs, &c., but still are no essential parts of our "self" or "soul," which continues to exist in spite of their amputation. Other parts, as the brain, heart, and blood, are so essential that they cannot be dispensed with, yet it is impossible to say that personality consists in any one of them.

Each one of these component members of our personality is continually dying and being born again, supported in this process by the food we eat, the water we drink, and the air we breathe; which three things link us on, and fetter us down, to the organic and inorganic world about us. For our meat and drink, though no part of our personality before we eat and drink, cannot, after we have done so, be separated entirely from us without the destruction of our personality altogether, so far as we can follow it; and who shall say at what precise moment our food has or has not become part of ourselves? A famished man eats food; after a short time his whole personality is so palpably affected that we know the food to have entered into him and taken, as it were, possession of him; but who can say at what precise moment it did so? Thus we find that we are rooted into outside things and melt away into them, nor can any man say he consists absolutely in this or that, nor define himself so certainly as to include neither more nor less than himself; many undoubted parts of his personality being more separable from it, and changing it less when so separated, both to his own senses and those of other people, than other parts which are strictly speaking no parts at all.

A man's clothes, for example, as they lie on a chair at night are no part of him, but when he wears them they would appear to be so, as being a kind of food which warms him and hatches him, and the loss of which may kill him of cold. If this be denied, and a man's clothes be considered as no part of his self, nevertheless they, with his money, and it may perhaps be added his religious opinions, stamp a man's individuality as strongly as any natural feature could stamp it. Change in style of dress, gain or loss of money, make a man feel and appear more changed than having his chin shaved or his nails cut. In fact, as soon as we leave common parlance on one side, and try for a scientific definition of personality, we find that there is none possible, any more than there can be a demonstration of the fact that we exist at all—a demonstration for which, as for that of a personal God, many have hunted but none have found. The only solid foundation is, as in the case of the earth's crust, pretty near the surface of things; the deeper we try to go, the damper and darker and altogether more uncongenial we find it. There is no knowing into what quagmire of superstition we may not find ourselves drawn, if we once cut ourselves adrift from those superficial aspects of things, in which alone our nature permits us to be comforted.

Common parlance, however, settles the difficulty readily enough (as indeed it settles most others if they show signs of awkwardness) by the simple process of ignoring it: we decline, and very properly, to go into the question of where personality begins and ends, but assume it to be known by every one, and throw the onus of not knowing it upon the over-curious, who had better think as their neighbours do, right or wrong, or there is no knowing into what villainy they may not presently fall.

Assuming, then, that every one knows what is meant by the word "person" (and such superstitious bases as this are the foundations upon which all action, whether of man, beast, or plant, is constructed and rendered possible; for even the corn in the fields grows upon a superstitious basis as to its own existence, and only turns the earth and moisture into wheat through the conceit of its own ability to do so, without which faith it were powerless; and the lichen only grows upon the granite rock by first saying to itself, "I think I can do it;" so that it would not be able to grow unless it thought it could grow, and would not think it could grow unless it found itself able to grow, and thus spends its life arguing in a most vicious circle, basing its action upon a hypothesis, which hypothesis is in turn based upon its action)—assuming that we know what is meant by the word "person," we say that we are one and the same from the moment of our birth to the moment of our death, so that whatever is done by or happens to any one between birth and death, is said to happen to or be done by one individual. This in practice is found to be sufficient for the law courts and the purposes of daily life, which, being full of hurry and the pressure of business, can only tolerate compromise, or conventional rendering of intricate phenomena. When facts of extreme complexity have to be daily and hourly dealt with by people whose time is money, they must be simplified, and treated much as a painter treats them, drawing them in squarely, seizing the more important features, and neglecting all that does not assert itself as too essential to be passed over—hence the slang and cant words of every profession, and indeed all language; for language at best is but a kind of "patter," the only way, it is true, in many cases, of expressing our ideas to one another, but still a very bad way, and not for one moment comparable to the unspoken speech which we may sometimes have recourse to. The metaphors and *façons de parler* to which even in the plainest speech we are perpetually recurring (as, for example, in this last two lines, "plain," "perpetually," and "recurring," are all words based on metaphor, and hence more or less liable to mislead) often deceive us, as though there were nothing more than what we see and say, and as though words, instead of being, as they are, the creatures of our convenience, had some claim to be the actual ideas themselves concerning which we are conversing.

This is so well expressed in a letter I have recently received from a friend, now in New Zealand, and certainly not intended by him for publication, that I shall venture to quote the passage, but should say that I do so without his knowledge or permission which I should not be able to receive before this book must be completed.

"Words, words, words," he writes, "are the stumbling-blocks in the way of truth. Until you think of things as they are, and not of the words that misrepresent them, you cannot think rightly. Words produce the appearance of hard and fast lines where there are none. Words divide; thus we call this a man, that an ape, that a monkey, while they are all only differentiations of the same thing. To think of a thing they must be got rid of: they are the clothes that thoughts wear—only the clothes. I say this over and over again, for there is nothing of more importance. Other men's words will stop you at the beginning of an investigation. A man may play with words all his life, arranging them and rearranging them like dominoes. If I could *think* to you without words you would understand me better."

If such remarks as the above hold good at all, they do so with the words "personal identity." The least reflection will show that personal identity in any sort of strictness is an impossibility. The expression is one of the many ways in which we are obliged to scamp our thoughts through pressure of other business which pays us better. For surely all reasonable people will feel that an infant an hour before birth, when in the eye of the law he has no existence, and could not be called a peer for another sixty minutes, though his father were a peer, and already dead,—surely such an embryo is more personally identical with the baby into which he develops within an hour's time than the born baby is so with itself (if the expression may be pardoned), one, twenty, or it may be eighty years after birth. There is more sameness of matter; there are fewer differences of any kind perceptible by a third person; there is more sense of continuity on the part of the person himself; and far more of all that goes to make up our sense of sameness of personality between an embryo an hour before birth and the child on being born, than there is between the child just born and the man of twenty. Yet there is no hesitation about admitting sameness of personality between these two last.

On the other hand, if that hazy contradiction in terms, "personal identity," be once allowed to retreat behind the threshold of the womb, it has eluded us once for all. What is true of one hour before birth is true of two, and so on till we get back to the impregnate ovum, which may fairly claim to have been personally identical with the man of eighty into which it ultimately developed, in spite of the fact that there is no particle of same matter nor sense of continuity between them, nor recognised community of instinct, nor indeed of anything which goes to the making up of that which we call identity.

There is far more of all these things common to the impregnate ovum and the ovum immediately before impregnation, or again between the impregnate ovum, and both the ovum before impregnation and the spermatozoon which impregnated it. Nor, if we admit personal identity between the ovum and the octogenarian, is there any sufficient reason why we should not admit it between the impregnate ovum and the two factors of which it is composed, which two factors are but offshoots from two distinct personalities, of which they are as much part as the apple is of the apple-tree; so that an impregnate ovum cannot without a violation of first principles be debarred from claiming personal identity with both its parents, and hence, by an easy chain of reasoning, *with each of the impregnate ova from which its parents were developed.*

So that each ovum when impregnate should be considered not as descended from its ancestors, but as being a continuation of the personality of every ovum in the chain of its ancestry, which every ovum *it actually is* quite as truly as the octogenarian *is* the same identity with the ovum from which he has been developed.

This process cannot stop short of the primordial cell, which again will probably turn out to be but a brief resting-place. We therefore prove each one of us to *be actually* the primordial cell which never died nor dies, but has differentiated itself into the life of the world, all living beings whatever, being one with it, and members one of another.

To look at the matter for a moment in another light, it will be admitted that if the primordial cell had been killed before leaving issue, all its possible descendants would have been killed at one and the same time. It is hard to see how this single fact does not establish at the point, as it were, of a logical bayonet, an identity, between any creature and all others that are descended from it.

In Bishop Butler's first dissertation on personality, we find expressed very much the same opinions as would follow from the above considerations, though they are mentioned by the Bishop only to be condemned, namely, "that personality is not a permanent but a transient thing; that it lives and dies, begins and ends continually; that no man can any more remain one and the same person two moments together, than two successive moments can be one and the same moment;" in which case, he continues, our present self would not be "in reality the same with the self of yesterday, but another like self or person coming up in its room and mistaken for it, to which another self will succeed to-morrow." This view the Bishop proceeds to reduce to absurdity by saying, "It must be a fallacy upon ourselves to charge our present selves with anything we did, or to imagine our present selves interested in anything which befell us yesterday; or that our present self will be interested in what will befall us to-morrow. This, I say, must follow, for if the self or person of to-day and that of to-morrow are not the same, but only like persons, the person of to-day is really no more interested in what will befall the person of to-morrow than in what will befall any other person. It may be thought, perhaps, that this is not a just representation of the opinion we are speaking of, because those who maintain it allow that a person is the same as far back as his remembrance reaches. And indeed they do use the words *identity* and *same person*. Nor will language permit these words to be laid aside, since, if they were, there must be I know not what ridiculous periphrasis substituted in the room of them. But they cannot consistently with themselves mean that the person is really the same. For it is self-evident that the personality cannot be really the same, if, as they expressly assert, that in which it consists is not the same. And as consistently with themselves they cannot, so I think it appears they do not mean that the person is really the same, but only that he is so in a fictitious sense; in such a sense only as they assert— for this they do assert—that any number of persons whatever may be the same person. The bare unfolding of this notion, and laying it thus naked and open, seems the best confutation of it."

This fencing, for it does not deserve the name of serious disputation, is rendered possible by the laxness with which the words "identical" and "identity" are commonly used. Bishop Butler would not seriously deny that personality undergoes great changes between infancy and old age, and hence that it must undergo some change from moment to moment. So universally is this recognised, that it is common to hear it said of such and such a man that he is not at all the person he was, or of such and such another that he is twice the man he used to be— expressions than which none nearer the truth can well be found. On the other hand, those whom Bishop Butler is intending to confute would be the first to admit that, though there are many changes between infancy and old age, yet they come about in any one individual under such circumstances as we are all agreed in considering as the factors of personal identity rather than as hindrances thereto—that is to say, there has been no death on the part of the individual between any two phases of his existence, and any one phase has had a permanent though perhaps imperceptible effect upon all succeeding ones. So that no one ever seriously argued in the manner supposed by Bishop Butler, unless with modifications and saving clauses, to which it does not suit his purpose to call attention.

Identical strictly means "one and the same;" and if it were tied down to its strictest usage, it would indeed follow very logically, as we have said already, that no such thing as personal identity is possible, but that the case actually is as Bishop Butler has supposed his opponents without qualification to maintain it. In common use, however, the word "identical" is taken to mean anything so like another that no vital or essential differences can be perceived between them; as in the case of two specimens of the same kind of plant, when we say they are identical in spite of considerable individual differences. So with two impressions of a print from the same plate; so with the plate itself, which is somewhat modified with every impression taken from it. In like manner "identity" is not held to its strict meaning— absolute sameness—but is predicated rightly of a past and present which are now very widely asunder, provided they have been continuously connected by links so small as not to give too sudden a sense of change at any one point; as, for instance, in the case of the Thames at Oxford and Windsor or again at Greenwich, we say the same river flows by all three places, by which we mean that much of the water at Greenwich has come down from Oxford and Windsor in a continuous stream. How sudden a change at any one point, or how great a difference between the two extremes is sufficient to bar identity, is one of the most uncertain things imaginable, and seems to be decided on different grounds in different cases, sometimes very intelligibly, and again at others arbitrarily and capriciously.

Personal identity is barred at one end, in the common opinion, by birth, and at the other by death. Before birth, a child cannot complain either by himself or another, in such way as to set the law in motion; after death he is in like manner powerless to make himself felt by society, except in so far as he can do so by acts done before the breath has left his body. At any point between birth and death he is liable, either by himself or another, to affect his fellow-creatures; hence, no two other epochs can be found of equal convenience for social purposes, and therefore they have been seized by society as settling the whole question of when personal identity begins and ends—society being rightly concerned with its own practical convenience, rather than with the abstract truth concerning its individual members. No one who is capable of reflection will deny that the limitation of personality is certainly arbitrary to a degree as regards birth, nor yet that it is very possibly arbitrary as regards death; and as for intermediate points, no doubt it would be more strictly accurate to say, "you are the now phase of the person I met last night," or "you are the being which has been evolved from the being I met last night," than "you are the person I met last night." But life is too short for the pen-phrases which would crowd upon us from every quarter, if we did not set our face against all that is under the surface of things, unless, that is to say, the going beneath the surface is, for some special chance of profit, excusable or capable of extenuation.

CHAPTER VI—PERSONAL IDENTITY— (Continued)

How arbitrary current notions concerning identity really are, may perhaps be perceived by reflecting upon some of the many different phases of reproduction.

Direct reproduction in which a creation reproduces another, the *facsimile*, or nearly so, of itself may perhaps occur among the lowest forms of animal life; but it is certainly not the rule among beings of a higher order.

A hen lays an egg, which egg becomes a chicken, which chicken, in the course of time, becomes a hen.

A moth lays an egg, which egg becomes a caterpillar, which caterpillar, after going through several stages, becomes a chrysalis, which chrysalis becomes a moth.

A medusa begets a ciliated larva, the larva begets a polyp, the polyp begets a strobila, and the strobila begets a medusa again; the cycle of reproduction being completed in the fourth generation.

A frog lays an egg, which egg becomes a tadpole; the tadpole, after more or fewer intermediate stages, becomes a frog.

The mammals lay eggs, which they hatch inside their own bodies, instead of outside them; but the difference is one of degree and not of kind. In all these cases how difficult is it to say where identity begins or ends, or again where death begins or ends, or where reproduction begins or ends.

How small and unimportant is the difference between the changes which a caterpillar undergoes before becoming a moth, and those of a strobila before becoming a medusa. Yet in the one case we say the caterpillar does not die, but is changed (though, if the various changes in its existence be produced metagenetically, as is the case with many insects, it would appear to make a clean sweep of every organ of its existence, and start *de novo*, growing a head where its feet were, and so on—at least twice between its lives as caterpillar and butterfly); in this case, however, we say the caterpillar does not die, but is changed; being, nevertheless, one personality with the moth, into which it is developed. But in the case of the strobila we say that it is not changed, but dies, and is no part of the personality of the medusa.

We say the egg becomes the caterpillar, not by the death of the egg and birth of the caterpillar, but by the ordinary process of nutrition and waste—waste and repair—waste and repair continually. In like manner we say the caterpillar becomes the chrysalis, and the chrysalis the moth, not through the death of either one or the other, but by the development of the same creature, and the ordinary processes of waste and repair. But the medusa after three or four cycles becomes the medusa again, not, we say, by these same processes of nutrition and waste, but by a series of generations, each one involving an actual birth and an actual death. Why this difference? Surely only because the changes in the offspring of the medusa are marked by the leaving a little more husk behind them, and that husk less shrivelled, than is left on the occasion of each change between the caterpillar and the butterfly. A little more residuum, which residuum, it may be, can move about; and though shrivelling from hour to hour, may yet leave a little more offspring before it is reduced to powder; or again, perhaps, because in the one case, though the actors are changed, they are changed behind the scenes, and come on in parts and dresses, more nearly resembling those of the original actors, than in the other.

When the caterpillar emerges from the egg, almost all that was inside the egg has become caterpillar; the shell is nearly empty, and cannot move; therefore we do not count it, and call the caterpillar a continuation of the egg's existence, and personally identical with the egg. So with the chrysalis and the moth; but after the moth has laid her eggs she can still move her wings about, and she looks nearly as large as she did before she laid them; besides, she may yet lay a few more, therefore we do not consider the moth's life as continued in the life of her eggs, but rather in their husk, which we still call the moth, and which we say dies in a day or two, and there is an end of it. Moreover, if we hold the moth's life to be continued in that of her eggs, we shall be forced to admit her to be personally identical with each single egg, and, hence, each egg to be identical with every other egg, as far as the past, and community of memories, are concerned; and it is not easy at first to break the spell which words have cast around us, and to feel that one person may become many persons, and that many different persons may be practically one and the same person, as far as their past experience is concerned; and again, that two or more persons may unite and become one person, with the memories and experiences of both, though this has been actually the case with every one of us.

Our present way of looking at these matters is perfectly right and reasonable, so long as we bear in mind that it is a *façon de parler* , a sort of hieroglyphic which shall stand for the course of nature, but nothing more. Repair (as is now universally admitted by physiologists) is only a phase of reproduction, or rather reproduction and repair are only phases of the same power; and again, death and the ordinary daily waste of tissue, are phases of the same thing. As for identity it is determined in any true sense of the word, not by death alone, but by a combination of death and failure of issue, whether of mind or body.

To repeat. Wherever there is a separate centre of thought and action, we see that it is connected with its successive stages of being, by a series of infinitely small changes from moment to moment, with, perhaps, at times more startling and rapid changes, but, nevertheless, with no such sudden, complete, and unrepaired break up of the preceding condition, as we shall agree in calling death. The branching out from it at different times of new centres of thought and action, has commonly as little appreciable effect upon the parent-stock as the fall of an apple full of ripe seeds has upon an apple-tree; and though the life of the parent, from the date of the branching off of such personalities, is more truly continued in these than in the residuum of its own life, we should find ourselves involved in a good deal of trouble if we were commonly to take this view of the matter. The residuum has generally the upper hand. He has more money, and can eat up his new life more easily than his new life, him. A moral residuum will therefore prefer to see the remainder of his life in his own person, than in that of his descendants, and will act accordingly. Hence we, in common with most other living beings, ignore the offspring as forming part of the personality of the parent, except in so far as that we make the father liable for its support and for its extravagances (than which no greater proof need be wished that the law is at heart a philosopher, and perceives the completeness of the personal identity between father and son) for twenty-one years from birth. In other respects we are accustomed, probably rather from considerations of practical convenience than as the result of pure reason, to ignore the identity between parent and offspring as completely as we ignore personality before birth. With these exceptions, however, the common opinion concerning personal identity is reasonable enough, and is found to consist neither in consciousness of such identity, nor yet in the power of recollecting its various phases (for it is plain that identity survives the distinction or suspension of both these), but in the fact that the various stages appear to the majority of people to have been in some way or other linked together.

For a very little reflection will show that identity, as commonly predicated of living agents, does not consist in identity of matter, of which there is no same particle in the infant, we will say, and the octogenarian into whom he has developed. Nor, again, does it depend upon sameness of form or fashion; for personality is felt to survive frequent and radical modification of structure, as in the case of caterpillars and other insects. Mr. Darwin, quoting from Professor Owen, tells us (Plants and Animals under Domestication, vol. ii. p. 362, ed. 1875), that in the case of what is called metagenetic development, "the new parts are not moulded upon the inner surfaces of the old ones. The plastic force has changed its mode of operation. *The outer case, and all that gave form and character to the precedent individual, perish, and are cast off; they are not changed* into the corresponding parts of the same individual. These are due to a new and distinct developmental process." Assuredly, there is more birth and death in the world than is dreamt of by the greater part of us; but it is so masked, and on the whole, so little to our purpose, that we fail to see it. Yet radical and sweeping as the changes of organism above described must be, we do not feel them to be more a bar to personal identity than the considerable changes which take place in the structure of our own bodies between youth and old age.

Perhaps the most striking illustration of this is to be found in the case of some Echinoderms, concerning which Mr. Darwin tells us, that "the animal in the second stage of development is formed almost like a bud within the animal of the first stage, the latter being then cast off like an old vestment, yet sometimes maintaining for a short period an independent vitality" ("Plants and Animals under Domestication," vol. ii. p. 362, ed. 1875).

Nor yet does personality depend upon any consciousness or sense of such personality on the part of the creature itself—it is not likely that the moth remembers having been a caterpillar, more than we ourselves remember having been children of a day old. It depends simply upon the fact that the various phases of existence have been linked together, by links which we agree in considering sufficient to cause identity, and that they have flowed the one out of the other in what we see as a continuous, though it may be at times, a troubled stream. This is the very essence of personality, but it involves the probable unity of all animal and vegetable life, as being, in reality, nothing but one single creature, of which the component members are but, as it were, blood corpuscles or individual cells; life being a sort of leaven, which, if once introduced into the world, will leaven it altogether; or of fire, which will consume all it can burn; or of air or water, which will turn most things into themselves. Indeed, no difficulty would probably be felt about admitting the continued existence of personal identity between parents and their offspring through all time (there being no *sudden* break at any time between the existence of any maternal parent and that of its offspring), were it not that after a certain time the changes in outward appearance between descendants and ancestors become very great, the two seeming to stand so far apart, that it seems absurd in any way to say that they are one and the same being; much in the same way as after a time—though exactly when no one can say—the Thames becomes the sea. Moreover, the separation of the identity is practically of far greater importance to it than its continuance. We want to be ourselves; we do not want any one else to claim part and parcel of our identity. This community of identities is not found to answer in everyday life. When then our love of independence is backed up by the fact that continuity of life between parents and offspring is a matter which depends on things which are a good deal hidden, and that thus birth gives us an opportunity of pretending that there has been a sudden leap into a separate life; when also we have regard to the utter ignorance of embryology, which prevailed till quite recently, it is not surprising that our ordinary language should be found to have regard to what is important and obvious, rather than to what is not quite obvious, and is quite unimportant.

Personality is the creature of time and space, changing, as time changes, imperceptibly; we are therefore driven to deal with it as with all continuous and blending things; as with time, for example, itself, which we divide into days, and seasons, and times, and years, into divisions that are often arbitrary, but coincide, on the whole, as nearly as we can make them do so, with the more marked changes which we can observe. We lay hold, in fact, of anything we can catch; the most important feature in any existence as regards ourselves being that which we can best lay hold of rather than that which is most essential to the existence itself. We can lay hold of the continued personality of the egg and the moth into which the egg develops, but it is less easy to catch sight of the continued personality between the moth and the eggs which she lays; yet the one continuation of personality is just as true and free from quibble as the other. A moth becomes each egg that she lays, and that she does so, she will in good time show by doing, now that she has got a fresh start, as near as may be what she did when first she was an egg, and then a moth, before; and this I take it, so far as I can gather from looking at life and things generally, she would not be able to do if she had not travelled the same road often enough already, to be able to know it in her sleep and blindfold, that is to say, to remember it without any conscious act of memory.

So also a grain of wheat is linked with an ear, containing, we will say, a dozen grains, by a series of changes so subtle that we cannot say at what moment the original grain became the blade, nor when each ear of the head became possessed of an individual centre of action. To say that each grain of the head is personally identical with the original grain would perhaps be an abuse of terms; but it can be no abuse to say that each grain is a continuation of the personality of the original grain, and if so, of every grain in the chain of its own ancestry; and that, as being such a continuation, it must be stored with the memories and experiences of its past existences, to be recollected under the circumstances most favourable to recollection, *i.e.*, when under similar conditions to those when the impression was last made and last remembered. Truly, then, in each case the new egg and the new grain *is* the egg, and the grain from which its parent sprang, as completely as the full-grown ox is the calf from which it has grown.

Again, in the case of some weeping trees, whose boughs spring up into fresh trees when they have reached the ground, who shall say at what time they cease to be members of the parent tree? In the case of cuttings from plants it is easy to elude the difficulty by making a parade of the sharp and sudden act of separation from the parent stock, but this is only a piece of mental sleight of hand; the cutting remains as much part of its parent plant as though it had never been severed from it; it goes on profiting by the experience which it had before it was cut off, as much as though it had never been cut off at all. This will be more readily seen in the case of worms which have been cut in half. Let a worm be cut in half, and the two halves will become fresh worms; which of them is the original worm? Surely both. Perhaps no simpler case than this could readily be found of the manner in which personality eludes us, the moment we try to investigate its real nature. There are few ideas which on first consideration appear so simple, and none which becomes more utterly incapable of limitation or definition as soon as it is examined closely.

Finally, Mr. Darwin ("Plants and Animals under Domestication," vol. ii. p. 38, ed. 1875), writes—

"Even with plants multiplied by bulbs, layers, &c., which may *in one sense* be said to form part of the same individual," &c., &c.; and again, p. 58, "The same rule holds good with plants when propagated by bulbs, offsets, &c., which *in one sense* still form parts of the same individual," &c. In each of these passages it is plain that the difficulty of separating the personality of the offspring from that of the parent plant is present to his mind. Yet, p. 351 of the same volume as above, he tells us that asexual generation "is effected in many ways—by the formation of buds of various kinds, and by fissiparous generation, that is, by spontaneous or artificial division." The multiplication of plants by bulbs and layers clearly comes under this head, nor will any essential difference be felt between one kind of asexual generation and another; if, then, the offspring formed by bulbs and layers is in one sense part of the original plant, so also, it would appear, is all offspring developed by asexual generation in its manifold phrases.

If we now turn to p. 357, we find the conclusion arrived at, as it would appear, on the most satisfactory evidence, that "sexual and asexual reproduction are not seen to differ essentially; and . . . . that asexual reproduction, the power of regrowth, and development are all parts of one and the same great law." Does it not then follow, quite reasonably and necessarily, that all offspring, however generated, is *in one sense* part of the individuality of its parent or parents. The question, therefore, turns upon "in what sense" this may be said to be the case? To which I would venture to reply, "In the same sense as the parent plant (which is but the representative of the outside matter which it has assimilated during growth, and of its own powers of development) is the same individual that it was when it was itself an offset, or a cow the same individual that it was when it was a calf—but no otherwise."

Not much difficulty will be felt about supposing the offset of a plant, to be imbued with the memory of the past history of the plant of which it is an offset. It is part of the plant itself; and will know whatever the plant knows. Why, then, should there be more difficulty in supposing the offspring of the highest mammals, to remember in a profound but unselfconscious way, the anterior history of the creatures of which they too have been part and parcel?

Personal identity, then, is much like species itself. It is now, thanks to Mr. Darwin, generally held that species blend or have blended into one another; so that any possibility of arrangement and apparent subdivision into definite groups, is due to the suppression by death both of individuals and whole genera, which, had they been now existing, would have linked all living beings by a series of gradations so subtle that little classification could have been attempted. How it is that the one great personality of life as a whole, should have split itself up into so many centres of thought and action, each one of which is wholly, or at any rate nearly, unconscious of its connection with the other members, instead of having grown up into a huge polyp, or as it were coral reef or compound animal over the whole world, which should be conscious but of its own one single existence; how it is that the daily waste of this creature should be carried on by the conscious death of its individual members, instead of by the unconscious waste of tissue which goes on in the bodies of each individual (if indeed the tissue which we waste daily in our own bodies is so unconscious of its birth and death as we suppose); how, again, that the daily repair of this huge creature life should have become decentralised, and be carried on by conscious reproduction on the part of its component items, instead of by the unconscious nutrition of the whole from a single centre, as the nutrition of our own bodies would appear (though perhaps falsely) to be carried on; these are matters upon which I dare not speculate here, but on which some reflections may follow in subsequent chapters.

CHAPTER VII—OUR SUBORDINATE PERSONALITIES

We have seen that we can apprehend neither the beginning nor the end of our personality, which comes up out of infinity as an island out of the sea, so gently, that none can say when it is first visible on our mental horizon, and fades away in the case of those who leave offspring, so imperceptibly that none can say when it is out of sight. But, like the island, whether we can see it or no, it is always there. Not only are we infinite as regards time, but we are so also as regards extension, being so linked on to the external world that we cannot say where we either begin or end. If those who so frequently declare that man is a finite creature would point out his boundaries, it might lead to a better understanding.

Nevertheless, we are in the habit of considering that our personality, or soul, no matter where it begins or ends, and no matter what it comprises, is nevertheless a single thing, uncompounded of other souls. Yet there is nothing more certain than that this is not at all the case, but that every individual person is a compound creature, being made up of an infinite number of distinct centres of sensation and will, each one of which is personal, and has a soul and individual existence, a reproductive system, intelligence, and memory of its own, with probably its hopes and fears, its times of scarcity and repletion, and a strong conviction that it is itself the centre of the universe.

True, no one is aware of more than one individuality in his own person at one time. We are, indeed, often greatly influenced by other people, so much so, that we act on many occasions in accordance with their will rather than our own, making our actions answer to their sensations, and register the conclusions of their cerebral action and not our own; for the time being, we become so completely part of them, that we are ready to do things most distasteful and dangerous to us, if they think it for their advantage that we should do so. Thus we sometimes see people become mere processes of their wives or nearest relations. Yet there is a something which blinds us, so that we cannot see how completely we are possessed by the souls which influence us upon these occasions. We still think we are ourselves, and ourselves only, and are as certain as we can be of any fact, that we are single sentient beings, uncompounded of other sentient beings, and that our action is determined by the sole operation of a single will.

But in reality, over and above this possession of our souls by others of our own species, the will of the lower animals often enters into our bodies and possesses them, making us do as they will, and not as we will; as, for example, when people try to drive pigs, or are run away with by a restive horse, or are attacked by a savage animal which masters them. It is absurd to say that a person is a single "ego" when he is in the clutches of a lion. Even when we are alone, and uninfluenced by other people except in so far as we remember their wishes, we yet generally conform to the usages which the current feeling of our peers has taught us to respect; their will having so mastered our original nature, that, do what we may, we can never again separate ourselves and dwell in the isolation of our own single personality. And even though we succeeded in this, and made a clean sweep of every mental influence which had ever been brought to bear upon us, and though at the same time we were alone in some desert where there was neither beast nor bird to attract our attention or in any way influence our action, yet we could not escape the parasites which abound within us; whose action, as every medical man well knows, is often such as to drive men to the commission of grave crimes, or to throw them into convulsions, make lunatics of them, kill them—when but for the existence and course of conduct pursued by these parasites they would have done no wrong to any man.

These parasites—are they part of us or no? Some are plainly not so in any strict sense of the word, yet their action may, in cases which it is unnecessary to detail, affect us so powerfully that we are irresistibly impelled to act in such or such a manner; and yet we are as wholly unconscious of any impulse outside of our own "ego" as though they were part of ourselves; others again are essential to our very existence, as the corpuscles of the blood, which the best authorities concur in supposing to be composed of an infinite number of living souls, on whose welfare the healthy condition of our blood, and hence of our whole bodies, depends. We breathe that they may breathe, not that we may do so; we only care about oxygen in so far as the infinitely small beings which course up and down in our veins care about it: the whole arrangement and mechanism of our lungs may be our doing, but is for their convenience, and they only serve us because it suits their purpose to do so, as long as we serve them. Who shall draw the line between the parasites which are part of us, and the parasites which are not part of us? Or again, between the influence of those parasites which are within us, but are yet not *us*, and the external influence of other sentient beings and our fellow-men? There is no line possible. Everything melts away into everything else; there are no hard edges; it is only from a little distance that we see the effect as of individual features and existences. When we go close up, there is nothing but a blur and confused mass of apparently meaningless touches, as in a picture by Turner.

The following passage from Mr. Darwin's provisional theory of Pangenesis, will sufficiently show that the above is no strange and paradoxical view put forward wantonly, but that it follows as a matter of course from the conclusions arrived at by those who are acknowledged leaders in the scientific world. Mr. Darwin writes thus:-

"The functional independence of the elements or units of the body .— Physiologists agree that the whole organism consists of a multitude of elemental parts, which are to a great extent independent of one another. Each organ, says Claude Bernard, has its proper life, its autonomy; it can develop and reproduce itself independently of the adjoining tissues. A great German authority, Virchow, asserts still more emphatically that each system consists of 'an enormous mass of minute centres of action. . . . Every element has its own special action, and even though it derive its stimulus to activity from other parts, yet alone effects the actual performance of duties. . . . Every single epithelial and muscular fibre-cell leads a sort of parasitical existence in relation to the rest of the body. . . . Every single bone corpuscle really possesses conditions of nutrition peculiar to itself.' Each element, as Sir J. Paget remarks, lives its appointed time, and then dies, and is replaced after being cast off and absorbed. I presume that no physiologist doubts that, for instance, each bone corpuscle of the finger differs from the corresponding corpuscle of the corresponding joint of the toe," &c., &c. ("Plants and Animals under Domestication," vol ii. pp. 364, 365, ed. 1875).

In a work on heredity by M. Ribot, I find him saying, "Some recent authors attribute a memory" (and if so, surely every attribute of complete individuality) "to every organic element of the body;" among them Dr. Maudsley, who is quoted by M. Ribot, as saying, "The permanent effects of a particular virus, such as that of the variola, in the constitution, shows that the organic element remembers for the remainder of its life certain modifications it has received. The manner in which a cicatrix in a child's finger grows with the growth of the body, proves, as has been shown by Paget, that the organic element of the part does not forget the impression it has received. What has been said about the different nervous centres of the body demonstrates the existence of a memory in the nerve cells diffused through the heart and intestines; in those of the spinal cord, in the cells of the motor ganglia, and in the cells of the cortical substance of the cerebal hemispheres."

Now, if words have any meaning at all, it must follow from the passages quoted above, that each cell in the human body is a person with an intelligent soul, of a low class, perhaps, but still differing from our own more complex soul in degree, and not in kind; and, like ourselves, being born, living, and dying. So that each single creature, whether man or beast, proves to be as a ray of white light, which, though single, is compounded of the red, blue, and yellow rays. It would appear, then, as though "we," "our souls," or "selves," or "personalities," or by whatever name we may prefer to be called, are but the *consensus* and full flowing stream of countless sensations and impulses on the part of our tributary souls or "selves," who probably know no more that we exist, and that they exist as part of us, than a microscopic water-flea knows the results of spectrum analysis, or than an agricultural labourer knows the working of the British constitution: and of whom we know no more, until some misconduct on our part, or some confusion of ideas on theirs, has driven them into insurrection, than we do of the habits and feelings of some class widely separated from our own.

These component souls are of many and very different natures, living in territories which are to them vast continents, and rivers, and seas, but which are yet only the bodies of our other component souls; coral reefs and sponge-beds within us; the animal itself being a kind of mean proportional between its house and its soul, and none being able to say where house ends and animal begins, more than they can say where animal ends and soul begins. For our bones within us are but inside walls and buttresses, that is to say, houses constructed of lime and stone, as it were, by coral insects; and our houses without us are but outside bones, a kind of exterior skeleton or shell, so that we perish of cold if permanently and suddenly deprived of the coverings which warm us and cherish us, as the wing of a hen cherishes her chickens. If we consider the shells of many living creatures, we shall find it hard to say whether they are rather houses, or part of the animal itself, being, as they are, inseparable from the animal, without the destruction of its personality.

Is it possible, then, to avoid imagining that if we have within us so many tributary souls, so utterly different from the soul which they unite to form, that they neither can perceive us, nor we them, though it is in us that they live and move and have their being, and though we are what we are, solely as the result of their co-operation—is it possible to avoid imagining that we may be ourselves atoms, undesignedly combining to form some vaster being, though we are utterly incapable of perceiving that any such being exists, or of realising the scheme or scope of our own combination? And this, too, not a spiritual being, which, without matter, or what we think matter of some sort, is as complete nonsense to us as though men bade us love and lean upon an intelligent vacuum, but a being with what is virtually flesh and blood and bones; with organs, senses, dimensions, in some way analogous to our own, into some other part of which being, at the time of our great change we must infallibly re-enter, starting clean anew, with bygones bygones, and no more ache for ever from either age or antecedents. Truly, sufficient for the life is the evil thereof. Any speculations of ours concerning the nature of such a being, must be as futile and little valuable as those of a blood corpuscle might be expected to be concerning the nature of man; but if I were myself a blood corpuscle, I should be amused at making the discovery that I was not only enjoying life in my own sphere, but was *bonâ fide* part of an animal which would not die with myself, and in which I might thus think of myself as continuing to live to all eternity, or to what, as far as my power of thought would carry me, must seem practically eternal. But, after all, the amusement would be of a rather dreary nature.

On the other hand, if I were the being of whom such an introspective blood corpuscle was a component item, I should conceive he served me better by attending to my blood and making himself a successful corpuscle, than by speculating about my nature. He would serve me best by serving himself best, without being over curious. I should expect that my blood might suffer if his brain were to become too active. If, therefore, I could discover the vein in which he was, I should let him out to begin life anew in some other and, *quâ* me, more profitable capacity.

With the units of our bodies it is as with the stars of heaven: there is neither speech nor language, but their voices are heard among them. Our will is the *fiat* of their collective wisdom, as sanctioned in their parliament, the brain; it is they who make us do whatever we do—it is they who should be rewarded if they have done well, or hanged if they have committed murder. When the balance of power is well preserved among them, when they respect each other's rights and work harmoniously together, then we thrive and are well; if we are ill, it is because they are quarrelling with themselves, or are gone on strike for this or that addition to their environment, and our doctor must pacify or chastise them as best he may. They are we and we are they; and when we die it is but a redistribution of the balance of power among them or a change of dynasty, the result, it may be, of heroic struggle, with more epics and love romances than we could read from now to the Millennium, if they were so written down that we could comprehend them.

It is plain, then, that the more we examine the question of personality the more it baffles us, the only safeguard against utter confusion and idleness of thought being to fall back upon the superficial and common sense view, and refuse to tolerate discussions which seem to hold out little prospect of commercial value, and which would compel us, if logically followed, to be at the inconvenience of altering our opinions upon matters which we have come to consider as settled.

And we observe that this is what is practically done by some of our ablest philosophers, who seem unwilling, if one may say so without presumption, to accept the conclusions to which their own experiments and observations would seem to point.

Dr. Carpenter, for example, quotes the well-known experiments upon headless frogs. If we cut off a frog's head and pinch any part of its skin, the animal at once begins to move away with the same regularity as though the brain had not been removed. Flourens took guinea-pigs, deprived them of the cerebral lobes, and then irritated their skin; the animals immediately walked, leaped, and trotted about, but when the irritation was discontinued they ceased to move. Headless birds, under excitation, can still perform with their wings the rhythmic movements of flying. But here are some facts more curious still, and more difficult of explanation. If we take a frog or a strong and healthy triton, and subject it to various experiments; if we touch, pinch, or burn it with acetic acid, and if then, after decapitating the animal, we subject it to the same experiments, it will be seen that the reactions are exactly the same; it will strive to be free of the pain, and to shake off the acetic acid that is burning it; it will bring its foot up to the part of its body that is irritated, and this movement of the member will follow the irritation wherever it may be produced.

The above is mainly taken from M. Ribot's work on heredity rather than Dr. Carpenter's, because M. Ribot tells us that the head of the frog was actually cut off, a fact which does not appear so plainly in Dr. Carpenter's allusion to the same experiments. But Dr. Carpenter tells us that *after the brain of a frog has been removed*—which would seem to be much the same thing as though its head were cut off— "if acetic acid be applied over the upper and under part of the thigh, the foot of the same side will wipe it away; *but if that foot be cut off, after some ineffectual efforts and a short period of inaction ,*" during which it is hard not to surmise that the headless body is considering what it had better do under the circumstances, *"the same movement will be made by the foot of the opposite side,"* which, to ordinary people, would convey the impression that the headless body was capable of feeling the impressions it had received, and of reasoning upon them by a psychological act; and this of course involves the possession of a soul of some sort.

Here is a frog whose right thigh you burn with acetic acid. Very naturally it tries to get at the place with its right foot to remove the acid. You then cut off the frog's head, and put more acetic acid on the some place: the headless frog, or rather the body of the late frog, does just what the frog did before its head was cut off—it tries to get at the place with its right foot. You now cut off its right foot: the headless body deliberates, and after a while tries to do with its left foot what it can no longer do with its right. Plain matter-of-fact people will draw their own inference. They will not be seduced from the superficial view of the matter. They will say that the headless body can still, to some extent, feel, think, and act, and if so, that it must have a living soul.

Dr. Carpenter writes as follows:- "Now the performance of these, as well as of many other movements, that show a most remarkable adaptation to a purpose, might be supposed to indicate that sensations are called up by the *impressions*, and that the animal can not only *feel* , but can voluntarily direct its movements so as to get rid of the irritation which annoys it. But such an inference would be inconsistent with other facts. In the first place, the motions performed under such circumstances are never spontaneous, but are always excited by a stimulus of some kind."

Here we pause to ask ourselves whether any action of any creature under any circumstances is ever excited without "stimulus of some kind," and unless we can answer this question in the affirmative, it is not easy to see how Dr. Carpenter's objection is valid.

"Thus," he continues, "a decapitated frog" (here then we have it that the frog's head was actually cut off) "after the first violent convulsive moments occasioned by the operation have passed away, remains at rest until it is touched; and then the leg, or its whole body may be thrown into sudden action, which suddenly subsides again." (How does this quiescence when it no longer feels anything show that the "leg or whole body" had not perceived something which made it feel when it was not quiescent?) —"Again we find that such movements may be performed not only when the brain has been removed, the spinal cord remaining entire, but also when the spinal cord has been itself cut across, so as to be divided into two or more portions, each of them completely isolated from each other, and from other parts of the nervous centres. Thus, if the head of a frog be cut off, and its spinal cord be divided in the middle of the back, so that its fore legs remain connected with the upper part, and its hind legs with the lower, each pair of members may be excited to movements by stimulants applied to itself; but the two pairs will not exhibit any consentaneous motions, as they will do when the spinal cord is undivided."

This may be put perhaps more plainly thus. If you take a frog and cut it into three pieces—say, the head for one piece, the fore legs and shoulder for another, and the hind legs for a third—and then irritate any one of these pieces, you will find it move much as it would have moved under like irritation if the animal had remained undivided, but you will no longer find any concert between the movements of the three pieces; that is to say, if you irritate the head, the other two pieces will remain quiet, and if you irritate the hind legs, you will excite no action in the fore legs or head.

Dr. Carpenter continues: "Or if the spinal cord be cut across without the removal of the brain, the lower limbs may be *excited* to movement by an appropriate stimulant, though the animal has clearly no power over them, whilst the upper part remains under its control as completely as before."

Why are the head and shoulders "the animal" more than the hind legs under these circumstances? Neither half can exist long without the other; the two parts, therefore, being equally important to each other, we have surely as good a right to claim the title of "the animal" for the hind legs, and to maintain that they have no power over the head and shoulders, as any one else has to claim the animalship for these last. What we say is, that the animal has ceased to exist as a frog on being cut in half, and that the two halves are no longer, either of them, the frog, but are simply pieces of still living organism, each of which has a soul of its own, being capable of sensation, and of intelligent psychological action as the consequence of sensations, though the one part has probably a much higher and more intelligent soul than the other, and neither part has a soul for a moment comparable in power and durability to that of the original frog.

"Now it is scarcely conceivable," continues Dr Carpenter, "that in this last case sensations should be felt and volition exercised through the instrumentality of that portion of the spinal cord which remains connected with the nerves of the posterior extremities, but which is cut off from the brain. For if it were so, there must be two distinct centres of sensation and will in the same animal, the attributes of the brain not being affected; and by dividing the spinal cord into two or more segments we might thus create in the body of one animal two or more such independent centres in addition to that which holds its proper place in the head."

In the face of the facts before us, it does not seen far-fetched to suppose that there *are* two, or indeed an infinite number of centres of sensation and will in an animal, the attributes of whose brain are not affected but that these centres, while the brain is intact, habitually act in connection with and in subordination to that central authority; as in the ordinary state of the fish trade, fish is caught, we will say, at Yarmouth, sent up to London, and then sent down to Yarmouth again to be eaten, instead of being eaten at Yarmouth when caught. But from the phenomena exhibited by three pieces of an animal, it is impossible to argue that the causes of the phenomena were present in the quondam animal itself; the memory of an infinite series of generations having so habituated the local centres of sensation and will, to act in concert with the central government, that as long as they can get at that government, they are absolutely incapable of acting independently. When thrown on their own resources, they are so demoralised by ages of dependence on the brain, that they die after a few efforts at self-assertion, from sheer unfamiliarity with the position, and inability to recognise themselves when disjointed rudely from their habitual associations.

In conclusion, Dr. Carpenter says, "To say that two or more distinct centres of sensation and will are present in such a case, would really be the same as saying that we have the power of constituting two or more distinct egos in one body, *which is manifestly absurd.*" One sees the absurdity of maintaining that we can make one frog into two frogs by cutting a frog into two pieces, but there is no absurdity in believing that the two pieces have minor centres of sensation and intelligence within themselves, which, when the animal is entire, act in much concert with the brain, and with each other, that it is not easy to detect their originally autonomous character, but which, when deprived of their power of acting in concert, are thrown back upon earlier habit, now too long forgotten to be capable of permanent resumption.

Illustrations are apt to mislead, nevertheless they may perhaps be sometimes tolerated. Suppose, for example, that London to the extent, say, of a circle with a six-mile radius from Charing Cross, were utterly annihilated in the space of five minutes during the Session of Parliament. Suppose, also, that two entirely impassable barriers, say of five miles in width, half a mile high, and red hot, were thrown across England; one from Gloucester to Harwich, and another from Liverpool to Hull, and at the same time the sea were to become a mass of molten lava, so no water communication should be possible; the political, mercantile, social, and intellectual life of the country would be convulsed in a manner which it is hardly possible to realise. Hundreds of thousands would die through the dislocation of existing arrangements. Nevertheless, each of the three parts into which England was divided would show signs of provincial life for which it would find certain imperfect organisms ready to hand. Bristol, Birmingham, Liverpool, and Manchester, accustomed though they are to act in subordination to London, would probably take up the reins of government in their several sections; they would make their town councils into local governments, appoint judges from the ablest of their magistrates, organise relief committees, and endeavour as well as they could to remove any acetic acid that might be now poured on Wiltshire, Warwickshire, or Northumberland, but no concert between the three divisions of the country would be any longer possible. Should we be justified, under these circumstances, in calling any of the three parts of England, England? Or, again, when we observed the provincial action to be as nearly like that of the original undivided nation as circumstances would allow, should we be justified in saying that the action, such as it was, was not political? And, lastly, should we for a moment think that an admission that the provincial action was of a *bonâ fide* political character would involve the supposition that England, undivided, had more than one "ego" as England, no matter how many subordinate "egos" might go to the making of it, each one of which proved, on emergency, to be capable of a feeble autonomy?

M. Ribot would seem to take a juster view of the phenomenon when he says (p. 222 of the English translation)—

"We can hardly say that here the movements are co-ordinated like those of a machine; the acts of the animal are adapted to a special end; we find in them the characters of intelligence and will, a knowledge and choice of means, since they are as variable as the cause which provokes them.

"If these, then, and similar acts, were such that both the impressions which produced them and the acts themselves were perceived by the animal, would they not be called psychological? Is there not in them all that constitutes an intelligent act—adaptation of means to ends; not a general and vague adaptation, but a determinate adaptation to a determinate end? In the reflex action we find all that constitutes in some sort the very groundwork of an intelligent act— that is to say, the same series of stages, in the same order, with the same relations between them. We have thus, in the reflex act, all that constitutes the psychological act except consciousness. The reflex act, which is physiological, differs in nothing from the psychological act, save only in this—that it is without consciousness."

The only remark which suggests itself upon this, is that we have no right to say that the part of the animal which moves does not also perceive its own act of motion, as much as it has perceived the impression which has caused it to move. It is plain "the animal" cannot do so, for the animal cannot be said to be any longer in existence. Half a frog is not a frog; nevertheless, if the hind legs are capable, as M. Ribot appears to admit, of "perceiving the impression" which produces their action, and if in that action there is (and there would certainly appear to be so) "all that constitutes an intelligent act, . . . a determinate adaptation to a determinate end," one fails to see on what ground they should be supposed to be incapable of perceiving their own action, in which case the action of the hind legs becomes distinctly psychological.

Secondly, M. Ribot appears to forget that it is the tendency of all psychological action to become unconscious on being frequently repeated, and that no line can be drawn between psychological acts and those reflex acts which he calls physiological. All we can say is, that there are acts which we do without knowing that we do them; but the analogy of many habits which we have been able to watch in their passage from laborious consciousness to perfect unconsciousness, would suggest that all action is really psychological, only that the soul's action becomes invisible to ourselves after it has been repeated sufficiently often—that there is, in fact, a law as simple as in the case of optics or gravitation, whereby conscious perception of any action shall vary inversely as the square, say, of its being repeated.

It is easy to understand the advantage to the individual of this power of doing things rightly without thinking about them; for were there no such power, the attention would be incapable of following the multitude of matters which would be continually arresting it; those animals which had developed a power of working automatically, and without a recurrence to first principles when they had once mastered any particular process, would, in the common course of events, stand a better chance of continuing their species, and thus of transmitting their new power to their descendants.

M. Ribot declines to pursue the subject further, and has only cursorily alluded to it. He writes, however, that, on the "obscure problem" of the difference between reflex and psychological actions, some say, "when there can be no consciousness, because the brain is wanting, there is, in spite of appearances, only mechanism," whilst others maintain, that "when there is selection, reflection, psychical action, there must also be consciousness in spite of appearances." A little later (p. 223), he says, "It is quite possible that if a headless animal could live a sufficient length of time" (that is to say, if *the hind legs of an animal* could live a sufficient length of time without the brain), "there would be found in it" (*them*) "a consciousness like that of the lower species, which would consist merely in the faculty of apprehending the external world." (Why merely? It is more than apprehending the outside world to be able to try to do a thing with one's left foot, when one finds that one cannot do it with one's right.) "It would not be correct to say that the amphioxus, the only one among fishes and vertebrata which has a spinal cord without a brain, has no consciousness because it has no brain; and if it be admitted that the little ganglia of the invertebrata can form a consciousness, the same may hold good for the spinal cord."

We conclude, therefore, that it is within the common scope and meaning of the words "personal identity," not only that one creature can become many as the moth becomes manifold in her eggs, but that each individual may be manifold in the sense of being compounded of a vast number of subordinate individualities which have their separate lives within him, with their hopes, and fears, and intrigues, being born and dying within us, many generations, of them during our single lifetime.

"An organic being," writes Mr. Darwin, "is a microcosm, a little universe, formed of a host of self-propagating organisms, inconceivably minute, and numerous as the stars in heaven."

As these myriads of smaller organisms are parts and processes of us, so are we but parts and processes of life at large.

CHAPTER VIII—APPLICATION OF THE FOREGOING CHAPTERS - THE ASSIMILATION OF OUTSIDE MATTER

Let us now return to the position which we left at the end of the fourth chapter. We had then concluded that the self-development of each new life in succeeding generations—the various stages through which it passes (as it would appear, at first sight, without rhyme or reason)—the manner in which it prepares structures of the most surpassing intricacy and delicacy, for which it has no use at the time when it prepares them—and the many elaborate instincts which it exhibits immediately on, and indeed before, birth—all point in the direction of habit and memory, as the only causes which could produce them.

Why should the embryo of any animal go through so many stages—embryological allusions to forefathers of a widely different type? And why, again, should the germs of the same kind of creature always go through the same stages? If the germ of any animal now living is, in its simplest state, but part of the personal identity of one of the original germs of all life whatsoever, and hence, if any now living organism must be considered without quibble as being itself millions of years old, and as imbued with an intense though unconscious memory of all that it has done sufficiently often to have made a permanent impression; if this be so, we can answer the above questions perfectly well. The creature goes through so many intermediate stages between its earliest state as life at all, and its latest development, for the simplest of all reasons, namely, because this is the road by which it has always hitherto travelled to its present differentiation; this is the road it knows, and into every turn and up or down of which, it has been guided by the force of circumstances and the balance of considerations. These, acting in such a manner for such and such a time, caused it to travel in such and such fashion, which fashion having been once sufficiently established, becomes a matter of trick or routine to which the creature is still a slave, and in which it confirms itself by repetition in each succeeding generation.

Thus I suppose, as almost every one else, so far as I can gather, supposes, that we are descended from ancestors of widely different characters to our own. If we could see some of our forefathers a million years back, we should find them unlike anything we could call man; if we were to go back fifty million years, we should find them, it may be, fishes pure and simple, breathing through gills, and unable to exist for many minutes in air.

It is admitted on all hands that there is more or less analogy between the embryological development of the individual, and the various phases or conditions of life through which his forefathers have passed. I suppose, then, that the fish of fifty million years back and the man of to-day are one single living being, in the same sense, or very nearly so, as the octogenarian is one single living being with the infant from which he has grown; and that the fish has lived himself into manhood, not as we live out our little life, living, and living, and living till we die, but living by pulsations, so to speak; living so far, and after a certain time going into a new body, and throwing off the old; making his body much as we make anything that we want, and have often made already, that is to say, as nearly as may be in the same way as he made it last time; also that he is as unable as we ourselves are, to make what he wants without going through the usual processes with which he is familiar, even though there may be other better ways of doing the same thing, which might not be far to seek, if the creature thought them better, and had not got so accustomed to such and such a method, that he would only be baffled and put out by any attempt to teach him otherwise.

And this oneness of personality between ourselves and our supposed fishlike ancestors of many millions of years ago, must hold also between each individual one of us and the single pair of fishes from which we are each (on the present momentary hypothesis) descended; and it must also hold between such pair of fishes and all their descendants besides man, it may be some of them birds, and others fishes; all these descendants, whether human or otherwise, being but the way in which the creature (which was a pair of fishes when we first took it in hand though it was a hundred thousand other things as well, and had been all manner of other things before any part of it became fishlike) continues to exist—its manner, in fact, of growing. As the manner in which the human body grows is by the continued birth and death, in our single lifetime, of many generations of cells which we know nothing about, but say that we have had only one hand or foot all our lives, when we have really had many, one after another; so this huge compound creature, LIFE, probably thinks itself but one single animal whose component cells, as it may imagine, grow, and it may be waste and repair, but do not die.

It may be that the cells of which we are built up, and which we have already seen must be considered as separate persons, each one of them with a life and memory of its own—it may be that these cells reckon time in a manner inconceivable by us, so that no word can convey any idea of it whatever. What may to them appear a long and painful process may to us be so instantaneous as to escape us altogether, we wanting some microscope to show us the details of time. If, in like manner, we were to allow our imagination to conceive the existence of a being as much in need of a microscope for our time and affairs as we for those of our own component cells, the years would be to such a being but as the winkings or the twinklings of an eye. Would he think, then, that all the ants and flies of one wink were different from those of the next? or would he not rather believe that they were always the same flies, and, again, always the same men and women, if he could see them at all, and if the whole human race did not appear to him as a sort of spreading and lichen-like growth over the earth, not differentiated at all into individuals? With the help of a microscope and the intelligent exercise of his reason, he would in time conceive the truth. He would put Covent Garden Market on the field of his microscope, and would perhaps write a great deal of nonsense about the unerring "instinct" which taught each costermonger to recognise his own basket or his own donkey-cart; and this, *mutatis mutandis*, is what we are getting to do as regards our own bodies. What I wish is, to make the same sort of step in an upward direction which has already been taken in a downward one, and to show reason for thinking that we are only component atoms of a single compound creature, LIFE, which has probably a distinct conception of its own personality though none whatever of ours, more than we of our own units. I wish also to show reason for thinking that this creature, LIFE, has only come to be what it is, by the same sort of process as that by which any human art or manufacture is developed, *i.e.*, through constantly doing the same thing over and over again, beginning from something which is barely recognisable as faith, or as the desire to know, or do, or live at all, and as to the origin of which we are in utter darkness,—and growing till it is first conscious of effort, then conscious of power, then powerful with but little consciousness, and finally, so powerful and so charged with memory as to be absolutely without all self-consciousness whatever, except as regards its latest phases in each of its many differentiations, or when placed in such new circumstances as compel it to choose between death and a reconsideration of its position.

No conjecture can be hazarded as to how the smallest particle of matter became so imbued with faith that it must be considered as the beginning of LIFE, or as to what such faith is, except that it is the very essence of all things, and that it has no foundation.

In this way, then, I conceive we can fairly transfer the experience of the race to the individual, without any other meaning to our words than what they would naturally suggest; that is to say, that there is in every impregnate ovum a *bonâ fide* memory, which carries it back not only to the time when it was last an impregnate ovum, but to that earlier date when it was the very beginning of life at all, which same creature it still is, whether as man or ovum, and hence imbued, so far as time and circumstance allow, with all its memories. Surely this is no strained hypothesis; for the mere fact that the germ, from the earliest moment that we are able to detect it, appears to be so perfectly familiar with its business, acts with so little hesitation and so little introspection or reference to principles, this alone should incline us to suspect that it must be armed with that which, so far as we observe in daily life, can alone ensure such a result—to wit, long practice, and the memory of many similar performances.

The difficulty is, that we are conscious of no such memory in our own persons, and beyond the one great proof of memory given by the actual repetition of the performance—and of some of the latest deviations from the ordinary performance (and this proof ought in itself, one would have thought, to outweigh any save the directest evidence to the contrary) we can detect no symptom of any such mental operation as recollection on the part of the embryo. On the other hand, we have seen that we know most intensely those things that we are least conscious of knowing; we will most intensely what we are least conscious of willing; we feel continually without knowing that we feel, and our attention is hourly arrested without our attention being arrested by the arresting of our attention. Memory is no less capable of unconscious exercise, and on becoming intense through frequent repetition, vanishes no less completely as a conscious action of the mind than knowledge and volition. We must all be aware of instances in which it is plain we must have remembered, without being in the smallest degree conscious of remembering. Is it then absurd to suppose that our past existences have been repeated on such a vast number of occasions that the germ, linked on to all preceding germs, and, by once having become part of their identity, imbued with all their memories, remembers too intensely to be conscious of remembering, and works on with the same kind of unconsciousness with which we play, or walk, or read, until something unfamiliar happens to us? and is it not singularly in accordance with this view that consciousness should begin with that part of the creature's performance with which it is least familiar, as having repeated it least often —that is to say, in our own case, with the commencement of our human life —at birth, or thereabouts?

It is certainly noteworthy that the embryo is never at a loss, unless something happens to it which has not usually happened to its forefathers, and which in the nature of things it cannot remember.

When events are happening to it which have ordinarily happened to its forefathers, and which it would therefore remember, if it was possessed of the kind of memory which we are here attributing to it, *it acts precisely as it would act if it were possessed of such memory.*

When, on the other hand, events are happening to it which, if it has the kind of memory we are attributing to it, would baffle that memory, or which have rarely or never been included in the category of its recollections, *it acts precisely as a creature acts when its recollection is disturbed, or when it is required to do something which it has never done before.*

We cannot remember having been in the embryonic stage, but we do not on that account deny that we ever were in such a stage at all. On a little reflection it will appear no more reasonable to maintain that, when we were in the embryonic stage, we did not remember our past existences, than to say that we never were embryos at all. We cannot remember what we did or did not recollect in that state; we cannot now remember having grown the eyes which we undoubtedly did grow, much less can we remember whether or not we then remembered having grown them before; but it is probable that our memory was then, in respect of our previous existences as embryos, as much more intense than it is now in respect of our childhood, as our power of acquiring a new language was greater when we were one or two years old, than when we were twenty. And why should this power of acquiring languages be greater at two years than at twenty, but that for many generations we have learnt to speak at about this age, and hence look to learn to do so again on reaching it, just as we looked to making eyes, when the time came at which we were accustomed to make them.

If we once had the memory of having been infants (which we had from day to day during infancy), and have lost it, we may well have had other and more intense memories which we have lost no less completely. Indeed, there is nothing more extraordinary in the supposition that the impregnate ovum has an intense sense of its continuity with, and therefore of its identity with, the two impregnate ova from which it has sprung, than in the fact that we have no sense of our continuity with ourselves as infants. If then, there is no *à priori* objection to this view, and if the impregnate ovum acts in such a manner as to carry the strongest conviction that it must have already on many occasions done what it is doing now, and that it has a vivid though unconscious recollection of what all, and more especially its nearer, ancestral ova did under similar circumstances, there would seem to be little doubt what conclusion we ought to come to.

A hen's egg, for example, as soon as the hen begins to sit, sets to work immediately to do as nearly as may be what the two eggs from which its father and mother were hatched did when hens began to sit upon them. The inference would seem almost irresistible,—that the second egg remembers the course pursued by the eggs from which it has sprung, and of whose present identity it is unquestionably a part-phase; it also seems irresistibly forced upon us to believe that the intensity of this memory is the secret of its easy action.

It has, I believe, been often remarked, that a hen is only an egg's way of making another egg. Every creature must be allowed to "run" its own development in its own way; the egg's way may seem a very roundabout manner of doing things; but it *is* its way, and it is one of which man, upon the whole, has no great reason to complain. Why the fowl should be considered more alive than the egg, and why it should be said that the hen lays the egg, and not that the egg lays the hen, these are questions which lie beyond the power of philosophic explanation, but are perhaps most answerable by considering the conceit of man, and his habit, persisted in during many ages, of ignoring all that does not remind him of himself, or hurt him, or profit him; also by considering the use of language, which, if it is to serve at all, can only do so by ignoring a vast number of facts which gradually drop out of mind from being out of sight. But, perhaps, after all, the real reason is, that the egg does not cackle when it has laid the hen, and that it works towards the hen with gradual and noiseless steps, which we can watch if we be so minded; whereas, we can less easily watch the steps which lead from the hen to the egg, but hear a noise, and see an egg where there was no egg. Therefore, we say, the development of the fowl from the egg bears no sort of resemblance to that of the egg from the fowl, whereas, in truth, a hen, or any other living creature, is only the primordial cell's way of going back upon itself.

But to return. We see an egg, A, which evidently knows its own meaning perfectly well, and we know that a twelvemonth ago there were two other such eggs, B and C, which have now disappeared, but from which we know A to have been so continuously developed as to be part of the present form of their identity. A's meaning is seen to be precisely the same as B and C's meaning; A's personal appearance is, to all intents and purposes, B and C's personal appearance; it would seem, then, unreasonable to deny that A is only B and C come back, with such modification as they may have incurred since their disappearance; and that, in spite of any such modification, they remember in A perfectly well what they did as B and C.

We have considered the question of personal identity so as to see whether, without abuse of terms, we can claim it as existing between any two generations of living agents (and if between two, then between any number up to infinity), and we found that we were not only at liberty to claim this, but that we are compelled irresistibly to do so, unless, that is to say, we would think very differently concerning personal identity than we do at present. We found it impossible to hold the ordinary common sense opinions concerning personal identity, without admitting that we are personally identical with all our forefathers, who have successfully assimilated outside matter to themselves, and by assimilation imbued it with all their own memories; we being nothing else than this outside matter so assimilated and imbued with such memories. This, at least, will, I believe, balance the account correctly.

A few remarks upon the assimilation of outside matter by living organisms may perhaps be hazarded here.

As long as any living organism can maintain itself in a position to which it has been accustomed, more or less nearly, both in its own life and in those of its forefathers, nothing can harm it. As long as the organism is familiar with the position, and remembers its antecedents, nothing can assimilate it.

It must be first dislodged from the position with which it is familiar, as being able to remember it, before mischief can happen to it. Nothing can assimilate living organism.

On the other hand, the moment living organism loses sight of its own position and antecedents, it is liable to immediate assimilation, and to be thus familiarised with the position and antecedents of some other creature. If any living organism be kept for but a very short time in a position wholly different from what it has been accustomed to in its own life, and in the lives of its forefathers, it commonly loses its memories completely, once and for ever; but it must immediately acquire new ones, for nothing can know nothing; everything must remember either its own antecedents, or some one else's. And as nothing can know nothing, so nothing can believe in nothing.

A grain of corn, for example, has never been accustomed to find itself in a hen's stomach—neither it nor its forefathers. For a grain so placed leaves no offspring, and hence cannot transmit its experience. The first minute or so after being eaten, it may think it has just been sown, and begin to prepare for sprouting, but in a few seconds, it discovers the environment to be unfamiliar; it therefore gets frightened, loses its head, is carried into the gizzard, and comminuted among the gizzard stones. The hen succeeded in putting it into a position with which it was unfamiliar; from this it was an easy stage to assimilating it entirely. Once assimilated, the grain ceases to remember any more as a grain, but becomes initiated into all that happens to, and has happened to, fowls for countless ages. Then it will attack all other grains whenever it sees them; there is no such persecutor of grain, as another grain when it has once fairly identified itself with a hen.

We may remark in passing, that if anything be once familiarised with anything, it is content. The only things we really care for in life are familiar things; let us have the means of doing what we have been accustomed to do, of dressing as we have been accustomed to dress, of eating as we have been accustomed to eat, and let us have no less liberty than we are accustomed to have, and last, but not least, let us not be disturbed in thinking as we have been accustomed to think, and the vast majority of mankind will be very fairly contented—all plants and animals will certainly be so. This would seem to suggest a possible doctrine of a future state; concerning which we may reflect that though, after we die, we cease to be familiar with ourselves, we shall nevertheless become immediately familiar with many other histories compared with which our present life must then seem intolerably uninteresting.

This is the reason why a very heavy and sudden shock to the nervous system does not pain, but kills outright at once; while one with which the system can, at any rate, try to familiarise itself is exceedingly painful. We cannot bear unfamiliarity. The part that is treated in a manner with which it is not familiar cries immediately to the brain— its central government—for help, and makes itself generally as troublesome as it can, till it is in some way comforted. Indeed, the law against cruelty to animals is but an example of the hatred we feel on seeing even dumb creatures put into positions with which they are not familiar. We hate this so much for ourselves, that we will not tolerate it for other creatures if we can possibly avoid it. So again, it is said, that when Andromeda and Perseus had travelled but a little way from the rock where Andromeda had so long been chained, she began upbraiding him with the loss of her dragon, who, on the whole, she said, had been very good to her. The only things we really hate are unfamiliar things, and though nature would not be nature if she did not cross our love of the familiar with a love also of the unfamiliar, yet there can be no doubt which of the two principles is master.

Let us return, however, to the grain of corn. If the grain had had presence of mind to avoid being carried into the gizzard stones, as many seeds do which are carried for hundreds of miles in birds' stomachs, and if it had persuaded itself that the novelty of the position was not greater than it could very well manage to put up with - if, in fact, it had not known when it was beaten—it might have stuck in the hen's stomach and begun to grow; in this case it would have assimilated a good part of the hen before many days were over; for hens are not familiar with grains that grow in their stomachs, and unless the one in question was as strongminded for a hen, as the grain that could avoid being assimilated would be for a grain, the hen would soon cease to take an interest in her antecedents. It is to be doubted, however, whether a grain has ever been grown which has had strength of mind enough to avoid being set off its balance on finding itself inside a hen's gizzard. For living organism is the creature of habit and routine, and the inside of a gizzard is not in the grain's programme.

Suppose, then, that the grain, instead of being carried into the gizzard, had stuck in the hen's throat and choked her. It would now find itself in a position very like what it had often been in before. That is to say, it would be in a damp, dark, quiet place, not too far from light, and with decaying matter around it. It would therefore know perfectly well what to do, and would begin to grow until disturbed, and again put into a position with which it might, very possibly, be unfamiliar.

The great question between vast masses of living organism is simply this: "Am I to put you into a position with which your forefathers have been unfamiliar, or are you to put me into one about which my own have been in like manner ignorant?" Man is only the dominant animal on the earth, because he can, as a general rule, settle this question in his own favour.

The only manner in which an organism, which has once forgotten its antecedents, can ever recover its memory, is by being assimilated by a creature of its own kind; one, moreover, which knows its business, or is not in such a false position as to be compelled to be aware of being so. It was, doubtless, owing to the recognition of this fact, that some Eastern nations, as we are told by Herodotus, were in the habit of eating their deceased parents—for matter which has once been assimilated by any identity or personality, becomes for all practical purposes part of the assimilating personality.

The bearing of the above will become obvious when we return, as we will now do, to the question of personal identity. The only difficulty would seem to lie in our unfamiliarity with the real meanings which we attach to words in daily use. Hence, while recognising continuity without sudden break as the underlying principle of identity, we forget that this involves personal identity between all the beings who are in one chain of descent, the numbers of such beings, whether in succession, or contemporaneous, going for nothing at all. Thus we take two eggs, one male and one female, and hatch them; after some months the pair of fowls so hatched, having succeeded in putting a vast quantity of grain and worms into false positions, become full-grown, breed, and produce a dozen new eggs.

Two live fowls and a dozen eggs are the present phase of the personality of the two original eggs. They are also part of the present phase of the personality of all the worms and grain which the fowls have assimilated from their leaving the eggshell; but the personalities of these last do not count; they have lost their grain and worm memories, and are instinct with the memorises of the whole ancestry of the creature which has assimilated them.

We cannot, perhaps, strictly say that the two fowls and the dozen new eggs actually *are* the two original eggs; these two eggs are no longer in existence, and we see the two birds themselves which were hatched from them. A bird cannot be called an egg without an abuse of terms. Nevertheless, it is doubtful how far we should not say this, for it is only with a mental reserve—and with no greater mental reserve—that we predicate absolute identity concerning any living being for two consecutive moments; and it is certainly as free from quibble to say to two fowls and a dozen eggs, "you are the two eggs I had on my kitchen shelf twelve months ago," as to say to a man, "you are the child whom I remember thirty years ago in your mother's arms." In either case we mean, "you have been continually putting other organisms into a false position, and then assimilating them, ever since I last saw you, while nothing has yet occurred to put *you* into such a false position as to have made you lose the memory of your antecedents."

It would seem perfectly fair, therefore, to say to any egg of the twelve, or to the two fowls and the whole twelve eggs together, "you were a couple of eggs twelve months ago; twelve months before that you were four eggs;" and so on, *ad infinitum*, the number neither of the ancestors nor of the descendants counting for anything, and continuity being the sole thing looked to. From daily observation we are familiar with the fact that identity does both unite with other identities, so that a single new identity is the result, and does also split itself up into several identities, so that the one becomes many. This is plain from the manner in which the male and female sexual elements unite to form a single ovum, which we observe to be instinct with the memories of both the individuals from which it has been derived; and there is the additional consideration, that each of the elements whose fusion goes to make up the impregnate ovum, is held by some to be itself composed of a fused mass of germs, which stand very much in the same relation to the spermatozoon and ovum, as the living cellular units of which we are composed do to ourselves—that is to say, are living independent organisms, which probably have no conception of the existence of the spermatozoon nor of the ovum, more than the spermatozoon or ovum have of theirs.

This, at least, is what I gather from Mr. Darwin's provisional theory of Pangenesis; and, again, from one of the concluding sentences in his "Effects of Cross and Self Fertilisation," where, asking the question why two sexes have been developed, he replies that the answer seems to lie "in the great good which is derived from the fusion of two somewhat differentiated individuals. With the exception," he continues, "or the lowest organisms this is possible only by means of the sexual elements—*these consisting of cells separated from the body*" (*i.e.*, separated from the bodies of each parent) " *containing the germs of every part*" (*i.e.*, consisting of the seeds or germs from which each individual cell of the coming organism will be developed—these seeds or germs having been shed by each individual cell of the parent forms), "*and capable of being fused completely together*" (*i.e.*, so at least I gather, capable of being fused completely, in the same way as the cells of our own bodies are fused, and thus, of forming a single living personality in the case of both the male and female element; which elements are themselves capable of a second fusion so as to form the impregnate ovum). This single impregnate ovum, then, is a single identity that has taken the place of and come up in the room of two distinct personalities, each of whose characteristics it, to a certain extent, partakes, and which consist, each one of them, of the fused germs of a vast mass of other personalities.

As regards the dispersion of one identity into many, this also is a matter of daily observation in the case of all female creatures that are with egg or young; the identity of the young with the female parent is in many respects so complete, as to need no enforcing, in spite of the entrance into the offspring of all the elements derived from the male parent, and of the gradual separation of the two identities, which becomes more and more complete, till in time it is hard to conceive that they can ever have been united.

Numbers, therefore, go for nothing; and, as far as identity or continued personality goes, it is as fair to say to the two fowls, above referred to, "you were four fowls twelve months ago," as it is to say to a dozen eggs, "you were two eggs twelve months ago." But here a difficulty meets us; for if we say, "you were two eggs twelve months ago," it follows that we mean, "you are now those two eggs;" just as when we say to a person, "you were such and such a boy twenty years ago," we mean, "you are now that boy, or all that represents him;" it would seem, then, that in like manner we should say to the two fowls, "you *are* the four fowls who between them laid the two eggs from which you sprung." But it may be that all these four fowls are still to be seen running about; we should be therefore saying, "you two fowls are really not yourselves only, but you are also the other four fowls into the bargain;" and this might be philosophically true, and might, perhaps, be considered so, but for the convenience of the law courts.

The difficulty would seem to arise from the fact that the eggs must disappear before fowls can be hatched from them, whereas, the hens so hatched may outlive the development of other hens, from the eggs which they in due course have laid. The original eggs being out of sight are out of mind, and it is without an effort that we acquiesce in the assertion,—that the dozen new eggs actually are the two original ones. But the original four fowls being still in sight, cannot be ignored, we only, therefore, see the new ones as growths from the original ones.

The strict rendering of the facts should be, "you are part of the present phase of the identity of such and such a past identity," *i.e* ., either of the two eggs or the four fowls, as the case may be; this will put the eggs and the fowls, as it were, into the same box, and will meet both the philosophical and legal requirement of the case, only it is a little long.

So far then, as regards actual identity of personality; which, we find, will allow us to say, that eggs are part of the present phase of a certain past identity, whether of other eggs, or of fowls, or chickens, and in like, manner that chickens are part of the present phase of certain other chickens, or eggs, or fowls; in fact, that anything is part of the present phase of any past identity in the line of its ancestry. But as regards the actual memory of such identity (unconscious memory, but still clearly memory), we observe that the egg, as long as it is an egg, appears to have a very distinct recollection of having been an egg before, and the fowl of having been a fowl before, but that neither egg nor fowl appear to have any recollection of any other stage of their past existences, than the one corresponding to that in which they are themselves at the moment existing.

So we, at six or seven years old, have no recollection of ever having been infants, much less of having been embryos; but the manner in which we shed our teeth and make new ones, and the way in which we grow generally, making ourselves for the most part exceedingly like what we made ourselves, in the person of some one of our nearer ancestors, and not unfrequently repeating the very blunders which we made upon that occasion when we come to a corresponding age, proves most incontestably that we remember our past existences, though too utterly to be capable of introspection in the matter. So, when we grow wisdom teeth, at the age it may be of one or two and twenty, it is plain we remember our past existences at that age, however completely we may have forgotten the earlier stages of our present existence. It may be said that it is the jaw which remembers, and not we, but it seems hard to deny the jaw a right of citizenship in our personality; and in the case of a growing boy, every part of him seems to remember equally well, and if every part of him combined does not make *him* , there would seem but little use in continuing the argument further.

In like manner, a caterpillar appears not to remember having been an egg, either in its present or any past existence. It has no concern with eggs as soon as it is hatched, but it clearly remembers not only having been a caterpillar before, but also having turned itself into a chrysalis before; for when the time comes for it to do this, it is at no loss, as it would certainly be if the position was unfamiliar, but it immediately begins doing what it did when last it was in a like case, repeating the process as nearly as the environment will allow, taking every step in the same order as last time, and doing its work with that ease and perfection which we observe to belong to the force of habit, and to be utterly incompatible with any other supposition than that of long long practice.

Once having become a chrysalis, its memory of its caterpillarhood appears to leave it for good and all, not to return until it again assumes the shape of a caterpillar by process of descent. Its memory now overleaps all past modifications, and reverts to the time when it was last what it is now, and though it is probable that both caterpillar and chrysalis, on any given day of their existence in either of these forms, have some sort of dim power of recollecting what happened to them yesterday, or the day before; yet it is plain their main memory goes back to the corresponding day of their last existence in their present form, the chrysalis remembering what happened to it on such a day far more practically, though less consciously, than what happened to it yesterday; and naturally, for yesterday is but once, and its past existences have been legion. Hence, it prepares its wings in due time, doing each day what it did on the corresponding day of its last chrysalishood and at length becoming a moth; whereon its circumstances are so changed that it loses all sense of its identity as a chrysalis (as completely as we, for precisely the same reason, lose all sense of our identity with ourselves as infants), and remembers nothing but its past existences as a moth.

We observe this to hold throughout the animal and vegetable kingdoms. In any one phase of the existence of the lower animals, we observe that they remember the corresponding stage, and a little on either side of it, of all their past existences for a very great length of time. In their present existence they remember a little behind the present moment (remembering more and more the higher they advance in the scale of life), and being able to foresee about as much as they could foresee in their past existences, sometimes more and sometimes less. As with memory, so with prescience. The higher they advance in the scale of life the more prescient they are. It must, of course, be remembered, and will later on be more fully dwelt upon, that no offspring can remember anything which happens to its parents after it and its parents have parted company; and this is why there is, perhaps, more irregularity as regards our wisdom-teeth than about anything else that we grow; inasmuch as it must not uncommonly have happened in a long series of generations, that the offspring has been born before the parents have grown their wisdom-teeth, and thus there will be faults in the memory.

Is there, then, anything in memory, as we observe it in ourselves and others, under circumstances in which we shall agree in calling it memory pure and simple without ambiguity of terms—is there anything in memory which bars us from supposing it capable of overleaping a long time of abeyance, and thus of enabling each impregnate ovum, or each grain, to remember what it did when last in a like condition, and to go on remembering the corresponding period of its prior developments throughout the whole period of its present growth, though such memory has entirely failed as regards the interim between any two corresponding periods, and is not consciously recognised by the individual as being exercised at all?

CHAPTER IX—ON THE ABEYANCE OF MEMORY

Let us assume, for the moment, that the action of each impregnate germ is due to memory, which, as it were, pulsates anew in each succeeding generation, so that immediately on impregnation, the germ's memory reverts to the last occasion on which it was in a like condition, and recognising the position, is at no loss what to do. It is plain that in all cases where there are two parents, that is to say, in the greater number of cases, whether in the vegetable or animal kingdoms, there must be two such last occasions, each of which will have an equal claim upon the attention of the new germ. Its memory would therefore revert to both, and though it would probably adhere more closely to the course which it took either as its father or its mother, and thus come out eventually male or female, yet it would be not a little influenced by the less potent memory.

And not only this, but each of the germs to which the memory of the new germ reverts, is itself imbued with the memories of its own parent germs, and these again with the memories of preceding generations, and so on *ad infinitum*; so that, *ex hypothesi*, the germ must become instinct with all these memories, epitomised as after long time, and unperceived though they may well be, not to say obliterated in part or entirely so far as many features are concerned, by more recent impressions. In this case, we must conceive of the impregnate germ as of a creature which has to repeat a performance already repeated before on countless different occasions, but with no more variation on the more recent ones than is inevitable in the repetition of any performance by an intelligent being.

Now if we take the most parallel case to this which we can find, and consider what we should ourselves do under such circumstances, that is to say, if we consider what course is actually taken by beings who are influenced by what we all call memory, when they repeat an already often-repeated performance, and if we find a very strong analogy between the course so taken by ourselves, and that which from whatever cause we observe to be taken by a living germ, we shall surely be much inclined to think that there must be a similarity in the causes of action in each case; and hence, to conclude, that the action of the germ is due to memory.

It will, therefore, be necessary to consider the general tendency of our minds in regard to impressions made upon us, and the memory of such impressions.

Deep impressions upon the memory are made in two ways, differing rather in degree than kind, but with two somewhat widely different results. They are made:-

I. By unfamiliar objects, or combinations, which come at comparatively long intervals, and produce their effect, as it were, by one hard blow. The effect of these will vary with the unfamiliarity of the impressions themselves, and the manner in which they seem likely to lead to a further development of the unfamiliar, *i.e.*, with the question, whether they seem likely to compel us to change our habits, either for better or worse.

Thus, if an object or incident be very unfamiliar, as, we will say, a whale or an iceberg to one travelling to America for the first time, it will make a deep impression, though but little affecting our interests; but if we struck against the iceberg and were shipwrecked, or nearly so, it would produce a much deeper impression, we should think much more about icebergs, and remember much more about them, than if we had merely seen one. So, also, if we were able to catch the whale and sell its oil, we should have a deep impression made upon us. In either case we see that the amount of unfamiliarity, either present or prospective, is the main determinant of the depth of the impression.

As with consciousness and volition, so with sudden unfamiliarity. It impresses us more and more deeply the more unfamiliar it is, until it reaches such a point of impressiveness as to make no further impression at all; on which we then and there die. For death only kills through unfamiliarity—that is to say, because the new position, whatever it is, is so wide a cross as compared with the old one, that we cannot fuse the two so as to understand the combination; hence we lose all recognition of, and faith in, ourselves and our surroundings.

But however much we imagine we remember concerning the details of any remarkable impression which has been made us by a single blow, we do not remember as much or nearly as much as we think we do. The subordinate details soon drop out of mind. Those who think they remember even such a momentous matter as the battle of Waterloo recall now probably but half-a-dozen episodes, a gleam here, and a gleam there, so that what they call remembering the battle of Waterloo, is, in fact, little more than a kind of dreaming—so soon vanishes the memory of any unrepeated occurrence.

As for smaller impressions, there is very little of what happens to us in each week that will be in our memories a week hence; a man of eighty remembers few of the unrepeated incidents of his life beyond those of the last fortnight, a little here, and a little there, forming a matter of perhaps six weeks or two months in all, if everything that he can call to mind were acted over again with no greater fulness than he can remember it. As for incidents that have been often repeated, his mind strikes a balance of its past reminiscences, remembering the two or three last performances, and a general method of procedure, but nothing more.

If, then, the recollection of all that is not very novel, or very often repeated, so soon fades from our own minds, during what we consider as our single lifetime, what wonder that the details of our daily experience should find no place in that brief epitome of them which is all we can give in so small a volume as offspring?

If we cannot ourselves remember the hundred-thousandth part of what happened to us during our own childhood, how can we expect our offspring to remember more than what, through frequent repetition, they can now remember as a residuum, or general impression. On the other hand, whatever we remember in consequence of but a single impression, we remember consciously. We can at will recall details, and are perfectly well aware, when we do so, that we are recollecting. A man who has never seen death looks for the first time upon the dead face of some near relative or friend. He gazes for a few short minutes, but the impression thus made does not soon pass out of his mind. He remembers the room, the hour of the day or night, and if by day, what sort of a day. He remembers in what part of the room, and how disposed the body of the deceased was lying. Twenty years afterwards he can, at will, recall all these matters to his mind, and picture to himself the scene as he originally witnessed it.

The reason is plain; the impression was very unfamiliar, and affected the beholder, both as regards the loss of one who was dear to him, and as reminding him with more than common force that he will one day die himself. Moreover the impression was a simple one, not involving much subordinate detail; we have in this case, therefore, an example of the most lasting kind of impression that can be made by a single unrepeated event. But if we examine ourselves closely, we shall find that after a lapse of years we do not remember as much as we think we do, even in such a case as this; and that beyond the incidents above mentioned, and the expression upon the face of the dead person, we remember little of what we can so consciously and vividly recall.

II. Deep impressions are also made by the repetition, more or less often, of a feeble impression which, if unrepeated, would have soon passed out of our minds. We observe, therefore, that we remember best what we have done least often—any unfamiliar deviation, that is to say, from our ordinary method of procedure—and what we have done most often, with which, therefore, we are most familiar; our memory being mainly affected by the force of novelty and the force of routine—the most unfamiliar, and the most familiar, incidents or objects.

But we remember impressions which have been made upon us by force of routine, in a very different way to that in which we remember a single deep impression. As regards this second class, which comprises far the most numerous and important of the impressions with which our memory is stored, it is often only by the fact of our performance itself that we are able to recognise or show to others that we remember at all. We often do not remember how, or when, or where we acquired our knowledge. All we remember is, that we did learn, and that at one time and another we have done this or that very often.

As regards this second class of impressions we may observe:-

1. That as a general rule we remember only the individual features of the last few repetitions of the act—if, indeed, we remember this much. The influence of preceding ones is to be found only in the general average of the procedure, which is modified by them, but unconsciously to ourselves. Take, for example, some celebrated singer, or pianoforte player, who has sung the same air, or performed the same sonata several hundreds or, it may be, thousands of times: of the details of individual performances, he can probably call to mind none but those of the last few days, yet there can be no question that his present performance is affected by, and modified by, all his previous ones; the care he has bestowed on these being the secret of his present proficiency.

In each performance (the performer being supposed in the same state of mental and bodily health), the tendency will be to repeat the immediately preceding performances more nearly than remoter ones. It is the common tendency of living beings to go on doing what they have been doing most recently. The last habit is the strongest. Hence, if he took great pains last time, he will play better now, and will take a like degree of pains, and play better still next time, and so go on improving while life and vigour last. If, on the other hand, he took less pains last time, he will play worse now, and be inclined to take little pains next time, and so gradually deteriorate. This, at least, is the common everyday experience of mankind.

So with painters, actors, and professional men of every description; after a little while the memory of many past performances strikes a sort of fused balance in the mind, which results in a general method of procedure with but little conscious memory of even the latest performances, and with none whatever of by far the greater number of the remoter ones.

Still, it is noteworthy, that the memory of some even of these will occasionally assert itself, so far as we can see, arbitrarily, the reason why this or that occasion should still haunt us, when others like them are forgotten, depending on some cause too subtle for our powers of observation.

Even with such a simple matter as our daily dressing and undressing, we may remember some few details of our yesterday's toilet, but we retain nothing but a general and fused recollection of the many thousand earlier occasions on which we have dressed, or gone to bed. Men invariably put the same leg first into their trousers—this is the survival of memory in a residuum; but they cannot, till they actually put on a pair of trousers, remember which leg they *do* put in first; this is the rapid fading away of any small individual impression.

The seasons may serve as another illustration; we have a general recollection of the kind of weather which is seasonable for any month in a year; what flowers are due about what time, and whether the spring is on the whole backward or early; but we cannot remember the weather on any particular day a year ago, unless some unusual incident has impressed it upon our memory. We can remember, as a general rule, what kind of season it was, upon the whole, a year ago, or perhaps, even two years; but more than this, we rarely remember, except in such cases as the winter of 1854-1855, or the summer of 1868; the rest is all merged.

We observe, then, that as regards small and often repeated impressions, our tendency is to remember best, and in most detail, what we have been doing most recently, and what in general has occurred most recently, but that the earlier impressions though forgotten individually, are nevertheless, not wholly lost.

2. When we have done anything very often, and have got into the habit of doing it, we generally take the various steps in the same order; in many cases this seems to be a *sine quâ non* for our repetition of the action at all. Thus, there is probably no living man who could repeat the words of "God save the Queen" backwards, without much hesitation and many mistakes; so the musician and the singer must perform their pieces in the order of the notes as written, or at any rate as they ordinarily perform them; they cannot transpose bars or read them backwards, without being put out, nor would the audience recognise the impressions they have been accustomed to, unless these impressions are made in the accustomed order.

3. If, when we have once got well into the habit of doing anything in a certain way, some one shows us some other way of doing it, or some way which would in part modify our procedure, or if in our endeavours to improve, we have hit upon some new idea which seems likely to help us, and thus we vary our course, on the next occasion we remember this idea by reason of its novelty, but if we try to repeat it, we often find the residuum of our old memories pulling us so strongly into our old groove, that we have the greatest difficulty in repeating our performance in the new manner; there is a clashing of memories, a conflict, which if the idea is very new, and involves, so to speak, too sudden a cross—too wide a departure from our ordinary course—will sometimes render the performance monstrous, or baffle us altogether, the new memory failing to fuse harmoniously with the old. If the idea is not too widely different from our older ones, we can cross them with it, but with more or less difficulty, as a general rule in proportion to the amount of variation. The whole process of understanding a thing consists in this, and, so far as I can see at present, in this only.

Sometimes we repeat the new performance for a few times, in a way which shows that the fusion of memories is still in force; and then insensibly revert to the old, in which case the memory of the new soon fades away, leaving a residuum too feeble to contend against that of our many earlier memories of the same kind. If, however, the new way is obviously to our advantage, we make an effort to retain it, and gradually getting into the habit of using it, come to remember it by force of routine, as we originally remembered it by force of novelty. Even as regards our own discoveries, we do not always succeed in remembering our most improved and most striking performances, so as to be able to repeat them at will immediately: in any such performance we may have gone some way beyond our ordinary powers, owing to some unconscious action of the mind. The supreme effort has exhausted us, and we must rest on our oars a little, before we make further progress; or we may even fall back a little, before we make another leap in advance.

In this respect, almost every conceivable degree of variation is observable, according to differences of character and circumstances. Sometimes the new impression has to be made upon us many times from without, before the earlier strain of action is eliminated; in this case, there will long remain a tendency to revert to the earlier habit. Sometimes, after the impression has been once made, we repeat our old way two or three times, and then revert to the new, which gradually ousts the old; sometimes, on the other hand, a single impression, though involving considerable departure from our routine, makes its mark so deeply that we adopt the new at once, though not without difficulty, and repeat it in our next performance, and henceforward in all others; but those who vary their performance thus readily will show a tendency to vary subsequent performances according as they receive fresh ideas from others, or reason them out independently. They are men of genius.

This holds good concerning all actions which we do habitually, whether they involve laborious acquirement or not. Thus, if we have varied our usual dinner in some way that leaves a favourable impression upon our minds, so that our dinner may, in the language of the horticulturist, be said to have "sported," our tendency will be to revert to this particular dinner either next day, or as soon as circumstances will allow, but it is possible that several hundred dinners may elapse before we can do so successfully, or before our memory reverts to this particular dinner.

4. As regards our habitual actions, however unconsciously we remember them, we, nevertheless, remember them with far greater intensity than many individual impressions or actions, it may be of much greater moment, that have happened to us more recently. Thus, many a man who has familiarised himself, for example, with the odes of Horace, so as to have had them at his fingers' ends as the result of many repetitions, will be able years hence to repeat a given ode, though unable to remember any circumstance in connection with his having learnt it, and no less unable to

remember when he repeated it last. A host of individual circumstances, many of them not unimportant, will have dropped out of his mind, along with a mass of literature read but once or twice, and not impressed upon the memory by several repetitions; but he returns to the well-known ode with so little effort, that he would not know that he was remembering unless his reason told him so. The ode seems more like something born with him.

We observe, also, that people who have become imbecile, or whose memory is much impaired, yet frequently retain their power of recalling impression which have been long ago repeatedly made upon them.

In such cases, people are sometimes seen to forget what happened last week, yesterday, or an hour ago, without even the smallest power of recovering their recollection; but the oft repeated earlier impression remains, though there may be no memory whatever of how it came to be impressed so deeply. The phenomena of memory, therefore, are exactly like those of consciousness and volition, in so far as that the consciousness of recollection vanishes, when the power of recollection has become intense. When we are aware that we are recollecting, and are trying, perhaps hard, to recollect, it is a sign that we do not recollect utterly. When we remember utterly and intensely, there is no conscious effort of recollection; our recollection can only be recognised by ourselves and others, through our performance itself, which testifies to the existence of a memory, that we could not otherwise follow or detect.

5. When circumstances have led us to change our habits of life—as when the university has succeeded school, or professional life the university —we get into many fresh ways, and leave many old ones. But on revisiting the old scene, unless the lapse of time has been inordinately great, we experience a desire to revert to old habits. We say that old associations crowd upon us. Let a Trinity man, after thirty years absence from Cambridge, pace for five minutes in the cloister of Neville's Court, and listen to the echo of his footfall, as it licks up against the end of the cloister, or let an old Johnian stand wherever he likes in the third Court of St. John's, in either case he will find the thirty years drop out of his life, as if they were half-an-hour; his life will have rolled back upon itself, to the date when he was an undergraduate, and his instinct will be to do almost mechanically, whatever it would have come most natural to him to do, when he was last there at the same season of the year, and the same hour of the day; and it is

plain this is due to similarity of environment, for if the place he revisits be much changed, there will be little or no association.

So those who are accustomed at intervals to cross the Atlantic, get into certain habits on board ship, different to their usual ones. It may be that at home they never play whist; on board ship they do nothing else all the evening. At home they never touch spirits; on the voyage they regularly take a glass of something before they go to bed. They do not smoke at home; here they are smoking all day. Once the voyage is at an end, they return without an effort to their usual habits, and do not feel any wish for cards, spirits, or tobacco. They do not remember yesterday, when they did want all these things; at least, not with such force as to be influenced by it in their desires and actions; their true memory—the memory which makes them want, and do, reverts to the last occasion on which they were in circumstances like their present; they therefore want now what they wanted then, and nothing more; but when the time comes for them to go on shipboard again, no sooner do they smell the smell of the ship, than their real memory reverts to the times when they were last at sea, and striking a balance of their recollections, they smoke, play cards, and drink whisky and water.

We observe it then as a matter of the commonest daily occurrence within our own experience, that memory does fade completely away, and recur with the recurrence of surroundings like those which made any particular impression in the first instance. We observe that there is hardly any limit to the completeness and the length of time during which our memory may remain in abeyance. A smell may remind an old man of eighty of some incident of his childhood, forgotten for nearly as many years as he has lived. In other words, we observe that when an impression has been repeatedly made in a certain sequence on any living organism—that impression not having been prejudicial to the creature itself—the organism will have a tendency, on reassuming the shape and conditions in which it was when the impression was last made, to remember the impression, and therefore to do again now what it did then; all intermediate memories dropping clean out of mind, so far as they have any effect upon action.

6. Finally, we should note the suddenness and apparent caprice with which memory will assert itself at odd times; we have been saying or doing this or that, when suddenly a memory of something which happened to us, perhaps in infancy, comes into our head; nor can we in the least connect this

recollection with the subject of which we have just been thinking, though doubtless there has been a connection, too rapid and subtle for our apprehension.

The foregoing phenomena of memory, so far as we can judge, would appear to be present themselves throughout the animal and vegetable kingdoms. This will be readily admitted as regards animals; as regards plants it may be inferred from the fact that they generally go on doing what they have been doing most lately, though accustomed to make certain changes at certain points in their existence. When the time comes for these changes, they appear to know it, and either bud forth into leaf or shed their leaves, as the case may be. If we keep a bulb in a paper bag it seems to remember having been a bulb before, until the time comes for it to put forth roots and grow. Then, if we supply it with earth and moisture, it seems to know where it is, and to go on doing now whatever it did when it was last planted; but if we keep it in the bag too long, it knows that it ought, according to its last experience, to be treated differently, and shows plain symptoms of uneasiness; it is distracted by the bag, which makes it remember its bulbhood, and also by the want of earth and water, without which associations its memory of its previous growth cannot be duly kindled. Its roots, therefore, which are most accustomed to earth and water, do not grow; but its leaves, which do not require contact with these things to jog their memory, make a more decided effort at development— a fact which would seem to go strongly in favour of the functional independence of the parts of all but the very simplest living organisms, if, indeed, more evidence were wanted in support of this.

CHAPTER X—WHAT WE SHOULD EXPECT TO FIND IF DIFFERENTIATIONS OF STRUCTURE AND INSTINCT ARE MAINLY DUE TO MEMORY

To repeat briefly;—we remember best our last few performances of any given kind, and our present performance is most likely to resemble one or other of these; we only remember our earlier performances by way of residuum; nevertheless, at times, some older feature is liable to reappear.

We take our steps in the same order on each successive occasion, and are for the most part incapable of changing that order.

The introduction of slightly new elements into our manner is attended with benefit; the new can be fused with the old, and the monotony of our action is relieved. But if the new element is too foreign, we cannot fuse the old and new—nature seeming equally to hate too wide a deviation from our ordinary practice, and no deviation at all. Or, in plain English—if any one gives us a new idea which is not too far ahead of us, such an idea is often of great service to us, and may give new life to our work—in fact, we soon go back, unless we more or less frequently come into contact with new ideas, and are capable of understanding and making use of them; if; on the other hand, they are too new, and too little led up to, so that we find them too strange and hard to be able to understand them and adopt them, then they put us out, with every degree of completeness—from simply causing us to fail in this or that particular part, to rendering us incapable of even trying to do our work at all, from pure despair of succeeding.

It requires many repetitions to fix an impression firmly; but when it is fixed, we cease to have much recollection of the manner in which it came to be so, or of any single and particular recurrence.

Our memory is mainly called into action by force of association and similarity in the surroundings. We want to go on doing what we did when we were last as we are now, and we forget what we did in the meantime.

These rules, however, are liable to many exceptions; as for example, that a single and apparently not very extraordinary occurrence may sometimes produce a lasting impression, and be liable to return with sudden force at some distant time, and then to go on returning to us at intervals. Some incidents, in fact, we know not how nor why, dwell with us much longer than others which were apparently quite as noteworthy or perhaps more so.

Now I submit that if the above observations are just, and if, also, the offspring, after having become a new and separate personality, yet retains so much of the old identity of which it was once indisputably part, that it remembers what it did when it was part of that identity as soon as it finds itself in circumstances which are calculated to refresh its memory owing to their similarity to certain antecedent ones, then we should expect to find:-

I. That offspring should, as a general rule, resemble its own most immediate progenitors; that is to say, that it should remember best what it has been doing most recently. The memory being a fusion of its recollections of what it did, both when it was its father and also when it was its mother, the offspring should have a very common tendency to resemble both parents, the one in some respects, and the other in others; but it might also hardly less commonly show a more marked recollection of the one history than of the other, thus more distinctly resembling one parent than the other. And this is what we observe to be the case. Not only so far as that the offspring is almost invariably either male or female, and generally resembles rather the one parent than the other, but also that in spite of such preponderance of one set of recollections, the sexual characters and instincts of the *opposite* sex appear, whether in male or female, though undeveloped and incapable of development except by abnormal treatment, such as has occasionally caused milk to be developed in the mammary glands of males; or by mutilation, or failure of sexual instinct through age, upon which, male characteristics frequently appear in the females of any species.

Brothers and sisters, each giving their own version of the same story, though in different words, should resemble each other more closely than more distant relations. This too we see.

But it should frequently happen that offspring should resemble its penultimate rather than its latest phase, and should thus be more like a grand-parent than a parent; for we observe that we very often repeat a performance in a manner resembling that of some earlier, but still recent, repetition; rather than on the precise lines of our very last performance. First-cousins may in this case resemble each other more closely than brothers and sisters.

More especially, we should not expect very successful men to be fathers of particularly gifted children; for the best men are, as it were, the happy thoughts and successes of the race—nature's "flukes," so to speak, in her onward progress. No creature can repeat at will, and immediately, its highest flight. It needs repose. The generations are the essays of any given race towards the highest ideal which it is as yet able to see ahead of itself, and this, in the nature of things, cannot be very far; so that we should expect to see success followed by more or less failure, and failure by success—a very successful creature being a *great* "fluke." And this is what we find.

In its earlier stages the embryo should be simply conscious of a general method of procedure on the part of its forefathers, and should, by reason of long practice, compress tedious and complicated histories into a very narrow compass, remembering no single performance in particular. For we observe this in nature, both as regards the sleight-of-hand which practice gives to those who are thoroughly familiar with their business, and also as regards the fusion of remoter memories into a general residuum.

II. We should expect to find that the offspring, whether in its embryonic condition, or in any stage of development till it has reached maturity, should adopt nearly the same order in going through all its various stages. There should be such slight variations as are inseparable from the repetition of any performance by a living being (as contrasted with a machine), but no more. And this is what actually happens. A man may cut his wisdom-teeth a little later than he gets his beard and whiskers, or a little earlier; but on the whole, he adheres to his usual order, and is completely set off his balance, and upset in his performance, if that order be interfered with suddenly. It is, however, likely that gradual modifications of order have been made and then adhered to.

After any animal has reached the period at which it ordinarily begins to continue its race, we should expect that it should show little further power of development, or, at any rate, that few great changes of structure or fresh features should appear; for we cannot suppose offspring to remember anything that happens to the parent subsequently to the parent's ceasing to contain the offspring within itself; from the average age, therefore, of reproduction, offspring would cease to have any further experience on which to fall back, and would thus continue to make the best use of what it already knew, till memory failing either in one part or another, the organism would begin to decay.

To this cause must be referred the phenomena of old age, which interesting subject I am unable to pursue within the limits of this volume.

Those creatures who are longest in reaching maturity might be expected also to be the longest lived; I am not certain, however, how far what is called alternate generation militates against this view, but I do not think it does so seriously.

Lateness of marriage, provided the constitution of the individuals marrying is in no respect impaired, should also tend to longevity.

I believe that all the above will be found sufficiently well supported by facts. If so, when we feel that we are getting old we should try and give our cells such treatment as they will find it most easy to understand, through their experience of their own individual life, which, however, can only guide them inferentially, and to a very small extent; and throughout life we should remember the important bearing which memory has upon health, and both occasionally cross the memories of our component cells with slightly new experiences, and be careful not to put them either suddenly or for long together into conditions which they will not be able to understand. Nothing is so likely to make our cells forget themselves, as neglect of one or other of these considerations. They will either fail to recognise themselves completely, in which case we shall die; or they will go on strike, more or less seriously as the case may be, or perhaps, rather, they will try and remember their usual course, and fail; they will therefore try some other, and will probably make a mess of it, as people generally do when they try to do things which they do not understand, unless indeed they have very exceptional capacity.

It also follows that when we are ill, our cells being in such or such a state of mind, and inclined to hold a corresponding opinion with more or less unreasoning violence, should not be puzzled more than they are puzzled already, by being contradicted too suddenly; for they will not be in a frame of mind which can understand the position of an open opponent: they should therefore either be let alone, if possible, without notice other than dignified silence, till their spleen is over, and till they have remembered themselves; or they should be reasoned with as by one who agrees with them, and who is anxious to see things as far as possible from their own point of view. And this is how experience teaches that we must deal with monomaniacs, whom we simply infuriate by contradiction, but whose delusion we can sometimes persuade to hang itself if we but give it sufficient rope. All which has its bearing upon politics, too, at much sacrifice, it may be, of political principles, but a politician who cannot see principles where principle-mongers fail to see them, is a dangerous person.

I may say, in passing, that the reason why a small wound heals, and leaves no scar, while a larger one leaves a mark which is more or less permanent, may be looked for in the fact that when the wound is only small, the damaged cells are snubbed, so to speak, by the vast majority of the unhurt cells in their own neighbourhood. When the wound is more serious they can stick to it, and bear each other out that they were hurt.

III. We should expect to find a predominance of sexual over asexual generation, in the arrangements of nature for continuing her various species, inasmuch as two heads are better than one, and a *locus pnitentiæ* is thus given to the embryo—an opportunity of correcting the experience of one parent by that of the other. And this is what the more intelligent embryos may be supposed to do; for there would seem little reason to doubt that there are clever embryos and stupid embryos, with better or worse memories, as the case may be, of how they dealt with their protoplasm before, and better or worse able to see how they can do better now; and that embryos differ as widely in intellectual and moral capacity, and in a general sense of the fitness of things, and of what will look well into the bargain, as those larger embryos—to wit, children—do. Indeed it would seem probable that all our mental powers must go through a quasi-embryological condition, much as the power of keeping, and wisely spending, money must do so, and that all the qualities of human thought and character are to be found in the embryo.

Those who have observed at what an early age differences of intellect and temper show themselves in the young, for example, of cats and dogs, will find it difficult to doubt that from the very moment of impregnation, and onward, there has been a corresponding difference in the embryo—and that of six unborn puppies, one, we will say, has been throughout the whole process of development more sensible and better looking—a nicer embryo, in fact—than the others.

IV. We should expect to find that all species, whether of plants or animals, are occasionally benefited by a cross; but we should also expect that a cross should have a tendency to introduce a disturbing element, if it be too wide, inasmuch as the offspring would be pulled hither and thither by two conflicting memories or advices, much as though a number of people speaking at once were without previous warning to advise an unhappy performer to vary his ordinary performance - one set of people telling him he has always hitherto done thus, and the other saying no less loudly that he did it thus;—and he were suddenly to become convinced that they each spoke the truth. In such a case he will either completely break down, if the advice be too conflicting, or if it be less conflicting, he may yet be so exhausted by the one supreme effort of fusing these experiences that he will never be able to perform again; or if the conflict of experience be not great enough to produce such a permanent effect as this, it will yet, if it be at all serious, probably damage his performances on their next several occasions, through his inability to fuse the experiences into a harmonious whole, or, in other words, to understand the ideas which are prescribed to him; for to fuse is only to understand.

And this is absolutely what we find in fact. Mr. Darwin writes concerning hybrids and first crosses:- "The male element may reach the female element, but be incapable of causing an embryo to be developed, as seems to have been the case with some of Thuret's experiments on Fuci. No explanation can be given of these facts any more than why certain trees cannot be grafted on others."

I submit that what I have written above supplies a very fair *primâ facie* explanation.

Mr. Darwin continues:-

"Lastly, an embryo may be developed, and then perish at an early period. This latter alternative has not been sufficiently attended to; but I believe, from observations communicated to me by Mr. Hewitt, who has had great experience in hybridising pheasants and fowls, that the early death of the embryo is a very frequent cause of sterility in first crosses. Mr. Salter has recently given the results of an examination of about five hundred eggs produced from various crosses between three species of Gallus and their hybrids; the majority of these eggs had been fertilised; and in the majority of the fertilised eggs, the embryos had either been partially developed, and had then perished, or had become nearly mature, but the young chickens had been unable to break through the shell. Of the chickens which were born more than four-fifths died within the first few days, or at latest weeks, 'without any obvious cause, apparently from mere inability to live,' so that from the five hundred eggs only twelve chickens were reared" ("Origin of Species," 249, ed. 1876).

No wonder the poor creatures died, distracted as they were by the internal tumult of conflicting memories. But they must have suffered greatly; and the Society for the Prevention of Cruelty to Animals may perhaps think it worth while to keep an eye even on the embryos of hybrids and first crosses. Five hundred creatures puzzled to death is not a pleasant subject for contemplation. Ten or a dozen should, I think, be sufficient for the future.

As regards plants, we read:-

"Hybridised embryos probably often perish in like manner . . . of which fact Max Wichura has given some striking cases with hybrid willows . . . It may be here worth noticing, that in some cases of parthenogenesis, the embryos within the eggs of silk moths, which have not been fertilised, pass through their early stages of development, and then perish like the embryos produced by a cross between distinct species" *(Ibid)*.

This last fact would at first sight seem to make against me, but we must consider that the presence of a double memory, provided it be not too conflicting, would be a part of the experience of the silk moth's egg, which might be then as fatally puzzled by the monotony of a single memory as it would be by two memories which were not sufficiently like each other. So that failure here must be referred to the utter absence of that little internal stimulant of slightly conflicting memory which the creature has always hitherto experienced, and without which it fails to recognise itself. In either case, then, whether with hybrids or in cases of parthenogenesis, the early death of the embryo is due to inability to recollect, owing to a fault in the chain of associated ideas. All the facts here given are an excellent illustration of the principle, elsewhere insisted upon by Mr. Darwin, that *any* great and sudden change of surroundings has a tendency to induce sterility; on which head he writes ("Plants and Animals under Domestication," vol. ii. p. 143, ed. 1875):-

"It would appear that any change in the habits of life, whatever their habits may be, if great enough, tends to affect in an inexplicable manner the powers of reproduction."

And again on the next page:-

"Finally, we must conclude, limited though the conclusion is, that changed conditions of life have an especial power of acting injuriously on the reproductive system. The whole case is quite peculiar, for these organs, though not diseased, are thus rendered incapable of performing their proper functions, or perform them imperfectly."

One is inclined to doubt whether the blame may not rest with the inability on the part of the creature reproduced to recognise the new surroundings, and hence with its failing to know itself. And this seems to be in some measure supported—but not in such a manner as I can hold to be quite satisfactory—by the continuation of the passage in the "Origin of Species," from which I have just been quoting—for Mr. Darwin goes on to say:-

"Hybrids, however, are differently circumstanced before and after birth. When born, and living in a country where their parents live, they are generally placed under suitable conditions of life. But a hybrid partakes of only half of the nature and condition of its mother; it may therefore before birth, as long as it is nourished within its mother's womb, or within the egg or seed produced by its mother, be exposed to conditions in some degree unsuitable, and consequently be liable to perish at an early period . . . " After which, however, the conclusion arrived at is, that, "after all, the cause more probably lies in some imperfection in the original act of impregnation, causing the embryo to be imperfectly developed rather than in the conditions to which it is subsequently exposed." A conclusion which I am not prepared to accept.

Returning to my second alternative, that is to say, to the case of hybrids which are born well developed and healthy, but nevertheless perfectly sterile, it is less obvious why, having succeeded in understanding the conflicting memories of their parents, they should fail to produce offspring; but I do not think the reader will feel surprised that this should be the case. The following anecdote, true or false, may not be out of place here:-

"Plutarch tells us of a magpie, belonging to a barber at Rome, which could imitate to a nicety almost every word it heard. Some trumpets happened one day to be sounded before the shop, and for a day or two afterwards the magpie was quite mute, and seemed pensive and melancholy. All who knew it were greatly surprised at its silence; and it was supposed that the sound of the trumpets had so stunned it as to deprive it at once of both voice and hearing. It soon appeared, however, that this was far from being the case; for, says Plutarch, the bird had been all the time occupied in profound meditation, studying how to imitate the sound of the trumpets; and when at last master of it, the magpie, to the astonishment of all its friends, suddenly broke its long silence by a perfect imitation of the flourish of trumpets it had heard, observing with the greatest exactness all the repetitions, stops, and changes. *The acquisition of this lesson had, however, exhausted the whole of the magpie's stock of intellect, for it made it forget everything it had learned before*" ("Percy Anecdotes," Instinct, p. 166).

Or, perhaps, more seriously, the memory of every impregnate ovum from which every ancestor of a mule, for example, has sprung, has reverted to a very long period of time during which its forefathers have been creatures like that which it is itself now going to become: thus, the impregnate ovum from which the mule's father was developed remembered nothing but horse memories; but it felt its faith in these supported by the recollection of a *vast number* of previous generations, in which it was, to all intents and purposes, what it now is. In like manner, the impregnate ovum from which the mule's mother was developed would be backed by the assurance that it had done what it is going to do now a hundred thousand times already. All would thus be plain sailing. A horse and a donkey would result. These two are brought together; an impregnate ovum is produced which finds an unusual conflict of memory between the two lines of its ancestors, nevertheless, being accustomed to *some* conflict, it manages to get over the difficulty, *as on either side it finds itself backed by a very long series of sufficiently steady memory.* A mule results— a creature so distinctly different from either horse or donkey, that reproduction is baffled, owing to the creature's having nothing but its own knowledge of itself to fall back upon, behind which there comes an immediate dislocation, or fault of memory, which is sufficient to bar identity, and hence reproduction, by rendering too severe an appeal to reason necessary—for no creature can reproduce itself on the shallow foundation which reason can alone give. Ordinarily, therefore, the hybrid, or the spermatozoon or ovum, which it may throw off (as the case may be), finds one single experience too small to give it the necessary faith, on the strength of which even to try to reproduce itself. In other cases the hybrid itself has failed to be developed; in others the hybrid, or first cross, is almost fertile; in others it is fertile, but produces depraved issue. The result will vary with the capacities of the creatures crossed, and the amount of conflict between their several experiences.

The above view would remove all difficulties out of the way of evolution, in so far as the sterility of hybrids is concerned. For it would thus appear that this sterility has nothing to do with any supposed immutable or fixed limits of species, but results simply from the same principle which prevents old friends, no matter how intimate in youth, from returning to their old intimacy after a lapse of years, during which they have been subjected to widely different influences, inasmuch as they will each have contracted new habits, and have got into new ways, which they do not like now to alter.

We should expect that our domesticated plants and animals should vary most, inasmuch as these have been subjected to changed conditions which would disturb the memory, and, breaking the chain of recollection, through failure of some one or other of the associated ideas, would thus directly and most markedly affect the reproductive system. Every reader of Mr. Darwin will know that this is what actually happens, and also that when once a plant or animal begins to vary, it will probably vary a good deal further; which, again, is what we should expect—the disturbance of the memory introducing a fresh factor of disturbance, which has to be dealt with by the offspring as it best may. Mr. Darwin writes: "All our domesticated productions, with the rarest exceptions, vary far more than natural species" ("Plants and Animals," &c., vol ii. p. 241, ed. 1875).

On my third supposition, *i.e.*, when the difference between parents has not been great enough to baffle reproduction on the part of the first cross, but when the histories of the father and mother have been, nevertheless, widely different—as in the case of Europeans and Indians—we should expect to have a race of offspring who should seem to be quite clear only about those points, on which their progenitors on both sides were in accord before the manifold divergencies in their experiences commenced; that is to say, the offspring should show a tendency to revert to an early savage condition.

That this indeed occurs may be seen from Mr. Darwin's "Plants and Animals under Domestication" (vol ii. p. 21, ed. 1875), where we find that travellers in all parts of the world have frequently remarked " *on the degraded state and savage condition of crossed races of man* ." A few lines lower down Mr. Darwin tells us that he was himself "struck with the fact that, in South America, men of complicated descent between Negroes, Indians, and Spaniards seldom had, whatever the cause might be, a good expression." "Livingstone" (continues Mr. Darwin) "remarks, 'It is unaccountable why half-castes are so much more cruel than the Portuguese, but such is undoubtedly the case.' An inhabitant remarked to Livingstone, 'God made white men, and God made black men, but the devil made half-castes.'" A little further on Mr. Darwin says that we may "perhaps infer that the degraded state of so many half-castes *is in part due to reversion to a primitive and savage condition, induced by the act of crossing,* even if mainly due to the unfavourable moral conditions under which they are generally reared." Why the crossing should produce this particular tendency would seem to be intelligible enough, if the fashion and instincts of offspring are, in any case, nothing but the memories of its past existences; but it would hardly seem to be so upon any of the theories now generally accepted; as, indeed, is very readily admitted by Mr. Darwin himself, who even, as regards purely-bred animals and plants, remarks that "we are quite unable to assign any proximate cause" for their tendency to at times reassume long lost characters.

If the reader will follow for himself the remaining phenomena of reversion, he will, I believe, find them all explicable on the theory that they are due to memory of past experiences fused, and modified— at times specifically and definitely—by changed conditions. There is, however, one apparently very important phenomenon which I do not at this moment see how to connect with memory, namely, the tendency on the part of offspring to revert to an earlier impregnation. Mr. Darwin's "Provisional Theory of Pangenesis" seemed to afford a satisfactory explanation of this; but the connection with memory was not immediately apparent. I think it likely, however, that this difficulty will vanish on further consideration, so I will not do more than call attention to it here.

The instincts of certain neuter insects hardly bear upon reversion, but will be dealt with at some length in Chapter XII.

V. We should expect to find, as was insisted on in the preceding section in reference to the sterility of hybrids, that it required many, or at any rate several, generations of changed habits before a sufficiently deep impression could be made upon the living being (who must be regarded always as one person in his whole line of ascent or descent) for it to be unconsciously remembered by him, when making himself anew in any succeeding generation, and thus to make him modify his method of procedure during his next embryological development. Nevertheless, we should expect to find that sometimes a very deep single impression made upon a living organism, should be remembered by it, even when it is next in an embryonic condition.

That this is so, we find from Mr. Darwin, who writes ("Plants and Animals under Domestication," vol. ii. p. 57, ed. 1875)—"There is ample evidence that the effect of mutilations and of accidents, especially, or perhaps exclusively, when followed by disease" (which would certainly intensify the impression made), "are occasionally inherited. There can be no doubt that the evil effects of the long continued exposure of the parent to injurious conditions are sometimes transmitted to the offspring." As regards impressions of a less striking character, it is so universally admitted that they are not observed to be repeated in what is called the offspring, until they have been confirmed in what is called the parent, for several generations, but that after several generations, more or fewer as the case may be, they often are transmitted—that it seems unnecessary to say more upon the matter. Perhaps, however, the following passage from Mr. Darwin may be admitted as conclusive:-

"That they" (acquired actions) "are inherited, we see with horses in certain transmitted paces, such as cantering and ambling, which are not natural to them—in the pointing of young pointers, and the setting of young setters—in the peculiar manner of flight of certain breeds of the pigeon, &c. We have analogous cases with mankind in the inheritance of tricks or unusual gestures." . . . ("Expression of the Emotions," p. 29).

In another place Mr. Darwin writes:-

"How again can we explain *the inherited effects* of the use or disuse of particular organs? The domesticated duck flies less and walks more than the wild duck, and its limb bones have become diminished and increased in a corresponding manner in comparison with those of the wild duck. A horse is trained to certain paces, and the colt inherits similar consensual movements. The domesticated rabbit becomes tame from close confinement; the dog intelligent from associating with man; the retriever is taught to fetch and carry; and these mental endowments and bodily powers are all inherited" ("Plants and Animals," &c., vol. ii. p. 367, ed. 1875).

"Nothing," he continues, "in the whole circuit of physiology is more wonderful. How can the use or disuse of a particular limb, or of the brain, affect a small aggregate of reproductive cells, seated in a distant part of the body in such a manner that the being developed from these cells inherits the character of one or both parents? Even an imperfect answer to this question would be satisfactory" ("Plants and Animals," &c. vol. ii. p. 367, ed. 1875).

With such an imperfect answer will I attempt to satisfy the reader, as to say that there appears to be that kind of continuity of existence and sameness of personality, between parents and offspring, which would lead us to expect that the impressions made upon the parent should be epitomised in the offspring, when they have been or have become important enough, through repetition in the history of several so-called existences to have earned a place in that smaller edition, which is issued from generation to generation; or, in other words, when they have been made so deeply, either at one blow or through many, that the offspring can remember them. In practice we observe this to be the case—so that the answer lies in the assertion that offspring and parent, being in one sense but the same individual, there is no great wonder that, in one sense, the first should remember what had happened to the latter; and that too, much in the same way as the individual remembers the events in the earlier history of what he calls his own lifetime, but condensed, and pruned of detail, and remembered as by one who has had a host of other matters to attend to in the interim.

It is thus easy to understand why such a rite as circumcision, though practised during many ages, should have produced little, if any, modification tending to make circumcision unnecessary. On the view here supported such modification would be more surprising than not, for unless the impression made upon the parent was of a grave character— and probably unless also aggravated by subsequent confusion of memories in the cells surrounding the part originally impressed—the parent himself would not be sufficiently impressed to prevent him from reproducing himself, as he had already done upon an infinite number of past occasions. The child, therefore, in the womb would do what the father in the womb had done before him, nor should any trace of memory concerning circumcision be expected till the eighth day after birth, when, but for the fact that the impression in this case is forgotten almost as soon as made, some slight presentiment of coming discomfort might, after a large number of generations, perhaps be looked for as a general rule. It would not, however, be surprising, that the effect of circumcision should be occasionally inherited, and it would appear as though this was sometimes actually the case.

The question should turn upon whether the disuse of an organ has arisen:-

1. From an internal desire on the part of the creature disusing it, to be quit of an organ which it finds troublesome.

2. From changed conditions and habits which render the organ no longer necessary, or which lead the creature to lay greater stress on certain other organs or modifications.

3. From the wish of others outside itself; the effect produced in this case being perhaps neither very good nor very bad for the individual, and resulting in no grave impression upon the organism as a whole.

4. From a single deep impression on a parent, affecting both himself as a whole, and gravely confusing the memories of the cells to be reproduced, or his memories in respect of those cells—according as one adopts Pangenesis and supposes a memory to "run" each gemmule, or as one supposes one memory to "run" the whole impregnate ovum—a compromise between these two views being nevertheless perhaps possible, inasmuch as the combined memories of all the cells may possibly *be* the memory which "runs" the impregnate ovum, just as we *are* ourselves the combination of all our cells, each one of which is both autonomous, and also takes its share in the central government. But within the limits of this volume it is absolutely impossible for me to go into this question.

In the first case—under which some instances which belong more strictly to the fourth would sometimes, but rarely, come—the organ should soon go, and sooner or later leave no rudiment, though still perhaps to be found crossing the life of the embryo, and then disappearing.

In the second it should go more slowly, and leave, it may be, a rudimentary structure.

In the third it should show little or no sign of natural decrease for a very long time.

In the fourth there may be absolute and total sterility, or sterility in regard to the particular organ, or a scar which shall show that the memory of the wound and of each step in the process of healing has been remembered; or there may be simply such disturbance in the reproduced organ as shall show a confused recollection of injury. There may be infinite gradations between the first and last of these possibilities.

I think that the facts, as given by Mr. Darwin ("Plants and Animals," &c., vol i. pp. 466-472, ed. 1875), will bear out the above to the satisfaction of the reader. I can, however, only quote the following passage:-

" . . . Brown Séquard has bred during thirty years many thousand guinea-pigs, . . . nor has he ever seen a guinea-pig born without toes which was not the offspring of parents *which had gnawed off their own toes*, owing to the sciatic nerve having been divided. Of this fact thirteen instances were carefully recorded, and a greater number were seen; yet Brown Séquard speaks of such cases as among the rarer forms of inheritance. It is a still more interesting fact—'that the sciatic nerve in the congenitally toeless animal has inherited the power of passing through *all the different morbid states* which have occurred in one of its parents *from the time of division* till after its reunion with the peripheric end. It is not therefore the power of simply performing an action which is inherited, but the power of performing a whole series of actions in a certain order.'"

I feel inclined to say it is not merely the original wound that is remembered, but the whole process of cure which is now accordingly repeated. Brown Séquard concludes, as Mr. Darwin tells us, "that what is transmitted is the morbid state of the nervous system," due to the operation performed on the parents.

A little lower down Mr. Darwin writes that Professor Rolleston has given him two cases—"namely, of two men, one of whom had his knee, and the other his cheek, severely cut, and both had children born with exactly the same spot marked or scarred."

VI. When, however, an impression has once reached transmission point —whether it be of the nature of a sudden striking thought, which makes its mark deeply then and there, or whether it be the result of smaller impressions repeated until the nail, so to speak, has been driven home—we should expect that it should be remembered by the offspring as something which he has done all his life, and which he has therefore no longer any occasion to learn; he will act, therefore, as people say, *instinctively*. No matter how complex and difficult the process, if the parents have done it sufficiently often (that is to say, for a sufficient number of generations), the offspring will remember the fact when association wakens the memory; it will need no instruction, and—unless when it has been taught to look for it during many generations—will expect none. This may be seen in the case of the humming-bird sphinx moth, which, as Mr. Darwin writes, "shortly after its emergence from the cocoon, as shown by the bloom on its unruffled scales, may be seen poised stationary in the air with its long hair-like proboscis uncurled, and inserted into the minute orifices of flowers; *and no one I believe has ever seen* this moth learning to perform its difficult task, which requires such unerring aim" ("Expression of the Emotions," p. 30).

And, indeed, when we consider that after a time the most complex and difficult actions come to be performed by man without the least effort or consciousness—that offspring cannot be considered as anything but a continuation of the parent life, whose past habits and experiences it epitomises when they have been sufficiently often repeated to produce a lasting impression—that consciousness of memory vanishes on the memory's becoming intense, as completely as the consciousness of complex and difficult movements vanishes as soon as they have been sufficiently practised—and finally, that the real presence of memory is testified rather by performance of the repeated action on recurrence of like surroundings, than by consciousness of recollecting on the part of the individual—so that not only should there be no reasonable bar to our attributing the whole range of the more complex instinctive actions, from first to last, to memory pure and simple, no matter how marvellous they may be, but rather that there is so much to compel us to do so, that we find it difficult to conceive how any other view can have been ever taken—when, I say, we consider all these facts, we should rather feel surprise that the hawk and sparrow still teach their offspring to fly, than that the humming-bird sphinx moth should need no teacher.

The phenomena, then, which we observe are exactly those which we should expect to find.

VII. We should also expect that the memory of animals, as regards their earlier existences, was solely stimulated by association. For we find, from Prof. Bain, that "actions, sensations, and states of feeling occurring together, or in close succession, tend to grow together or cohere in such a way that when any one of them is afterwards presented to the mind, the others are apt to be brought up in idea" ("The Senses and the Intellect," 2d ed. 1864, p. 332). And Prof. Huxley says ("Elementary Lessons in Physiology," 5th ed. 1872, p. 306), "It may be laid down as a rule that if any two mental states be called up together, or in succession, with due frequency and vividness, the subsequent production of the one of them will suffice to call up the other, *and that whether we desire it or not*." I would go one step further, and would say not only whether we desire it or not, but *whether we are aware that the idea has ever before been called up in our minds or not.* I should say that I have quoted both the above passages from Mr. Darwin's "Expression of the Emotions" (p. 30, ed. 1872).

We should, therefore, expect that when the offspring found itself in the presence of objects which had called up such and such ideas for a sufficient number of generations, that is to say, "with due frequency and vividness"— it being of the same age as its parents were, and generally in like case as when the ideas were called up in the minds of the parents—the same ideas should also be called up in the minds of the offspring *whether they desire it or not;*" and, I would say also, "whether they recognise the ideas as having ever before been present to them or not."

I think we might also expect that no other force, save that of association, should have power to kindle, so to speak, into the flame of action the atomic spark of memory, which we can alone suppose to be transmitted from one generation to another.

That both plants and animals do as we should expect of them in this respect is plain, not only from the performance of the most intricate and difficult actions—difficult both physically and intellectually— at an age, and under circumstances which preclude all possibility of what we call instruction, but from the fact that deviations from the parental instinct, or rather the recurrence of a memory, unless in connection with the accustomed train of associations, is of comparatively rare occurrence; the result, commonly, of some one of the many memories about which we know no more than we do of the memory which enables a cat to find her way home after a hundred-mile journey by train, and shut up in a hamper, or, perhaps even more commonly, of abnormal treatment.

VIII. If, then, memory depends on association, we should expect two corresponding phenomena in the case of plants and animals—namely, that they should show a tendency to resume feral habits on being turned wild after several generations of domestication, and also that peculiarities should tend to show themselves at a corresponding age in the offspring and in the parents. As regards the tendency to resume feral habits, Mr. Darwin, though apparently of opinion that the tendency to do this has been much exaggerated, yet does not doubt that such a tendency exists, as shown by well authenticated instances. He writes: "It has been repeatedly asserted in the most positive manner by various authors that feral animals and plants invariably return to their primitive specific type."

This shows, at any rate, that there is a considerable opinion to this effect among observers generally.

He continues: "It is curious on what little evidence this belief rests. Many of our domesticated animals could not subsist in a wild state,"—so that there is no knowing whether they would or would not revert. "In several cases we do not know the aboriginal parent species, and cannot tell whether or not there has been any close degree of reversion." So that here, too, there is at any rate no evidence *against* the tendency; the conclusion, however, is that, notwithstanding the deficiency of positive evidence to warrant the general belief as to the force of the tendency, yet "the simple fact of animals and plants becoming feral does cause some tendency to revert to the primitive state," and he tells us that "when variously-coloured tame rabbits are turned out in Europe, they generally re-acquire the colouring of the wild animal;" there can be no doubt," he says, "that this really does occur," though he seems inclined to account for it by the fact that oddly-coloured and conspicuous animals would suffer much from beasts of prey and from being easily shot. "The best known case of reversion:" he continues, "and that on which the widely-spread belief in its universality apparently rests, is that of pigs. These animals have run wild in the West Indies, South America, and the Falkland Islands, and have everywhere re-acquired the dark colour, the thick bristles, and great tusks of the wild boar; and the young have re-acquired longitudinal stripes." And on page 22 of "Plants and Animals under Domestication" (vol. ii. ed. 1875) we find that "the re-appearance of coloured, longitudinal stripes on young feral pigs cannot be attributed to the direct action of external conditions. In this case, and in many others, we can only say that any change in the habits of life apparently favours a tendency, inherent or latent, in the species to return to the primitive state." On which one cannot but remark that though any change may favour such tendency, yet the return to original habits and surroundings appears to do so in a way so marked as not to be readily referable to any other cause than that of association and memory—the creature, in fact, having got into its old groove, remembers it, and takes to all its old ways.

As regards the tendency to inherit changes (whether embryonic, or during post-natal development as ordinarily observed in any species), or peculiarities of habit or form which do not partake of the nature of disease, it must be sufficient to refer the reader to Mr. Darwin's remarks upon this subject ("Plants and Animals Under Domestication," vol. ii. pp. 51-57, ed. 1875). The existence of the tendency is not likely to be denied. The instances given by Mr. Darwin are strictly to the point as regards all ordinary developmental and metamorphic changes, and even as regards transmitted acquired actions, and tricks acquired before the time when the offspring has issued from the body of the parent, or on an average of many generations does so; but it cannot for a moment be supposed that the offspring knows by inheritance anything about what happens to the parent subsequently to the offspring's being born. Hence the appearance of diseases in the offspring, at comparatively late periods in life, but at the same age as, or earlier, than in the parents, must be regarded as due to the fact that in each case the machine having been made after the same pattern (which *is* due to memory), is liable to have the same weak points, and to break down after a similar amount of wear and tear; but after less wear and tear in the case of the offspring than in that of the parent, because a diseased organism is commonly a deteriorating organism, and if repeated at all closely, and without repentance and amendment of life, will be repeated for the worse. If we do not improve, we grow worse. This, at least, is what we observe daily.

Nor again can we believe, as some have fancifully imagined, that the remembrance of any occurrence of which the effect has been entirely, or almost entirely mental, should be remembered by offspring with any definiteness. The intellect of the offspring might be affected, for better or worse, by the general nature of the intellectual employment of the parent; or a great shock to a parent might destroy or weaken the intellect of the offspring; but unless a deep impression were made upon the cells of the body, and deepened by subsequent disease, we could not expect it to be remembered with any definiteness, or precision. We may talk as we will about mental pain, and mental scars, but after all, the impressions they leave are incomparably less durable than those made by an organic lesion. It is probable, therefore, that the feeling which so many have described, as though they remembered this or that in some past existence, is purely imaginary, and due rather to unconscious recognition of the fact that we certainly have lived before, than to any actual occurrence corresponding to the supposed recollection.

And lastly, we should look to find in the action of memory, as between one generation and another, a reflection of the many anomalies and exceptions to ordinary rules which we observe in memory, so far as we can watch its action in what we call our own single lives, and the single lives of others. We should expect that reversion should be frequently capricious—that is to say, give us more trouble to account for than we are either able or willing to take. And assuredly we find it so in fact. Mr. Darwin—from whom it is impossible to quote too much or too fully, inasmuch as no one else can furnish such a store of facts, so well arranged, and so above all suspicion of either carelessness or want of candour—so that, however we may differ from him, it is he himself who shows us how to do so, and whose pupils we all are—Mr. Darwin writes: "In every living being we may rest assured that a host of long-lost characters lie ready to be evolved under proper conditions" (does not one almost long to substitute the word "memories" for the word "characters?") "How can we make intelligible, and connect with other facts, this wonderful and common capacity of reversion—this power of calling back to life long-lost characters?" ("Plants and Animals," &c., vol. ii. p. 369, ed. 1875). Surely the answer may be hazarded, that we shall be able to do so when we can make intelligible the power of calling back to life long-lost memories. But I grant that this answer holds out no immediate prospect of a clear understanding.

One word more. Abundant facts are to be found which point inevitably, as will appear more plainly in the following chapter, in the direction of thinking that offspring inherits the memories of its parents; but I know of no single fact which suggests that parents are in the smallest degree affected (other than sympathetically) by the memories of their offspring *after that offspring has been born.* Whether the unborn offspring affects the memory of the mother in some particulars, and whether we have here the explanation of occasional reversion to a previous impregnation, is a matter on which I should hardly like to express an opinion now. Nor, again, can I find a single fact which seems to indicate any memory of the parental life on the part of offspring later than the average date of the offspring's quitting the body of the parent.

CHAPTER XI—INSTINCT AS INHERITED MEMORY

I have already alluded to M. Ribot's work on "Heredity," from which I will now take the following passages.

M. Ribot writes:-

"Instinct is innate, *i.e., anterior to all individual experience .*" This I deny on grounds already abundantly apparent; but let it pass. "Whereas intelligence is developed slowly by accumulated experience, instinct is perfect from the first" ("Heredity," p. 14).

Obviously the memory of a habit or experience will not commonly be transmitted to offspring in that perfection which is called "instinct," till the habit or experience has been repeated in several generations with more or less uniformity; for otherwise the impression made will not be strong enough to endure through the busy and difficult task of reproduction. This of course involves that the habit shall have attained, as it were equilibrium with the creature's sense of its own needs, so that it shall have long seemed the best course possible, leaving upon the whole and under ordinary circumstances little further to be desired, and hence that it should have been little varied during many generations. We should expect that it would be transmitted in a more or less partial, varying, imperfect, and intelligent condition before equilibrium had been attained; it would, however, continually tend towards equilibrium, for reasons which will appear more fully later on.

When this stage has been reached, as regards any habit, the creature will cease trying to improve; on which the repetition of the habit will become stable, and hence become capable of more unerring transmission— but at the same time improvement will cease; the habit will become fixed, and be perhaps transmitted at an earlier and earlier age, till it has reached that date of manifestation which shall be found most agreeable to the other habits of the creature. It will also be manifested, as a matter of course, without further consciousness or reflection, for people cannot be always opening up settled questions; if they thought a matter over yesterday they cannot think it all over again to-day, but will adopt for better or worse the conclusion then reached; and this, too, even in spite sometimes of considerable misgiving, that if they were to think still further they could find a still better course. It is not, therefore, to be expected that "instinct" should show signs of that hesitating and tentative action which results from knowledge that is still so imperfect as to be actively self-conscious; nor yet that it should grow or vary, unless under such changed conditions as shall baffle memory, and present the alternative of either invention—that is to say, variation—or death. But every instinct must have poised through the laboriously intelligent stages through which human civilisations *and mechanical inventions* are now passing; and he who would study the origin of an instinct with its development, partial transmission, further growth, further transmission, approach to more unreflecting stability, and finally, its perfection as an unerring and unerringly transmitted instinct, must look to laws, customs, *and machinery* as his best instructors. Customs and machines are instincts *and organs* now in process of development; they will assuredly one day reach the unconscious state of equilibrium which we observe in the structures and instincts of bees and ants, and an approach to which may be found among some savage nations. We may reflect, however, not without pleasure, that this condition—the true millennium—is still distant. Nevertheless the ants and bees seem happy; perhaps more happy than when so many social questions were in as hot discussion among them, as other, and not dissimilar ones, will one day be amongst ourselves.

And this, as will be apparent, opens up the whole question of the stability of species, which we cannot follow further here, than to say, that according to the balance of testimony, many plants and animals do appear to have reached a phase of being from which they are hard to move—that is to say, they will die sooner than be at the pains of altering their habits—true martyrs to their convictions. Such races refuse to see changes in their surroundings as long as they can, but when compelled to recognise them, they throw up the game because they cannot and will not, or will not and cannot, invent. And this is perfectly intelligible, for a race is nothing but a long-lived individual, and like any individual, or tribe of men whom we have yet observed, will have its special capacities and its special limitations, though, as in the case of the individual, so also with the race, it is exceedingly hard to say what those limitations are, and why, having been able to go so far, it should go no further. Every man and every race is capable of education up to a certain point, but not to the extent of being made from a sow's ear into a silk purse. The proximate cause of the limitation seems to lie in the absence of the wish to go further; the presence or absence of the wish will depend upon the nature and surroundings of the individual, which is simply a way of saying that one can get no further, but that as the song (with a slight alteration) says:-

"Some breeds do, and some breeds don't,
Some breeds will, but this breed won't,
I tried very often to see if it would,
But it said it really couldn't, and I don't think it could."

It may perhaps be maintained, that with time and patience, one might train a rather stupid plough-boy to understand the differential calculus. This might be done with the help of an inward desire on the part of the boy to learn, but never otherwise. If the boy wants to learn or to improve generally, he will do so in spite of every hindrance, till in time he becomes a very different being from what he was originally. If he does not want to learn, he will not do so for any wish of another person. If he feels that he has the power he will wish; or if he wishes, he will begin to think he has the power, and try to fulfil his wishes; one cannot say which comes first, for the power and the desire go always hand in hand, or nearly so, and the whole business is nothing but a most vicious circle from first to last. But it is plain that there is more to be said on behalf of such circles than we have been in the habit of thinking. Do what we will, we must each one of us argue in a circle of our own, from which, so long as we live at all, we can by no possibility escape. I am not sure whether the frank acceptation and recognition of this fact is not the best corrective for dogmatism that we are likely to find.

We can understand that a pigeon might in the course of ages grow to be a peacock if there was a persistent desire on the part of the pigeon through all these ages to do so. We know very well that this has not probably occurred in nature, inasmuch as no pigeon is at all likely to wish to be very different from what it is now. The idea of being anything very different from what it now is, would be too wide a cross with the pigeon's other ideas for it to entertain it seriously. If the pigeon had never seen a peacock, it would not be able to conceive the idea, so as to be able to make towards it; if, on the other hand, it had seen one, it would not probably either want to become one, or think that it would be any use wanting seriously, even though it were to feel a passing fancy to be so gorgeously arrayed; it would therefore lack that faith without which no action, and with which, every action, is possible.

That creatures have conceived the idea of making themselves like other creatures or objects which it was to their advantage or pleasure to resemble, will be believed by any one who turns to Mr. Mivart's "Genesis of Species," where he will find (chapter ii.) an account of some very showy South American butterflies, which give out such a strong odour that nothing will eat them, and which are hence mimicked both in appearance and flight by a very different kind of butterfly; and, again, we see that certain birds, without any particular desire of gain, no sooner hear any sound than they begin to mimick it, merely for the pleasure of mimicking; so we all enjoy to mimick, or to hear good mimicry, so also monkeys imitate the actions which they observe, from pure force of sympathy. To mimick, or to wish to mimick, is doubtless often one of the first steps towards varying in any given direction. Not less, in all probability, than a full twenty per cent. of all the courage and good nature now existing in the world, derives its origin, at no very distant date, from a desire to appear courageous and good-natured. And this suggests a work whose title should be "On the Fine Arts as bearing on the Reproductive System," of which the title must suffice here.

Against faith, then, and desire, all the "natural selection" in the world will not stop an amba from becoming an elephant, if a reasonable time be granted; without the faith and the desire, neither "natural selection" nor artificial breeding will be able to do much in the way of modifying any structure. When we have once thoroughly grasped the conception that we are all one creature, and that each one of us is many millions of years old, so that all the pigeons in the one line of an infinite number of generations are still one pigeon only—then we can understand that a bird, as different from a peacock as a pigeon is now, could yet have wandered on and on, first this way and then that, doing what it liked, and thought that it could do, till it found itself at length a peacock; but we cannot believe either that a bird like a pigeon should be able to apprehend any ideal so different from itself as a peacock, and make towards it, or that man, having wished to breed a bird anything like a peacock from a bird anything like a pigeon, would be able to succeed in accumulating accidental peacock-like variations till he had made the bird he was in search of, no matter in what number of generations; much less can we believe that the accumulation of small fortuitous variations by "natural selection" could succeed better. We can no more believe the above, than we can believe that a wish outside a plough-boy could turn him into a senior wrangler. The boy would prove to be too many for his teacher, and so would the pigeon for its breeder.

I do not forget that artificial breeding has modified the original type of the horse and the dog, till it has at length produced the dray-horse and the greyhound; but in each case man has had to get use and disuse—that is to say, the desires of the animal itself—to help him.

We are led, then, to the conclusion that all races have what for practical purposes may be considered as their limits, though there is no saying what those limits are, nor indeed why, in theory, there should be any limits at all, but only that there are limits in practice. Races which vary considerably must be considered as clever, but it may be speculative, people who commonly have a genius in some special direction, as perhaps for mimicry, perhaps for beauty, perhaps for music, perhaps for the higher mathematics, but seldom in more than one or two directions; while "inflexible organisations," like that of the goose, may be considered as belonging to people with one idea, and the greater tendency of plants and animals to vary under domestication may be reasonably compared with the effects of culture and education: that is to say, may be referred to increased range and variety of experience or perceptions, which will either cause sterility, if they be too unfamiliar, so as to be incapable of fusion with preceding ideas, and hence to bring memory to a sudden fault, or will open the door for all manner of further variation—the new ideas having suggested new trains of thought, which a clever example of a clever race will be only too eager to pursue.

Let us now return to M. Ribot. He writes (p. 14):- "The duckling hatched by the hen makes straight for water." In what conceivable way can we account for this, except on the supposition that the duckling knows perfectly well what it can, and what it cannot do with water, owing to its recollection of what it did when it was still one individuality with its parents, and hence, when it was a duckling before?

"The squirrel, before it knows anything of winter, lays up a store of nuts. A bird when hatched in a cage will, when given its freedom, build for itself a nest like that of its parents, out of the same materials, and of the same shape."

If this is not due to memory, even an imperfect explanation of what else it can be due to, "would be satisfactory."

"Intelligence gropes about, tries this way and that, misses its object, commits mistakes, and corrects them."

Yes. Because intelligence is of consciousness, and consciousness is of attention, and attention is of uncertainty, and uncertainty is of ignorance or want of consciousness. Intelligence is not yet thoroughly up to its business.

"Instinct advances with a mechanical certainty."

Why mechanical? Should not "with apparent certainty" suffice?

"Hence comes its unconscious character."

But for the word "mechanical" this is true, and is what we have been all along insisting on.

"It knows nothing either of ends, or of the means of attaining them; it implies no comparison, judgment, or choice."

This is assumption. What is certain is that instinct does not betray signs of self-consciousness as to its own knowledge. It has dismissed reference to first principles, and is no longer under the law, but under the grace of a settled conviction.

"All seems directed by thought."

Yes; because all *has been* in earlier existences directed by thought.

"Without ever arriving at thought."

Because it has *got past thought*, and though "directed by thought" originally, is now travelling in exactly the opposite direction. It is not likely to reach thought again, till people get to know worse and worse how to do things, the oftener they practise them.

"And if this phenomenon appear strange, it must be observed that analogous states occur in ourselves. *All that we do from habit— walking, writing, or practising a mechanical act, for instance—all these and many other very complex acts are performed without consciousness.*

"Instinct appears stationary. It does not, like intelligence, seem to grow and decay, to gain and to lose. It does not improve."

Naturally. For improvement can only as a general rule be looked for along the line of latest development, that is to say, in matters concerning which the creature is being still consciously exercised. Older questions are settled, and the solution must be accepted as final, for the question of living at all would be reduced to an absurdity, if everything decided upon one day was to be undecided again the next; as with painting or music, so with life and politics, let every man be fully persuaded in his own mind, for decision with wrong will be commonly a better policy than indecision—I had almost added with right; and a firm purpose with risk will be better than an infirm one with temporary exemption from disaster. Every race has made its great blunders, to which it has nevertheless adhered, inasmuch as the corresponding modification of other structures and instincts was found preferable to the revolution which would be caused by a radical change of structure, with consequent havoc among a legion of vested interests. Rudimentary organs are, as has been often said, the survivals of these interests—the signs of their peaceful and gradual extinction as living faiths; they are also instances of the difficulty of breaking through any cant or trick which we have long practised, and which is not sufficiently troublesome to make it a serious object with us to cure ourselves of the habit.

"If it does not remain perfectly invariable, at least it only varies within very narrow limits; and though this question has been warmly debated in our day, and is yet unsettled, we may yet say that in instinct immutability is the law, variation the exception."

This is quite as it should be. Genius will occasionally rise a little above convention, but with an old convention immutability will be the rule.

"Such," continues M. Ribot, "are the admitted characters of instinct."

Yes; but are they not also the admitted characters of actions that are due to memory?

At the bottom of p. 15, M. Ribot quotes the following from Mr. Darwin:-

"We have reason to believe that aboriginal habits are long retained under domestication. Thus with the common ass, we see signs of its original desert-life in its strong dislike to cross the smallest stream of water, and in its pleasure in rolling in the dust. The same strong dislike to cross a stream is common to the camel which has been domesticated from a very early period. Young pigs, though so tame, sometimes squat when frightened, and then try to conceal themselves, even in an open and bare place. Young turkeys, and occasionally even young fowls, when the hen gives the danger-cry, run away and try to hide themselves, like young partridges or pheasants, in order that their mother may take flight, of which she has lost the power. The musk duck in its native country often perches and roosts on trees, and our domesticated musk ducks, though sluggish birds, are fond of perching on the tops of barns, walls, &c. . . . We know that the dog, however well and regularly fed, often buries like the fox any superfluous food; we see him turning round and round on a carpet as if to trample down grass to form a bed. . . . In the delight with which lambs and kids crowd together and frisk upon the smallest hillock we see a vestige of their former alpine habits."

What does this delightful passage go to show, if not that the young in all these cases must still have a latent memory of their past existences, which is called into an active condition as soon as the associated ideas present themselves?

Returning to M. Ribot's own observations, we find he tells us that it usually requires three or four generations to fix the results of training, and to prevent a return to the instincts of the wild state. I think, however, it would not be presumptuous to suppose that if an animal after only three or four generations of training be restored to its original conditions of life, it will forget its intermediate training and return to its old ways, almost as readily as a London street Arab would forget the beneficial effects of a weeks training in a reformatory school, if he were then turned loose again on the streets. So if we hatch wild ducks' eggs under a tame duck, the ducklings "will have scarce left the egg-shell when they obey the instincts of their race and take their flight." So the colts from wild horses, and mongrel young between wild and domesticated horses, betray traces of their earlier memories.

On this M. Ribot says: "Originally man had considerable trouble in taming the animals which are now domesticated; and his work would have been in vain had not heredity" (memory) "come to his aid. It may be said that after man has modified a wild animal to his will, there goes on in its progeny a silent conflict between two heredities" (memories), "the one tending to fix the acquired modifications and the other to preserve the primitive instincts. The latter often get the mastery, and only after several generations is training sure of victory. But we may see that in either case heredity" (memory) "always asserts its rights."

How marvellously is the above passage elucidated and made to fit in with the results of our recognised experience, by the simple substitution of the word "memory" for "heredity."

"Among the higher animals"—to continue quoting—"which are possessed not only of instinct, but also of intelligence, nothing is more common than to see mental dispositions, which have evidently been acquired, so fixed by heredity, that they are confounded with instinct, so spontaneous and automatic do they become. Young pointers have been known to point the first time they were taken out, sometimes even better than dogs that had been for a long time in training. The habit of saving life is hereditary in breeds that have been brought up to it, as is also the shepherd dog's habit of moving around the flock and guarding it."

As soon as we have grasped the notion, that instinct is only the epitome of past experience, revised, corrected, made perfect, and learnt by rote, we no longer find any desire to separate "instinct" from "mental dispositions, which have evidently been acquired and fixed by heredity," for the simple reason that they are one and the same thing.

A few more examples are all that my limits will allow—they abound on every side, and the difficulty lies only in selecting—M. Ribot being to hand, I will venture to lay him under still further contributions.

On page 19 we find:- "Knight has shown experimentally the truth of the proverb, 'a good hound is bred so,' he took every care that when the pups were first taken into the field, they should receive no guidance from older dogs; yet the very first day, one of the pups stood trembling with anxiety, having his eyes fixed and all his muscles strained *at the partridges which their parents had been trained to point.* A spaniel belonging to a breed which had been trained to woodcock-shooting, knew perfectly well from the first how to act like an old dog, avoiding places where the ground was frozen, and where it was, therefore, useless to seek the game, as there was no scent. Finally, a young polecat terrier was thrown into a state of great excitement the first time he ever saw one of these animals, while a spaniel remained perfectly calm.

"In South America, according to Roulin, dogs belonging to a breed that has long been trained to the dangerous chase of the peccary, when taken for the first time into the woods, know the tactics to adopt quite as well as the old dogs, and that without any instruction. Dogs of other races, and unacquainted with the tactics, are killed at once, no matter how strong they may be. The American greyhound, instead of leaping at the stag, attacks him by the belly, and throws him over, as his ancestors had been trained to do in hunting the Indians.

"Thus, then, heredity transmits modification no less than natural instincts."

Should not this rather be—"thus, then, we see that not only older and remoter habits, but habits which have been practised for a comparatively small number of generations, may be so deeply impressed on the individual that they may dwell in his memory, surviving the so-called change of personality which he undergoes in each successive generation"?

"There is, however, an important difference to be noted: the heredity of instincts admits of no exceptions, while in that of modifications there are many."

It may be well doubted how far the heredity of instincts admits of no exceptions; on the contrary, it would seem probable that in many races geniuses have from time to time arisen who remembered not only their past experiences, as far as action and habit went, but have been able to rise in some degree above habit where they felt that improvement was possible, and who carried such improvement into further practice, by slightly modifying their structure in the desired direction on the next occasion that they had a chance of dealing with protoplasm at all. It is by these rare instances of intellectual genius (and I would add of moral genius, if many of the instincts and structures of plants and animals did not show that they had got into a region as far above morals—other than enlightened self-interest—as they are above articulate consciousness of their own aims in many other respects)—it is by these instances of either rare good luck or rare genius that many species have been, in all probability, originated or modified. Nevertheless inappreciable modification of instinct is, and ought to be, the rule.

As to M. Ribot's assertion, that to the heredity of modifications there are many exceptions, I readily agree with it, and can only say that it is exactly what I should expect; the lesson long since learnt by rote, and repeated in an infinite number of generations, would be repeated unintelligently, and with little or no difference, save from a rare accidental slip, the effect of which would be the culling out of the bungler who was guilty of it, or from the still rarer appearance of an individual of real genius; while the newer lesson would be repeated both with more hesitation and uncertainty, and with more intelligence; and this is well conveyed in M. Ribot's next sentence, for he says— "It is only when variations have been firmly rooted; when having become organic, they constitute a second nature, which supplants the first; when, like instinct, they have assumed a mechanical character, that they can be transmitted."

How nearly M. Ribot comes to the opinion which I myself venture to propound will appear from the following further quotation. After dealing with somnambulism, and saying, that if somnambulism were permanent and innate, it would be impossible to distinguish it from instinct, he continues:-

"Hence it is less difficult than is generally supposed, to conceive how intelligence may become instinct; we might even say that, leaving out of consideration the character of innateness, to which we will return, we have seen the metamorphosis take place. *There can then be no ground for making instinct a faculty apart, sui generis,* a phenomenon so mysterious, so strange, that usually no other explanation of it is offered but that of attributing it to the direct act of the Deity. This whole mistake is the result of a defective psychology which makes no account of the unconscious activity of the soul."

We are tempted to add—"and which also makes no account of the *bonâ fide* character of the continued personality of successive generations."

"But we are so accustomed," he continues, "to contrast the characters of instinct with those of intelligence—to say that instinct is innate, invariable, automatic, while intelligence is something acquired, variable, spontaneous —that it looks at first paradoxical to assert that instinct and intelligence are identical.

"It is said that instinct is innate. But if, on the one hand, we bear in mind that many instincts are acquired, and that, according to a theory hereafter to be explained" (which theory, I frankly confess, I never was able to get hold of), *"all instincts are only hereditary habits"* (italics mine); "if, on the other hand, we observe that intelligence is in some sense held to be innate by all modern schools of philosophy, which agree to reject the theory of the *tabula rasa* " (if there is no *tabula rasa,* there is continued psychological personality, or words have lost their meaning), "and to accept either latent ideas, or *à priori* forms of thought" (surely only a periphrasis for continued personality and memory) "or pre-ordination of the nervous system and of the organism; *it will be seen that this character of innateness does not constitute an absolute distinction between instinct and intelligence.*

"It is true that intelligence is variable, but so also is instinct, as we have seen. In winter, the Rhine beaver plasters his wall to windward; once he was a builder, now a burrower; once he lived in society, now he is solitary. Intelligence itself can scarcely be more variable . . . instinct may be modified, lost, reawakened.

"Although intelligence is, as a rule, conscious, it may also become unconscious and automatic, without losing its identity. Neither is instinct always so blind, so mechanical, as is supposed, for at times it is at fault. The wasp that has faultily trimmed a leaf of its paper begins again. The bee only gives the hexagonal form to its cell after many attempts and alterations. It is difficult to believe that the loftier instincts" (and surely, then, the more recent instincts) "of the higher animals are not accompanied *by at least a confused consciousness*. There is, therefore, no absolute distinction between instinct and intelligence; there is not a single characteristic which, seriously considered, remains the exclusive property of either. The contrast established between instinctive acts and intellectual acts is, nevertheless, perfectly true, but only when we compare the extremes. *As instinct rises it approaches intelligence—as intelligence descends it approaches instinct.*"

M. Ribot and myself (if I may venture to say so) are continually on the verge of coming to an understanding, when, at the very moment that we seem most likely to do so, we fly, as it were, to opposite poles. Surely the passage last quoted should be, "As instinct falls," *i.e* ., becomes less and less certain of its ground, "it approaches intelligence; as intelligence rises," *i.e.*, becomes more and more convinced of the truth and expediency of its convictions—"it approaches instinct."

Enough has been said to show that the opinions which I am advancing are not new, but I have looked in vain for the conclusions which, it appears to me, M. Ribot should draw from his facts; throughout his interesting book I find the facts which it would seem should have guided him to the conclusions, and sometimes almost the conclusions themselves, but he never seems quite to have reached them, nor has he arranged his facts so that others are likely to deduce them, unless they had already arrived at them by another road. I cannot, however, sufficiently express my obligations to M. Ribot.

I cannot refrain from bringing forward a few more instances of what I think must be considered by every reader as hereditary memory. Sydney

Smith writes:-

"Sir James Hall hatched some chickens in an oven. Within a few minutes after the shell was broken, a spider was turned loose before this very youthful brood; the destroyer of flies had hardly proceeded more than a few inches, before he was descried by one of these oven-born chickens, and, at one peck of his bill, immediately devoured. This certainly was not imitation. A female goat very near delivery died; Galen cut out the young kid, and placed before it a bundle of hay, a bunch of fruit, and a pan of milk; the young kid smelt to them all very attentively, and then began to lap the milk. This was not imitation. And what is commonly and rightly called instinct, cannot be explained away, under the notion of its being imitation" (Lecture xvii. on Moral Philosophy).

It cannot, indeed, be explained away under the notion of its being imitation, but I think it may well be so under that of its being memory.

Again, a little further on in the same lecture, as that above quoted from, we find:-

"Ants and beavers lay up magazines. Where do they get their knowledge that it will not be so easy to collect food in rainy weather, as it is in summer? Men and women know these things, because their grandpapas and grandmammas have told them so. Ants hatched from the egg artificially, or birds hatched in this manner, have all this knowledge by intuition, without the smallest communication with any of their relations. Now observe what the solitary wasp does; she digs several holes in the sand, in each of which she deposits an egg, though she certainly knows not (?) that an animal is deposited in that egg, and still less that this animal must be nourished with other animals. She collects a few green flies, rolls them up neatly in several parcels (like Bologna sausages), and stuffs one parcel into each hole where an egg is deposited. When the wasp worm is hatched, it finds a store of provision ready made; and what is most curious, the quantity allotted to each is exactly sufficient to support it, till it attains the period of wasphood, and can provide for itself. This instinct of the parent wasp is the more remarkable as it does not feed upon flesh itself. Here the little creature has never seen its parent; for by the time it is born, the parent is always eaten by sparrows; and yet, without the slightest education, or previous experience, it does everything that the parent did before it. Now the objectors to the doctrine of instinct may say what they please, but young tailors have no intuitive method of making pantaloons; a new-born mercer cannot measure diaper; nature teaches a cook's daughter nothing about sippets. All these things require with us seven years' apprenticeship; but insects are like Molière's persons of quality—they know everything (as Molière says), without having learnt anything. 'Les gens de qualité savent tout, sans avoir rien appris.'"

How completely all difficulty vanishes from the facts so pleasantly told in this passage when we bear in mind the true nature of personal identity, the ordinary working of memory, and the vanishing tendency of consciousness concerning what we know exceedingly well.

My last instance I take from M. Ribot, who writes:- "Gratiolet, in his *Anatomie Comparèe du Système Nerveux*, states that an old piece of wolf's skin, with the hair all worn away, when set before a little dog, threw the animal into convulsions of fear by the slight scent attaching to it. The dog had never seen a wolf, and we can only explain this alarm by the hereditary transmission of certain sentiments, coupled with a certain perception of the sense of smell" ("Heredity," p. 43).

I should prefer to say "we can only explain the alarm by supposing that the smell of the wolf's skin"—the sense of smell being, as we all know, more powerful to recall the ideas that have been associated with it than any other sense—"brought up the ideas with which it had been associated in the dog's mind during many previous existences"—he on smelling the wolf's skin remembering all about wolves perfectly well.

CHAPTER XII—INSTINCTS OF NEUTER INSECTS

In this chapter I will consider, as briefly as possible, the strongest argument that I have been able to discover against the supposition that instinct is chiefly due to habit. I have said "the strongest argument;" I should have said, the only argument that struck me as offering on the face of it serious difficulties.

Turning, then, to Mr. Darwin's chapter on instinct ("Natural Selection," ed. 1876, p. 205), we find substantially much the same views as those taken at a later date by M. Ribot, and referred to in the preceding chapter. Mr. Darwin writes:-

"An action, which we ourselves require experience to enable us to perform, when performed by an animal, more especially a very young one, without experience, and when performed by many animals in the same way without their knowing for what purpose it is performed, is usually said to be instinctive."

The above should strictly be, "without their being conscious of their own knowledge concerning the purpose for which they act as they do;" and though some may say that the two phrases come to the same thing, I think there is an important difference, as what I propose distinguishes ignorance from over-familiarity, both which states are alike unself-conscious, though with widely different results.

"But I could show," continues Mr. Darwin, "that none of these characters are universal. A little dose of judgement or reason, as Pierre Huber expresses it, often comes into play even with animals low in the scale of nature.

"Frederick Cuvier and several of the older metaphysicians have compared instinct with habit."

I would go further and would say, that instinct, in the great majority of cases, is habit pure and simple, contracted originally by some one or more individuals; practised, probably, in a consciously intelligent manner during many successive lives, until the habit has acquired the highest perfection which the circumstances admitted; and, finally, so deeply impressed upon the memory as to survive that effacement of minor impressions which generally takes place in every fresh life-wave or generation.

I would say, that unless the identity of offspring with their parents be so far admitted that the children be allowed to remember the deeper impressions engraved on the minds of those who begot them, it is little less than trifling to talk, as so many writers do, about inherited habit, or the experience of the race, or, indeed, accumulated variations of instincts.

When an instinct is not habit, as resulting from memory pure and simple, it is habit modified by some treatment, generally in the youth or embryonic stages of the individual, which disturbs his memory, and drives him on to some unusual course, inasmuch as he cannot recognise and remember his usual one by reason of the change now made in it. Habits and instincts, again, may be modified by any important change in the condition of the parents, which will then both affect the parent's sense of his own identity, and also create more or less fault, or dislocation of memory, in the offspring immediately behind the memory of his last life. Change of food may at times be sufficient to create a specific modification—that is to say, to affect all the individuals whose food is so changed, in one and the same way— whether as regards structure or habit. Thus we see that certain changes in food (and domicile), from those with which its ancestors have been familiar, will disturb the memory of a queen bee's egg, and set it at such disadvantage as to make it make itself into a neuter bee; but yet we find that the larva thus partly aborted may have its memories restored to it, if not already too much disturbed, and may thus return to its condition as a queen bee, if it only again be restored to the food and domicile, which its past memories can alone remember.

So we see that opium, tobacco, alcohol, hasheesh, and tea produce certain effects upon our own structure and instincts. But though capable of modification, and of specific modification, which may in time become inherited, and hence resolve itself into a true instinct or settled question, yet I maintain that the main bulk of the instinct (whether as affecting structure or habits of life) will be derived from memory pure and simple; the individual growing up in the shape he does, and liking to do this or that when he is grown up, simply from recollection of what he did last time, and of what on the whole suited him.

For it must be remembered that a drug which should destroy some one part at an early embryonic stage, and thus prevent it from development, would prevent the creature from recognising the surroundings which affected that part when he was last alive and unmutilated, as being the same as his present surroundings. He would be puzzled, for he would be viewing the position from a different standpoint. If any important item in a number of associated ideas disappears, the plot fails; and a great internal change is an exceedingly important item. Life and things to a creature so treated at an early embryonic stage would not be life and things as he last remembered them; hence he would not be able to do the same now as he did then; that is to say, he would vary both in structure and instinct; but if the creature were tolerably uniform to start with, and were treated in a tolerably uniform way, we might expect the effect produced to be much the same in all ordinary cases.

We see, also, that any important change in treatment and surroundings, if not sufficient to kill, would and does tend to produce not only variability but sterility, as part of the same story and for the same reason—namely, default of memory; this default will be of every degree of intensity, from total failure, to a slight disturbance of memory as affecting some one particular organ only; that is to say, from total sterility, to a slight variation in an unimportant part. So that even *the slightest conceivable variations should be referred to changed conditions, external or internal, and to their disturbing effects upon the memory*; and sterility, without any apparent disease of the reproductive system, may be referred not so much to special delicacy or susceptibility of the organs of reproduction as to inability on the part of the creature to know where it is, and to recognise itself as the same creature which it has been accustomed to reproduce.

Mr. Darwin thinks that the comparison of habit with instinct gives "an accurate notion of the frame of mind under which an instinctive action is performed, but not," he thinks, "of its origin."

"How unconsciously," Mr. Darwin continues, "many habitual actions are performed, indeed not rarely in direct opposition to our conscious will! Yet they may be modified by the will or by reason. Habits easily become associated with other habits, with certain periods of time and states of body. When once acquired, they often remain constant throughout life. Several other points of resemblance between instincts and habits could be pointed out. As in repeating a well-known song, so in instincts, one action follows another by a sort of rhythm. If a person be interrupted in a song or in repeating anything by rote, he is generally forced to go back to recover the habitual train of thought; so P. Huber found it was with a caterpillar, which makes a very complicated hammock. For if he took a caterpillar which had completed its hammock up to, say, the sixth stage of construction, and put it into a hammock completed up only to the third stage, the caterpillar simply re-performed the fourth, fifth, and sixth stages of construction. If, however, a caterpillar were taken out of a hammock made up, for instance, to the third stage, and were put into one finished up to the sixth stage, so that much of its work was already done for it, far from deriving any benefit from this, it was much embarrassed, and in order to complete its hammock, seemed forced to start from the third stage, where it had left off, and thus tried to complete the already finished work."

I see I must have unconsciously taken my first chapter from this passage, but it is immaterial. I owe Mr. Darwin much more than this. I owe it to him that I believe in evolution at all. I owe him for almost all the facts which have led me to differ from him, and which I feel absolutely safe in taking for granted, if he has advanced them. Nevertheless, I believe that the conclusion arrived at in the passage which I will next quote is a mistaken one, and that not a little only, but fundamentally. I shall therefore venture to dispute it.

The passage runs:-

"If we suppose any habitual action to become inherited—and it can be shown that this does sometimes happen—then the resemblance between what originally was a habit and an instinct becomes so close as not to be distinguished. . . . *But it would be a serious error to suppose that the greater number of instincts have been acquired by habit in one generation, and then transmitted by inheritance to succeeding generations. It can be clearly shown that the most wonderful instincts with which we are acquainted—namely, those of the hive-bee and of many ants, could not possibly have been acquired by habit.*" ("Origin of Species," p. 206, ed. 1876.) The italics in this passage are mine.

No difficulty is opposed to my view (as I call it, for the sake of brevity) by such an instinct as that of ants to milk aphids. Such instincts may be supposed to have been acquired in much the same way as the instinct of a farmer to keep a cow. Accidental discovery of the fact that the excretion was good, with "a little dose of judgement or reason" from time to time appearing in an exceptionally clever ant, and by him communicated to his fellows, till the habit was so confirmed as to be capable of transmission in full unself-consciousness (if indeed the instinct be unself-conscious in this case), would, I think, explain this as readily as the slow and gradual accumulations of instincts which had never passed through the intelligent and self-conscious stage, but had always prompted action without any idea of a why or a wherefore on the part of the creature itself.

For it must be remembered, as I am afraid I have already perhaps too often said, that even when we have got a slight variation of instinct, due to some cause which we know nothing about, but which I will not even for a moment call "spontaneous"—a word that should be cut out of every dictionary, or in some way branded as perhaps the most misleading in the language—we cannot see how it comes to be repeated in successive generations, so as to be capable of being acted upon by "natural selection" and accumulated, unless it be also capable of being remembered by the offspring of the varying creature. It may be answered that we cannot know anything about this, but that "like father like son" is an ultimate fact in nature. I can only answer that I never observe any "like father like son" without the son's both having had every opportunity of remembering, and showing every symptom of having remembered, in which case I decline to go further than memory (whatever memory may be) as the cause of the phenomenon.

But besides inheritance, teaching must be admitted as a means of at any rate modifying an instinct. We observe this in our own case; and we know that animals have great powers of communicating their ideas to one another, though their manner of doing this is as incomprehensible by us as a plant's knowledge of chemistry, or the manner in which an amba makes its test, or a spider its web, without having gone through a long course of mathematics. I think most readers will allow that our early training and the theological systems of the last eighteen hundred years are likely to have made us involuntarily under-estimate the powers of animals low in the scale of life, both as regards intelligence and the power of communicating their ideas to one another; but even now we admit that ants have great powers in this respect.

A habit, however, which is taught to the young or each successive generation, by older members of the community who have themselves received it by instruction, should surely rank as an inherited habit, and be considered as due to memory, though personal teaching be necessary to complete the inheritance.

An objection suggests itself that if such a habit as the flight of birds, which seems to require a little personal supervision and instruction before it is acquired perfectly, were really due to memory, the need of instruction would after a time cease, inasmuch as the creature would remember its past method of procedure, and would thus come to need no more teaching. The answer lies in the fact, that if a creature gets to depend upon teaching and personal help for any matter, its memory will make it look for such help on each repetition of the action; so we see that no man's memory will exert itself much until he is thrown upon memory as his only resource. We may read a page of a book a hundred times, but we do not remember it by heart unless we have either cultivated our powers of learning to repeat, or have taken pains to learn this particular page.

And whether we read from a book, or whether we repeat by heart, the repetition is still due to memory; only in the one case the memory is exerted to recall something which one saw only half a second ago, and in the other, to recall something not seen for a much longer period. So I imagine an instinct or habit may be called an inherited habit, and assigned to memory, even though the memory dates, not from the performance of the action by the learner when he was actually part of the personality of the teacher, but rather from a performance witnessed by, or explained by the teacher to, the pupil at a period subsequent to birth. In either case the habit is inherited in the sense of being acquired in one generation, and transmitted with such modifications as genius and experience may have suggested.

Mr. Darwin would probably admit this without hesitation; when, therefore, he says that certain instincts could not possibly have been acquired by habit, he must mean that they could not, under the circumstances, have been remembered by the pupil in the person of the teacher, and that it would be a serious error to suppose that the greater number of instincts can be thus remembered. To which I assent readily so far as that it is difficult (though not impossible) to see how some of the most wonderful instincts of neuter ants and bees can be due to the fact that the neuter ant or bee was ever in part, or in some respects, another neuter ant or bee in a previous generation. At the same time I maintain that this does not militate against the supposition that both instinct and structure are in the main due to memory. For the power of receiving any communication, and acting on it, is due to memory; and the neuter ant or bee may have received its lesson from another neuter ant or bee, who had it from another and modified it; and so back and back, till the foundation of the habit is reached, and is found to present little more than the faintest family likeness to its more complex descendant. Surely Mr. Darwin cannot mean that it can be shewn that the wonderful instincts of neuter ants and bees cannot have been acquired either, as above, by instruction, or by some not immediately obvious form of inherited transmission, but that they must be due to the fact that the ant or bee is, as it were, such and such a machine, of which if you touch such and such a spring, you will get a corresponding action. If he does, he will find, so far as I can see, no escape from a position very similar to the one which I put into the mouth of the first of the two professors, who dealt with the question of machinery in my earlier work, "Erewhon," and which I have since found that my great namesake made fun of in the following lines:-

. . . "They now begun
To spur their living engines on.
For as whipped tops and bandy'd balls,
The learned hold are animals:
So horses they affirm to be
Mere engines made by geometry,
And were invented first from engines
As Indian Britons were from Penguins."
- *Hudibras*, Canto ii. line 53, &c.

.

I can see, then, no difficulty in the development of the ordinary so-called instincts, whether of ants or bees, or the cuckoo, or any other animal, on the supposition that they were, for the most part, intelligently acquired with more or less labour, as the case may be, in much the same way as we see any art or science now in process of acquisition among ourselves, but were ultimately remembered by offspring, or communicated to it. When the limits of the race's capacity had been attained (and most races seem to have their limits, unsatisfactory though the expression may very fairly be considered), or when the creature had got into a condition, so to speak, of equilibrium with its surroundings, there would be no new development of instincts, and the old ones would cease to be improved, inasmuch as there would be no more reasoning or difference of opinion concerning them. The race, therefore, or species would remain in *statu quo* till either domesticated, and so brought into contact with new ideas and placed in changed conditions, or put under such pressure, in a wild state, as should force it to further invention, or extinguish it if incapable of rising to the occasion. That instinct and structure may be acquired by practice in one or more generations, and remembered in succeeding ones, is admitted by Mr. Darwin, for he allows ("Origin of Species," p. 206) that habitual action does sometimes become inherited, and, though he does not seem to conceive of such action as due to memory, yet it is inconceivable how it is inherited, if not as the result of memory.

It must be admitted, however, that when we come to consider the structures as well as the instincts of some of the neuter insects, our difficulties seem greatly increased. The neuter hive-bees have a cavity in their thighs in which to keep the wax, which it is their business to collect; but the drones and queen, which alone bear offspring, collect no wax, and therefore neither want, nor have, any such cavity. The neuter bees are also, if I understand rightly, furnished with a proboscis or trunk for extracting honey from flowers, whereas the fertile bees, who gather no honey, have no such proboscis. Imagine, if the reader will, that the neuter bees differ still more widely from the fertile ones; how, then, can they in any sense be said to derive organs from their parents, which not one of their parents for millions of generations has ever had? How, again, can it be supposed that they transmit these organs to the future neuter members of the community when they are perfectly sterile?

One can understand that the young neuter bee might be taught to make a hexagonal cell (though I have not found that any one has seen the lesson being given) inasmuch as it does not make the cell till after birth, and till after it has seen other neuter bees who might tell it much in, *quâ* us, a very little time; but we can hardly understand its growing a proboscis before it could possibly want it, or preparing a cavity in its thigh, to have it ready to put wax into, when none of its predecessors had ever done so, by supposing oral communication, during the larvahood. Nevertheless, it must not be forgotten that bees seem to know secrets about reproduction, which utterly baffle ourselves; for example, the queen bee appears to know how to deposit male or female, eggs at will; and this is a matter of almost inconceivable sociological importance, denoting a corresponding amount of sociological and physiological knowledge generally. It should not, then, surprise us if the race should possess other secrets, whose working we are unable to follow, or even detect at all.

Sydney Smith, indeed, writes:-

"The warmest admirers of honey, and the greatest friends to bees, will never, I presume, contend that the young swarm, who begin making honey three or four months after they are born, and immediately construct these mathematical cells, should have gained their geometrical knowledge as we gain ours, and in three months' time outstrip Mr. Maclaurin in mathematics as much as they did in making honey. It would take a senior wrangler at Cambridge ten hours a day for three years together to know enough mathematics for the calculation of these problems, with which not only every queen bee, but every undergraduate grub, is acquainted the moment it is born." This last statement may be a little too strong, but it will at once occur to the reader, that as we know the bees *do* surpass Mr. Maclaurin in the power of making honey, they may also surpass him in capacity for those branches of mathematics with which it has been their business to be conversant during many millions of years, and also in knowledge of physiology and psychology in so far as the knowledge bears upon the interests of their own community.

We know that the larva which develops into a neuter bee, and that again which in time becomes a queen bee, are the same kind of larva to start with; and that if you give one of these larvæ the food and treatment which all its foremothers have been accustomed to, it will turn out with all the structure and instincts of its foremothers—and that it only fails to do this because it has been fed, and otherwise treated, in such a manner as not one of its foremothers was ever yet fed or treated. So far, this is exactly what we should expect, on the view that structure and instinct are alike mainly due to memory, or to medicined memory. Give the larva a fair chance of knowing where it is, and it shows that it remembers by doing exactly what it did before. Give it a different kind of food and house, and it cannot be expected to be anything else than puzzled. It remembers a great deal. It comes out a bee, and nothing but a bee; but it is an aborted bee; it is, in fact, mutilated before birth instead of after—with instinct, as well as growth, correlated to its abortion, as we see happens frequently in the case of animals a good deal higher than bees that have been mutilated at a stage much later than that at which the abortion of neuter bees commences.

The larvæ being similar to start with, and being similarly mutilated - i.e., by change of food and dwelling, will naturally exhibit much similarity of instinct and structure on arriving at maturity. When driven from their usual course, they must take *some* new course or die. There is nothing strange in the fact that similar beings puzzled similarly should take a similar line of action. I grant, however, that it is hard to see how change of food and treatment can puzzle an insect into such "complex growth" as that it should make a cavity in its thigh, grow an invaluable proboscis, and betray a practical knowledge of difficult mathematical problems.

But it must be remembered that the memory of having been queen bees and drones—which is all that according to my supposition the larvæ can remember, (on a first view of the case), in their own proper persons—would nevertheless carry with it a potential recollection of all the social arrangements of the hive. They would thus potentially remember that the mass of the bees were always neuter bees; they would remember potentially the habits of these bees, so far as drones and queens know anything about them; and this may be supposed to be a very thorough acquaintance; in like manner, and with the same limitation, they would know from the very moment that they left the queen's body that neuter bees had a proboscis to gather honey with, and cavities in their thighs to put wax into, and that cells were to be made with certain angles—for surely it is not crediting the queen with more knowledge than she is likely to possess, if we suppose her to have a fair acquaintance with the phenomena of wax and cells generally, even though she does not make any; they would know (while still larvæ— and earlier) the kind of cells into which neuter bees were commonly put, and the kind of treatment they commonly received—they might therefore, as eggs—immediately on finding their recollection driven from its usual course, so that they must either find some other course, or die—know that they were being treated as neuter bees are treated, and that they were expected to develop into neuter bees accordingly; they might know all this, and a great deal more into the bargain, inasmuch as even before being actually deposited as eggs they would know and remember potentially, but unconsciously, all that their parents knew and remembered intensely. Is it, then, astonishing that they should adapt themselves so readily to the position which they know it is for the social welfare of the community, and hence of themselves, that they should occupy, and that they should know that they will want a cavity in their thighs and a proboscis, and hence make such implements out of their protoplasm as readily as they make their wings?

I admit that, under normal treatment, none of the above-mentioned potential memories would be kindled into such a state of activity that action would follow upon them, until the creature had attained a more or less similar condition to that in which its parent was when these memories were active within its mind: but the essence of the matter is, that these larvæ have been treated *abnormally*, so that if they do not die, there is nothing for it but that they must vary. One cannot argue from the normal to the abnormal. It would not, then, be strange if the potential memories should (owing to the margin for premature or tardy development which association admits) serve to give the puzzled larvæ a hint as to the course which they had better take, or that, at any rate, it should greatly supplement the instruction of the "nurse" bees themselves by rendering the larvæ so, as it were, inflammable on this point, that a spark should set them in a blaze. Abortion is generally premature. Thus the scars referred to in the last chapter as having appeared on the children of men who had been correspondingly wounded, should not, under normal circumstances, have appeared in the offspring till the children had got fairly near the same condition generally as that in which their fathers were when they were wounded, and even then, normally, there should have been an instrument to wound them, much as their fathers had been wounded. Association, however, does not always stick to the letter of its bond.

The line, again, might certainly be taken that the difference in structure and instincts between neuter and fertile bees is due to the specific effects of certain food and treatment; yet, though one would be sorry to set limits to the convertibility of food and genius, it seems hard to believe that there can be any untutored food which should teach a bee to make a hexagonal cell as soon as it was born, or which, before it was born, should teach it to prepare such structures as it would require in after life. If, then, food be considered as a direct agent in causing the structures and instinct, and not an indirect agent, merely indicating to the larva itself that it is to make itself after the fashion of neuter bees, then we should bear in mind that, at any rate, it has been leavened and prepared in the stomachs of those neuter bees into which the larva is now expected to develop itself, and may thus have in it more true germinative matter—gemmules, in fact— than is commonly supposed. Food, when sufficiently assimilated (the whole question turning upon what *is* "sufficiently"), becomes stored with all the experience and memories of the assimilating creature; corn becomes hen, and knows nothing but hen, when hen has eaten it. We know also that the neuter working-bees inject matter into the cell after the larva has been produced; nor would it seem harsh to suppose that though devoid of a reproductive system like that of their parents, they may yet be practically not so neuter as is commonly believed. One cannot say what gemmules of thigh and proboscis may not have got into the neutral bees' stomachs, if they assimilate their food sufficiently, and thus into the larva.

Mr. Darwin will be the first to admit that though a creature have no reproductive system, in any ordinary sense of the word, yet every unit or cell of its body may throw off gemmules which may be free to move over every part of the whole organism, and which "natural selection" might in time cause to stray into food which had been sufficiently prepared in the stomachs of the neuter bees.

I cannot say, then, precisely in what way, but I can see no reason for doubting that in some of the ways suggested above, or in some combination of them, the phenomena of the instincts of neuter ants and bees can be brought into the same category as the instincts and structure of fertile animals. At any rate, I see the great fact that when treated as they have been accustomed to be treated, these neuters act as though they remembered, and accordingly become queen bees; and that they only depart from their ancestral course on being treated in such fashion as their ancestors can never have remembered; also, that when they have been thrown off their accustomed line of thought and action, they only take that of their nurses, who have been about them from the moment of their being deposited as eggs by the queen bee, who have fed them from their own bodies, and between whom and them there may have been all manner of physical and mental communication, of which we know no more than we do of the power which enables a bee to find its way home after infinite shifting and turning among flowers, which no human powers could systematise so as to avoid confusion.

Or take it thus: We know that mutilation at an early age produces an effect upon the structure and instincts of cattle, sheep, and horses; and it might be presumed that if feasible at an earlier age, it would produce a still more marked effect. We observe that the effect produced is uniform, or nearly so. Suppose mutilation to produce a little more effect than it does, as we might easily do, if cattle, sheep, and horses had been for ages accustomed to a mutilated class living among them, which class had been always a caste apart, and had fed the young neuters from their own bodies, from an early embryonic stage onwards; would any one in this case dream of advancing the structure and instincts of this mutilated class against the doctrine that instinct is inherited habit? Or, if inclined to do this, would he not at once refrain, on remembering that the process of mutilation might be arrested, and the embryo be developed into an entire animal by simply treating it in the way to which all its ancestors had been accustomed? Surely he would not allow the difficulty (which I must admit in some measure to remain) to outweigh the evidence derivable from these very neuter insects themselves, as well as from such a vast number of other sources—all pointing in the direction of instinct as inherited habit. {5}

Lastly, it must be remembered that the instinct to make cells and honey is one which has no very great hold upon its possessors. Bees *can* make cells and honey, nor do they seem to have any very violent objection to doing so; but it is quite clear that there is nothing in their structure and instincts which urges them on to do these things for the mere love of doing them, as a hen is urged to sit upon a chalk stone, concerning which she probably is at heart utterly sceptical, rather than not sit at all. There is no honey and cell-making instinct so strong as the instinct to eat, if they are hungry, or to grow wings, and make themselves into bees at all. Like ourselves, so long as they can get plenty to eat and drink, they will do no work. Under these circumstances, not one drop of honey nor one particle of wax will they collect, except, I presume, to make cells for the rearing of their young.

Sydney Smith writes:-

"The most curious instance of a change of instinct is recorded by Darwin. The bees carried over to Barbadoes and the Western Isles ceased to lay up any honey after the first year, as they found it not useful to them. They found the weather so fine, and materials for making honey so plentiful, that they quitted their grave, prudent, and mercantile character, became exceedingly profligate and debauched, ate up their capital, resolved to work no more, and amused themselves by flying about the sugar-houses and stinging the blacks" (Lecture XVII. on Moral Philosophy). The ease, then, with which the honey-gathering and cell-making habits are relinquished, would seem to point strongly in the direction of their acquisition at a comparatively late period of development.

I have dealt with bees only, and not with ants, which would perhaps seem to present greater difficulty, inasmuch as in some families of these there are two, or even three, castes of neuters with well-marked and wide differences of structure and instinct; but I think the reader will agree with me that the ants are sufficiently covered by the bees, and that enough, therefore, has been said already. Mr. Darwin supposes that these modifications of structure and instinct have been effected by the accumulation of numerous slight, profitable, spontaneous variations on the part of the fertile parents, which has caused them (so, at least, I understand him) to lay this or that particular kind of egg, which should develop into a kind of bee or ant, with this or that particular instinct, which instinct is merely a co-ordination with structure, and in no way attributable to use or habit in preceding generations.

Even so, one cannot see that the habit of laying this particular kind of egg might not be due to use and memory in previous generations on the part of the fertile parents, "for the numerous slight spontaneous variations," on which "natural selection" is to work, must have had some cause than which none more reasonable than sense of need and experience presents itself; and there seems hardly any limit to what long-continued faith and desire, aided by intelligence, may be able to effect. But if sense of need and experience are denied, I see no escape from the view that machines are new species of life.

Mr. Darwin concludes: "I am surprised that no one has hitherto advanced this demonstrative case of neuter insects against the well-known doctrine of inherited habit as advanced by Lamarck" ("Natural Selection," p. 233, ed. 1876).

After reading this, one feels as though there was no more to be said. The well-known doctrine of inherited habit, as advanced by Lamarck, has indeed been long since so thoroughly exploded, that it is not worth while to go into an explanation of what it was, or to refute it in detail. Here, however, is an argument against it, which is so much better than anything advanced yet, that one is surprised it has never been made use of; so we will just advance it, as it were, to slay the slain, and pass on. Such, at least, is the effect which the paragraph above quoted produced upon myself, and would, I think, produce on the great majority of readers. When driven by the exigencies of my own position to examine the value of the demonstration more closely, I conclude, either that I have utterly failed to grasp Mr. Darwin's meaning, or that I have no less completely mistaken the value and bearing of the facts I have myself advanced in these few last pages. Failing this, my surprise is, not that "no one has hitherto advanced" the instincts of neuter insects as a demonstrative case against the doctrine of inherited habit, but rather that Mr. Darwin should have thought the case demonstrative; or again, when I remember that the neuter working bee is only an aborted queen, and may be turned back again into a queen, by giving it such treatment as it can alone be expected to remember—then I am surprised that the structure and instincts of neuter bees has never (if never) been brought forward in support of the doctrine of inherited habit as advanced by Lamarck, and against any theory which would rob such instincts of their foundation in intelligence, and of their connection with experience and memory.

As for the instinct to mutilate, that is as easily accounted for as any other inherited habit, whether of man to mutilate cattle, or of ants to make slaves, or of birds to make their nests. I can see no way of accounting for the existence of any one of these instincts, except on the supposition that they have arisen gradually, through perceptions of power and need on the part of the animal which exhibits them—these two perceptions advancing hand in hand from generation to generation, and being accumulated in time and in the common course of nature.

I have already sufficiently guarded against being supposed to maintain that very long before an instinct or structure was developed, the creature descried it in the far future, and made towards it. We do not observe this to be the manner of human progress. Our mechanical inventions, which, as I ventured to say in "Erewhon," through the mouth of the second professor, are really nothing but extra-corporaneous limbs—a wooden leg being nothing but a bad kind of flesh leg, and a flesh leg being only a much better kind of wooden leg than any creature could be expected to manufacture introspectively and consciously—our mechanical inventions have almost invariably grown up from small beginnings, and without any very distant foresight on the part of the inventors. When Watt perfected the steam engine, he did not, it seems, foresee the locomotive, much less would any one expect a savage to invent a steam engine. A child breathes automatically, because it has learnt to breathe little by little, and has now breathed for an incalculable length of time; but it cannot open oysters at all, nor even conceive the idea of opening oysters for two or three years after it is born, for the simple reason that this lesson is one which it is only beginning to learn. All I maintain is, that, give a child as many generations of practice in opening oysters as it has had in breathing or sucking, and it would on being born, turn to the oyster-knife no less naturally than to the breast. We observe that among certain families of men there has been a tendency to vary in the direction of the use and development of machinery; and that in a certain still smaller number of families, there seems to be an almost infinitely great capacity for varying and inventing still further, whether socially or mechanically; while other families, and perhaps the greater number, reach a certain point and stop; but we also observe that not even the most inventive races ever see very far ahead. I suppose the progress of plants and animals to be exactly analogous to this.

Mr. Darwin has always maintained that the effects of use and disuse are highly important in the development of structure, and if, as he has said, habits are sometimes inherited—then they should sometimes be important also in the development of instinct, or habit. But what does the development of an instinct or structure, or, indeed, any effect upon the organism produced by "use and disuse," imply? It implies an effect produced by a desire to do something for which the organism was not originally well adapted or sufficient, but for which it has come to be sufficient in consequence of the desire. The wish has been father to the power; but this again opens up the whole theory of Lamarck, that the development of organs has been due to the wants or desires of the animal in which the organ appears. So far as I can see, I am insisting on little more than this.

Once grant that a blacksmith's arm grows thicker through hammering iron, and you have an organ modified in accordance with a need or wish. Let the desire and the practice be remembered, and go on for long enough, and the slight alterations of the organ will be accumulated, until they are checked either by the creature's having got all that he cares about making serious further effort to obtain, or until his wants prove inconvenient to other creatures that are stronger than he, and he is hence brought to a standstill. Use and disuse, then, with me, and, as I gather also, with Lamarck, are the keys to the position, coupled, of course, with continued personality and memory. No sudden and striking changes would be effected, except that occasionally a blunder might prove a happy accident, as happens not unfrequently with painters, musicians, chemists, and inventors at the present day; or sometimes a creature, with exceptional powers of memory or reflection, would make his appearance in this race or in that. We all profit by our accidents as well as by our more cunning contrivances, so that analogy would point in the direction of thinking that many of the most happy thoughts in the animal and vegetable kingdom were originated much as certain discoveries that have been made by accident among ourselves. These would be originally blind variations, though even so, probably less blind than we think, if we could know the whole truth. When originated, they would be eagerly taken advantage of and improved upon by the animal in whom they appeared; but it cannot be supposed that they would be very far in advance of the last step gained, more than are those "flukes" which sometimes enable us to go so far beyond our own ordinary powers. For if they were, the animal would despair of repeating them. No creature hopes, or even wishes, for very much more than he has been accustomed to all his life, he and his family, and the others whom he can understand, around him. It has been well said that "enough" is always "a little more than one has." We do not try for things which we believe to be beyond our reach, hence one would expect that the fortunes, as it were, of animals should have been built up gradually. Our own riches grow with our desires and the pains we take in pursuit of them, and our desires vary and increase with our means of gratifying them; but unless with men of exceptional business aptitude, wealth grows gradually by the adding field to field and farm to farm; so with the limbs and instincts of animals; these are but the things they have made or bought with their money, or with money that has been left them by their forefathers, which, though it is neither silver nor gold, but faith and protoplasm only, is good money and capital notwithstanding.

I have already admitted that instinct may be modified by food or drugs, which may affect a structure or habit as powerfully as we see certain poisons affect the structure of plants by producing, as Mr. Darwin tells us, very complex galls upon their leaves. I do not, therefore, for a moment insist on habit as the sole cause of instinct. Every habit must have had its originating cause, and the causes which have started one habit will from time to time start or modify others; nor can I explain why some individuals of a race should be cleverer than others, any more than I can explain why they should exist at all; nevertheless, I observe it to be a fact that differences in intelligence and power of growth are universal in the individuals of all those races which we can best watch. I also most readily admit that the common course of nature would both cause many variations to arise independently of any desire on the part of the animal (much as we have lately seen that the moons of Mars were on the point of being discovered three hundred years ago, merely through Galileo sending to Kepler a Latin anagram which Kepler could not understand, and arranged into the line—"*Salve umbistineum geminatum Martia prolem,*" and interpreted to mean that Mars had two moons, whereas Galileo had meant to say "*Altissimum planetam tergeminum observavi,*" meaning that he had seen Saturn's ring), and would also preserve and accumulate such variations when they had arisen; but I can no more believe that the wonderful adaptation of structures to needs, which we see around us in such an infinite number of plants and animals, can have arisen without a perception of those needs on the part of the creature in whom the structure appears, than I can believe that the form of the dray-horse or greyhound—so well adapted both to the needs of the animal in his daily service to man, and to the desires of man, that the creature should do him this daily service—can have arisen without any desire on man's part to produce this particular structure, or without the inherited habit of performing the corresponding actions for man, on the part of the greyhound and dray-horse.

And I believe that this will be felt as reasonable by the great majority of my readers. I believe that nine fairly intelligent and observant men out of ten, if they were asked which they thought most likely to have been the main cause of the development of the various phases either of structure or instinct which we see around us, namely— sense of need, or even whim, and hence occasional discovery, helped by an occasional piece of good luck, communicated, it may be, and generally adopted, long practised, remembered by offspring, modified by changed surroundings, and accumulated in the course of time—or, the accumulation of small divergent, indefinite, and perfectly unintelligent variations, preserved through the survival of their possessor in the struggle for existence, and hence in time leading to wide differences from the original type—would answer in favour of the former alternative; and if for no other cause yet for this—that in the human race, which we are best able to watch, and between which and the lower animals no difference in kind will, I think, be supposed, but only in degree, we observe that progress must have an internal current setting in a definite direction, but whither we know not for very long beforehand; and that without such internal current there is stagnation. Our own progress— or variation—is due not to small, fortuitous inventions or modifications which have enabled their fortunate possessors to survive in times of difficulty, not, in fact, to strokes of luck (though these, of course, have had some effect—but not more, probably, than strokes of ill luck have counteracted) but to strokes of cunning—to a sense of need, and to study of the past and present which have given shrewd people a key with which to unlock the chambers of the future.

Further, Mr. Darwin himself says ("Plants and Animals under Domestication," ii. p. 237, ed. 1875):-

"But I think we must take a broader view and conclude that organic beings when subjected during several generations to any change whatever in their conditions tend to vary: *the kind of variation which ensues depending in most cases in a far higher degree on the nature or constitution of the being, than on the nature of the changed conditions .*" And this we observe in man. The history of a man prior to his birth is more important as far as his success or failure goes than his surroundings after birth, important though these may indeed be. The able man rises in spite of a thousand hindrances, the fool fails in spite of every advantage. "Natural selection," however, does not make either the able man or the fool. It only deals with him after other causes have made him, and would seem in the end to amount to little more than to a statement of the fact that when variations have arisen they will accumulate. One cannot look, as has already been said, for the origin of species in that part of the course of nature which settles the preservation or extinction of variations which have already arisen from some unknown cause, but one must look for it in the causes that have led to variation at all. These causes must get, as it were, behind the back of "natural selection," which is rather a shield and hindrance to our perception of our own ignorance than an explanation of what these causes are.

The remarks made above will apply equally to plants such as the misletoe and red clover. For the sake of brevity I will deal only with the misletoe, which seems to be the more striking case. Mr. Darwin writes:-

"Naturalists continually refer to external conditions, such as climate, food, &c., as the only possible cause of variation. In one limited sense, as we shall hereafter see, this may be true; but it is preposterous to attribute to mere external conditions, the structure, for instance, of the woodpecker, with its feet, tail, beak, and tongue, so admirably adapted to catch insects under the bark of trees. In the case of the misletoe, which draws its nourishment from certain trees, which has seeds that must be transported by certain birds, and which has flowers with separate sexes absolutely requiring the agency of certain insects to bring pollen from one flower to another, it is equally preposterous to account for the structure of this parasite with its relations to several distinct organic beings, by the effect of external conditions, or of habit, or of the volition of the plant itself" ("Natural Selection," p. 3, ed. 1876).

I cannot see this. To me it seems still more preposterous to account for it by the action of "natural selection" operating upon indefinite variations. It would be preposterous to suppose that a bird very different from a woodpecker should have had a conception of a woodpecker, and so by volition gradually grown towards it. So in like manner with the misletoe. Neither plant nor bird knew how far they were going, or saw more than a very little ahead as to the means of remedying this or that with which they were dissatisfied, or of getting this or that which they desired; but given perceptions at all, and thus a sense of needs and of the gratification of those needs, and thus hope and fear, and a sense of content and discontent—given also the lowest power of gratifying those needs—given also that some individuals have these powers in a higher degree than others—given also continued personality and memory over a vast extent of time—and the whole phenomena of species and genera resolve themselves into an illustration of the old proverb, that what is one man's meat is another man's poison. Life in its lowest form under the above conditions—and we cannot conceive of life at all without them—would be bound to vary, and to result after not so very many millions of years in the infinite forms and instincts which we see around us.

CHAPTER XIII—LAMARCK AND MR. DARWIN

It will have been seen that in the preceding pages the theory of evolution, as originally propounded by Lamarck, has been more than once supported, as against the later theory concerning it put forward by Mr. Darwin, and now generally accepted.

It is not possible for me, within the limits at my command, to do anything like justice to the arguments that may be brought forward in favour of either of these two theories. Mr. Darwin's books are at the command of every one; and so much has been discovered since Lamarck's day, that if he were living now, he would probably state his case very differently; I shall therefore content myself with a few brief remarks, which will hardly, however, aspire to the dignity of argument.

According to Mr. Darwin, differentiations of structure and instinct have mainly come about through the accumulation of small, fortuitous variations without intelligence or desire upon the part of the creature varying; modification, however, through desire and sense of need, is not denied entirely, inasmuch as considerable effect is ascribed by Mr. Darwin to use and disuse, which involves, as has been already said, the modification of a structure in accordance with the wishes of its possessor.

According to Lamarck, genera and species have been evolved, in the main, by exactly the same process as that by which human inventions and civilisations are now progressing; and this involves that intelligence, ingenuity, heroism, and all the elements of romance, should have had the main share in the development of every herb and living creature around us.

I take the following brief outline of the most important part of Lamarck's theory from vol. xxxvi. of the Naturalist's Library (Edinburgh, 1843):-

"The more simple bodies," says the editor, giving Lamarck's opinion without endorsing it, "are easily formed, and this being the case, it is easy to conceive how in the lapse of time animals of a more complex structure should be produced, *for it must be admitted as a fundamental law, that the production of a new organ in an animal body results from any new want or desire it may experience.* The first effort of a being just beginning to develop itself must be to procure subsistence, and hence in time there comes to be produced a stomach or alimentary cavity." (Thus we saw that the amba is in the habit of "extemporising" a stomach when it wants one.) "Other wants occasioned by circumstances will lead to other efforts, which in their turn will generate new organs."

Lamarck's wonderful conception was hampered by an unnecessary adjunct, namely, a belief in an inherent tendency towards progressive development in every low organism. He was thus driven to account for the presence of many very low and very ancient organisms at the present day, and fell back upon the theory, which is not yet supported by evidence, that such low forms are still continually coming into existence from inorganic matter. But there seems no necessity to suppose that all low forms should possess an inherent tendency towards progression. It would be enough that there should occasionally arise somewhat more gifted specimens of one or more original forms. These would vary, and the ball would be thus set rolling, while the less gifted would remain *in statu quo*, provided they were sufficiently gifted to escape extinction.

Nor do I gather that Lamarck insisted on continued personality and memory so as to account for heredity at all, and so as to see life as a single, or as at any rate, only a few, vast compound animals, but without the connecting organism between each component item in the whole creature, which is found in animals that are strictly called compound. Until continued personality and memory are connected with the idea of heredity, heredity of any kind is little more than a term for something which one does not understand. But there seems little *à priori* difficulty as regards Lamarck's main idea, now that Mr. Darwin has familiarised us with evolution, and made us feel what a vast array of facts can be brought forward in support of it.

Mr. Darwin tells us, in the preface to his last edition of the "Origin of Species," that Lamarck was partly led to his conclusions by the analogy of domestic productions. It is rather hard to say what these words imply; they may mean anything from a baby to an apple dumpling, but if they imply that Lamarck drew inspirations from the gradual development of the mechanical inventions of man, and from the progress of man's ideas, I would say that of all sources this would seem to be the safest and most fertile from which to draw.

Plants and animals under domestication are indeed a suggestive field for study, but machines are the manner in which man is varying at this moment. We know how our own minds work, and how our mechanical organisations—for, in all sober seriousness, this is what it comes to - have progressed hand in hand with our desires; sometimes the power a little ahead, and sometimes the desire; sometimes both combining to form an organ with almost infinite capacity for variation, and sometimes comparatively early reaching the limit of utmost development in respect of any new conception, and accordingly coming to a full stop; sometimes making leaps and bounds, and sometimes advancing sluggishly. Here we are behind the scenes, and can see how the whole thing works. We have man, the very animal which we can best understand, caught in the very act of variation, through his own needs, and not through the needs of others; the whole process is a natural one; the varying of a creature as much in a wild state as the ants and butterflies are wild. There is less occasion here for the continual "might be" and "may be," which we are compelled to put up with when dealing with plants and animals, of the workings of whose minds we can only obscurely judge. Also, there is more prospect of pecuniary profit attaching to the careful study of machinery than can be generally hoped for from the study of the lower animals; and though I admit that this consideration should not be carried too far, a great deal of very unnecessary suffering will be spared to the lower animals; for much that passes for natural history is little better than prying into other people's business, from no other motive than curiosity. I would, therefore, strongly advise the reader to use man, and the present races of man, and the growing inventions and conceptions of man, as his guide, if he would seek to form an independent judgement on the development of organic life. For all growth is only somebody making something.

Lamarck's theories fell into disrepute, partly because they were too startling to be capable of ready fusion with existing ideas; they were, in fact, too wide a cross for fertility; partly because they fell upon evil times, during the reaction that followed the French Revolution; partly because, unless I am mistaken, he did not sufficiently link on the experience of the race to that of the individual, nor perceive the importance of the principle that consciousness, memory, volition, intelligence, &c., vanish, or become latent, on becoming intense. He also appears to have mixed up matter with his system, which was either plainly wrong, or so incapable of proof as to enable people to laugh at him, and pooh-pooh him; but I believe it will come to be perceived, that he has received somewhat scant justice at the hands of his successors, and that his "crude theories," as they have been somewhat cheaply called, are far from having had their last say.

Returning to Mr. Darwin, we find, as we have already seen, that it is hard to say exactly how much Mr. Darwin differs from Lamarck, and how much he agrees with him. Mr. Darwin has always maintained that use and disuse are highly important, and this implies that the effect produced on the parent should be remembered by the offspring, in the same way as the memory of a wound is transmitted by one set of cells to succeeding ones, who long repeat the scar, though it may fade finally away. Also, after dealing with the manner in which one eye of a young flat-fish travels round the head till both eyes are on the same side of the fish, he gives ("Natural Selection," p. 188, ed. 1875) an instance of a structure "which apparently owes its origin exclusively to use or habit." He refers to the tail of some American monkeys "which has been converted into a wonderfully perfect prehensile organ, and serves as a fifth hand. A reviewer," he continues, . . . "remarks on this structure—'It is impossible to believe that in any number of ages the first slight incipient tendency to grasp, could preserve the lives of the individuals possessing it, or favour their chance of having and of rearing offspring.' But there is no necessity for any such belief. Habit, and this almost implies that some benefit, great or small, is thus derived, would in all probability suffice for the work." If, then, habit can do this—and it is no small thing to develop a wonderfully perfect prehensile organ which can serve as a fifth hand— how much more may not habit do, even though unaided, as Mr. Darwin supposes to have been the case in this instance, by "natural selection"? After attributing many of the structural and instinctive differences of plants and animals to the effects of use—as we may plainly do with Mr. Darwin's own consent—after attributing a good deal more to unknown causes, and a good deal to changed conditions, which are bound, if at all important, to result either in sterility or variation—how much of the work of originating species is left for natural selection?—which, as Mr. Darwin admits ("Natural Selection," p. 63, ed. 1876), does not *induce variability*, but "implies only the preservation of *such variations as arise, and are beneficial to the being under its conditions of life?*" An important part assuredly, and one which we can never sufficiently thank Mr. Darwin for having put so forcibly before us, but an indirect part only, like the part played by time and space, and not, I think, the one which Mr. Darwin would assign to it.

Mr. Darwin himself has admitted that in the earlier editions of his "Origin of Species" he "underrated, as it now seems probable, the frequency and importance of modifications due to spontaneous variability." And this involves the having over-rated the action of "natural selection" as an agent in the evolution of species. But one gathers that he still believes the accumulation of small and fortuitous variations through the agency of "natural selection" to be the main cause of the present divergencies of structure and instinct. I do not, however, think that Mr. Darwin is clear about his own meaning. I think the prominence given to "natural selection" in connection with the "origin of species" has led him, in spite of himself, and in spite of his being on his guard (as is clearly shown by the paragraph on page 63 "Natural Selection," above referred to), to regard "natural selection" as in some way accounting for variation, just as the use of the dangerous word "spontaneous,"—though he is so often on his guard against it, and so frequently prefaces it with the words "so-called,"— would seem to have led him into very serious confusion of thought in the passage quoted at the beginning of this paragraph.

For after saying that he had underrated "the frequency and importance of modifications due to spontaneous variability," he continues, "but it is impossible to attribute to this cause the innumerable structures which are so well adapted to the habits of life of each species." That is to say, it is impossible to attribute these innumerable structures to spontaneous variability.

What *is* spontaneous variability?

Clearly, from his preceding paragraph, Mr. Darwin means only "so-called spontaneous variations," such as "the appearance of a moss-rose on a common rose, or of a nectarine on a peach-tree," which he gives as good examples of so-called spontaneous variation.

And these variations are, after all, due to causes, but to unknown causes; spontaneous variation being, in fact, but another name for variation due to causes which we know nothing about, but in no possible sense a *cause of variation*. So that when we come to put clearly before our minds exactly what the sentence we are considering amounts to, it comes to this: that it is impossible to attribute the innumerable structures which are so well adapted to the habits of life of each species to *unknown causes*.

"I can no more believe in *this*," continues Mr. Darwin, "than that the well-adapted form of a race-horse or greyhound, which, before the principle of selection by man was well understood, excited so much surprise in the minds of the older naturalists, can *thus* be explained" ("Natural Selection," p. 171, ed. 1876).

Or, in other words, "I can no more believe that the well-adapted structures of species are due to unknown causes, than I can believe that the well-adapted form of a race-horse can be explained by being attributed to unknown causes.

I have puzzled over this paragraph for several hours with the sincerest desire to get at the precise idea which underlies it, but the more I have studied it the more convinced I am that it does not contain, or at any rate convey, any clear or definite idea at all. If I thought it was a mere slip, I should not call attention to it; this book will probably have slips enough of its own without introducing those of a great man unnecessarily; but I submit that it is necessary to call attention to it here, inasmuch as it is impossible to believe that after years of reflection upon his subject, Mr. Darwin should have written as above, especially in such a place, if his mind was really clear about his own position. Immediately after the admission of a certain amount of miscalculation, there comes a more or less exculpatory sentence which sounds so right that ninety-nine people out of a hundred would walk through it, unless led by some exigency of their own position to examine it closely but which yet upon examination proves to be as nearly meaningless as a sentence can be.

The weak point in Mr. Darwin's theory would seem to be a deficiency, so to speak, of motive power to originate and direct the variations which time is to accumulate. It deals admirably with the accumulation of variations in creatures already varying, but it does not provide a sufficient number of sufficiently important variations to be accumulated. Given the motive power which Lamarck suggested, and Mr. Darwin's mechanism would appear (with the help of memory, as bearing upon reproduction, of continued personality, and hence of inherited habit, and of the vanishing tendency of consciousness) to work with perfect ease. Mr. Darwin has made us all feel that in some way or other variations *are accumulated*, and that evolution is the true solution of the present widely different structures around us, whereas, before he wrote, hardly any one believed this. However we may differ from him in detail, the present general acceptance of evolution must remain as his work, and a more valuable work can hardly be imagined. Nevertheless, I cannot think that "natural selection," working upon small, fortuitous, indefinite, unintelligent variations, would produce the results we see around us. One wants something that will give a more definite aim to variations, and hence, at times, cause bolder leaps in advance. One cannot but doubt whether so many plants and animals would be being so continually saved "by the skin of their teeth," as must be so saved if the variations from which genera ultimately arise are as small in their commencement and at each successive stage as Mr. Darwin seems to believe. God—to use the language of the Bible—is not extreme to mark what is done amiss, whether with plant or beast or man; on the other hand, when towers of Siloam fall, they fall on the just as well as the unjust.

One feels, on considering Mr. Darwin's position, that if it be admitted that there is in the lowest creature a power to vary, no matter how small, one has got in this power as near the "origin of species" as one can ever hope to get. For no one professes to account for the origin of life; but if a creature with a power to vary reproduces itself at all, it must reproduce another creature *which shall also have the power to vary*; so that, given time and space enough, there is no knowing where such a creature could or would stop.

If the primordial cell had been only capable of reproducing itself once, there would have followed a single line of descendants, the chain of which might at any moment have been broken by casualty. Doubtless the millionth repetition would have differed very materially from the original— as widely, perhaps, as we differ from the primordial cell; but it would only have differed by addition, and could no more in any generation resume its latest development without having passed through the initial stage of being what its first forefather was, and doing what its first forefather did, and without going through all or a sufficient number of the steps whereby it had reached its latest differentiation, than water can rise above its own level.

The very idea, then, of reproduction involves, unless I am mistaken, that, no matter how much the creature reproducing itself may gain in power and versatility, it must still always begin *with itself again* in each generation. The primordial cell being capable of reproducing itself not only once, but many times over, each of the creatures which it produces must be similarly gifted; hence the geometrical ratio of increase and the existing divergence of type. In each generation it will pass rapidly and unconsciously through all the earlier stages of which there has been infinite experience, and for which the conditions are reproduced with sufficient similarity to cause no failure of memory or hesitation; but in each generation, when it comes to the part in which the course is not so clear, it will become conscious; still, however, where the course is plain, as in breathing, digesting, &c., retaining unconsciousness. Thus organs which present all the appearance of being designed—as, for example, the tip for its beak prepared by the embryo chicken—would be prepared in the end, as it were, by rote, and without sense of design, though none the less owing their origin to design.

The question is not concerning evolution, but as to the main cause which has led to evolution in such and such shapes. To me it seems that the "Origin of Variation," whatever it is, is the only true "Origin of Species," and that this must, as Lamarck insisted, be looked for in the needs and experiences of the creatures varying. Unless we can explain the origin of variations, we are met by the unexplained *at every step* in the progress of a creature from its original homogeneous condition to its differentiation, we will say, as an elephant; so that to say that an elephant has become an elephant through the accumulation of a vast number of small, fortuitous, but unexplained, variations in some lower creatures, is really to say that it has become an elephant owing to a series of causes about which we know nothing whatever, or, in other words, that one does not know how it came to be an elephant. But to say that an elephant has become an elephant owing to a series of variations, nine-tenths of which were caused by the wishes of the creature or creatures from which the elephant is descended—this is to offer a reason, and definitely put the insoluble one step further back. The question will then turn upon the sufficiency of the reason—that is to say, whether the hypothesis is borne out by facts.

The effects of competition would, of course, have an extremely important effect upon any creature, in the same way as any other condition of nature under which it lived, must affect its sense of need and its opinions generally. The results of competition would be, as it were, the decisions of an arbiter settling the question whether such and such variation was really to the animal's advantage or not—a matter on which the animal will, on the whole, have formed a pretty fair judgement for itself. *Undoubtedly the past decisions of such an arbiter would affect the conduct of the creature,* which would have doubtless had its shortcomings and blunders, and would amend them. The creature would shape its course according to its experience of the common course of events, but it would be continually trying and often successfully, to evade the law by all manner of sharp practice. New precedents would thus arise, so that the law would shift with time and circumstances; but the law would not otherwise direct the channels into which life would flow, than as laws, whether natural or artificial, have affected the development of the widely differing trades and professions among mankind. These have had their origin rather in the needs and experiences of mankind than in any laws.

To put much the same as the above in different words. Assume that small favourable variations are preserved more commonly, in proportion to their numbers, than is perhaps the case, and assume that considerable variations occur more rarely than they probably do occur, how account for any variation at all? "Natural selection" cannot *create* the smallest variation unless it acts through perception of its mode of operation, recognised inarticulately, but none the less clearly, by the creature varying. "Natural selection" operates on what it finds, and not on what it has made. Animals that have been wise and lucky live longer and breed more than others less wise and lucky. Assuredly. The wise and lucky animals transmit their wisdom and luck. Assuredly. They add to their powers, and diverge into widely different directions. Assuredly. What is the cause of this? Surely the fact that they were capable of feeling needs, and that they differed in their needs and manner of gratifying them, and that they continued to live in successive generations, rather than the fact that when lucky and wise they thrived and bred more descendants. This last is an accessory hardly less important for the *development* of species than the fact of the continuation of life at all; but it is an accessory of much the same kind as this, for if animals continue to live at all, they must live *in some way*, and will find that there are good ways and bad ways of living. An animal which discovers the good way will gradually develop further powers, and so species will get further and further apart; but the origin of this is to be looked for, not in the power which decides whether this or that way was good, but in the cause which determines the creature, consciously or unconsciously, to try this or that way.

But Mr. Darwin might say that this is not a fair way of stating the issue. He might say, "You beg the question; you assume that there is an inherent tendency in animals towards progressive development, whereas I say that there is no good evidence of any such tendency. I maintain that the differences that have from time to time arisen have come about mainly from causes so far beyond our ken, that we can only call them spontaneous; and if so, natural selection which you must allow to have at any rate played an important part in the *accumulation* of variations, must also be allowed to be the nearest thing to the cause of Specific differences, which we are able to arrive at."

Thus he writes ("Natural Selection," p. 176, ed. 1876): "Although we have no good evidence of the existence in organic beings of a tendency towards progressive development, yet this necessarily follows, as I have attempted to show in the fourth chapter, through the continued action of natural selection." Mr. Darwin does not say that organic beings have no tendency to vary at all, but only that there is no good evidence that they have a tendency to progressive development, which, I take it, means, to see an ideal a long way off, and very different to their present selves, which ideal they think will suit them, and towards which they accordingly make. I would admit this as contrary to all experience. I doubt whether plants and animals have any *innate tendency to vary* at all, being led to question this by gathering from "Plants and Animals under Domestication" that this is Mr. Darwin's own opinion. I am inclined rather to think that they have only an innate *power to vary* slightly, in accordance with changed conditions, and an innate capability of being affected both in structure and instinct, by causes similar to those which we observe to affect ourselves. But however this may be, they do vary somewhat, and unless they did, they would not in time have come to be so widely different from each other as they now are. The question is as to the origin and character of these variations.

We say they mainly originate in a creature through a sense of its needs, and vary through the varying surroundings which will cause those needs to vary, and through the opening up of new desires in many creatures, as the consequence of the gratification of old ones; they depend greatly on differences of individual capacity and temperament; they are communicated, and in the course of time transmitted, as what we call hereditary habits or structures, though these are only, in truth, intense and epitomised memories of how certain creatures liked to deal with protoplasm. The question whether this or that is really good or ill, is settled, as the proof of the pudding by the eating thereof, *i.e.*, by the rigorous competitive examinations through which most living organisms must pass. Mr. Darwin says that there is no good evidence in support of any great principle, or tendency on the part of the creature itself, which would steer variation, as it were, and keep its head straight, but that the most marvellous adaptations of structures to needs are simply the result of small and blind variations, accumulated by the operation of "natural selection," which is thus the main cause of the origin of species.

Enough has perhaps already been said to make the reader feel that the question wants reopening; I shall, therefore, here only remark that we may assume no fundamental difference as regards intelligence, memory, and sense of needs to exist between man and the lowest animals, and that in man we do distinctly see a tendency towards progressive development, operating through his power of profiting by and transmitting his experience, but operating in directions which man cannot foresee for any long distance. We also see this in many of the higher animals under domestication, as with horses which have learnt to canter and dogs which point; more especially we observe it along the line of latest development, where equilibrium of settled convictions has not yet been fully attained. One neither finds nor expects much *a priori* knowledge, whether in man or beast; but one does find some little in the beginnings of, and throughout the development of, every habit, at the commencement of which, and on every successive improvement in which, deductive and inductive methods are, as it were, fused. Thus the effect, where we can best watch its causes, seems mainly produced by a desire for a definite object—in some cases a serious and sensible desire, in others an idle one, in others, again, a mistaken one; and sometimes by a blunder which, in the hands of an otherwise able creature, has turned up trumps. In wild animals and plants the divergences have been accumulated, if they answered to the prolonged desires of the creature itself, and if these desires were to its true ultimate good; with plants or animals under domestication they have been accumulated if they answered a little to the original wishes of the creature, and much, to the wishes of man. As long as man continued to like them, they would be advantageous to the creature; when he tired of them, they would be disadvantageous to it, and would accumulate no longer. Surely the results produced in the adaptation of structure to need among many plants and insects are better accounted for on this, which I suppose to be Lamarck's view, namely, by supposing that what goes on amongst ourselves has gone on amongst all creatures, than by supposing that these adaptations are the results of perfectly blind and unintelligent variations.

Let me give two examples of such adaptations, taken from Mr. St. George Mivart's "Genesis of Species," to which work I would wish particularly to call the reader's attention. He should also read Mr. Darwin's answers to Mr. Mivart (p. 176, "Natural Selection," ed. 1876, and onwards).

Mr. Mivart writes:-

"Some insects which imitate leaves extend the imitation even to the very injuries on those leaves made by the attacks of insects or fungi. Thus speaking of the walking-stick insects, Mr. Wallace says, 'One of these creatures obtained by myself in Borneo (*ceroxylus laceratus*) was covered over with foliaceous excrescences of a clear olive green colour, so as exactly to resemble a stick grown over by a creeping moss or jungermannia. The Dyak who brought it me assured me it was grown over with moss, though alive, and it was only after a most minute examination that I could convince myself it was not so.' Again, as to the leaf butterfly, he says, 'We come to a still more extraordinary part of the imitation, for we find representations of leaves in every stage of decay, variously blotched, and mildewed, and pierced with holes, and in many cases irregularly covered with powdery black dots, gathered into patches and spots so closely resembling the various kinds of minute fungi that grow on dead leaves, that it is impossible to avoid thinking at first sight that the butterflies themselves have been attacked by real fungi.'"

I can no more believe that these artificial fungi in which the moth arrays itself are due to the accumulation of minute, perfectly blind, and unintelligent variations, than I can believe that the artificial flowers which a woman wears in her hat can have got there without design; or that a detective puts on plain clothes without the slightest intention of making his victim think that he is not a policeman.

Again Mr. Mivart writes:-

"In the work just referred to ('The Fertilisation of Orchids'), Mr. Darwin gives a series of the most wonderful and minute contrivances, by which the visits of insects are utilised for the fertilisation of orchids—structures so wonderful that nothing could well be more so, except the attribution of their origin to minute, fortuitous, and indefinite variations.

"The instances are too numerous and too long to quote, but in his 'Origin of Species' he describes two which must not be passed over. In one (*coryanthes*) the orchid has its lower lip enlarged into a bucket, above which stand two water-secreting horns. These latter replenish the bucket, from which, when half-filled, the water overflows by a spout on one side. Bees visiting the flower fall into the bucket and crawl out at the spout. By the peculiar arrangement of the parts of the flower, the first bee which does so, carries away the pollen mass glued to his back, and then when he has his next involuntary bath in another flower, as he crawls out, the pollen attached to him comes in contact with the stigma of that second flower and fertilises it. In the other example (*catasetum*), when a bee gnaws a certain part of the flower, he inevitably touches a long delicate projection which Mr. Darwin calls the 'antenna.' 'This antenna transmits a vibration to a membrane which is instantly ruptured; this sets free a spring by which the pollen mass is shot forth like an arrow in the right direction, and adheres by its viscid extremity to the back of the bee'" ("Genesis of Species," p. 63).

No one can tell a story so charmingly as Mr. Darwin, but I can no more believe that all this has come about without design on the part of the orchid, and a gradual perception of the advantages it is able to take over the bee, and a righteous determination to enjoy them, than I can believe that a mousetrap or a steam-engine is the result of the accumulation of blind minute fortuitous variations in a creature called man, which creature has never wanted either mousetraps or steam-engines, but has had a sort of promiscuous tendency to make them, and was benefited by making them, so that those of the race who had a tendency to make them survived and left issue, which issue would thus naturally tend to make more mousetraps and more steam-engines.

Pursuing this idea still further, can we for a moment believe that these additions to our limbs—for this is what they are—have mainly come about through the occasional birth of individuals, who, without design on their own parts, nevertheless made them better or worse, and who, accordingly, either survived and transmitted their improvement, or perished, they and their incapacity together?

When I can believe in this, then—and not till then—can I believe in an origin of species which does not resolve itself mainly into sense of need, faith, intelligence, and memory. Then, and not till then, can I believe that such organs as the eye and ear can have arisen in any other way than as the result of that kind of mental ingenuity, and of moral as well as physical capacity, without which, till then, I should have considered such an invention as the steam-engine to be impossible.

CHAPTER XIV—MR. MIVART AND MR. DARWIN

"A distinguished zoologist, Mr. St. George Mivart," writes Mr. Darwin, "has recently collected all the objections which have ever been advanced by myself and others against the theory of natural selection, as propounded by Mr. Wallace and myself, and has illustrated them with admirable art and force ("Natural Selection," p. 176, ed. 1876). I have already referred the reader to Mr. Mivart's work, but quote the above passage as showing that Mr. Mivart will not, probably, be found to have left much unsaid that would appear to make against Mr. Darwin's theory. It is incumbent upon me both to see how far Mr. Mivart's objections are weighty as against Mr. Darwin, and also whether or not they tell with equal force against the view which I am myself advocating. I will therefore touch briefly upon the most important of them, with the purpose of showing that they are serious as against the doctrine that small fortuitous variations are the origin of species, but that they have no force against evolution as guided by intelligence and memory.

But before doing this, I would demur to the words used by Mr. Darwin, and just quoted above, namely, "the theory of natural selection." I imagine that I see in them the fallacy which I believe to run through almost all Mr. Darwin's work, namely, that "natural selection" is a theory (if, indeed, it can be a theory at all), in some way accounting for the origin of variation, and so of species— "natural selection," as we have already seen, being unable to "induce variability," and being only able to accumulate what—on the occasion of each successive variation, and so during the whole process— must have been originated by something else.

Again, Mr. Darwin writes—"In considering the origin of species it is quite conceivable that a naturalist, reflecting on the mutual affinities of organic beings, or their embryological relations, their geographical distribution, geological succession, and other such facts, might come to the conclusion that species had not been independently created, but had descended, like varieties from other species. Nevertheless, such a conclusion, even if well founded, would be unsatisfactory, until it could be shown how the innumerable species inhabiting this world had been modified, so as to acquire that perfection of structure and co-adaptation which justly excites our admiration" ("Origin of Species," p. 2, ed. 1876).

After reading the above we feel that nothing more satisfactory could be desired. We are sure that we are in the hands of one who can indeed tell us "how the innumerable species inhabiting this world have been modified," and we are no less sure that though others may have written upon the subject before, there has been, as yet, no satisfactory explanation put forward of the grand principle upon which modification has proceeded. Then follows a delightful volume, with facts upon facts concerning animals, all showing that species is due to successive small modifications accumulated in the course of nature. But one cannot suppose that Lamarck ever doubted this; for he can never have meant to say, that a low form of life made itself into an elephant at one or two great bounds; and if he did not mean this, he must have meant that it made itself into an elephant through the accumulation of small successive modifications; these, he must have seen, were capable of accumulation in the scheme of nature, though he may not have dwelt on the manner in which this is accomplished, inasmuch as it is obviously a matter of secondary importance in comparison with the origin of the variations themselves. We believe, however, throughout Mr. Darwin's book, that we are being told what we expected to be told; and so convinced are we, by the facts adduced, that in some way or other evolution must be true, and so grateful are we for being allowed to think this, that we put down the volume without perceiving that, whereas Lamarck *did* adduce a great and general cause of variation, the insufficiency of which, in spite of errors of detail, has yet to be shown, Mr. Darwin's main cause of variation resolves itself into a confession of ignorance.

This, however, should detract but little from our admiration for Mr. Darwin's achievement. Any one can make people see a thing if he puts it in the right way, but Mr. Darwin made us see evolution, in spite of his having put it, in what seems to not a few, an exceedingly mistaken way. Yet his triumph is complete, for no matter how much any one now moves the foundation, he cannot shake the superstructure, which has become so currently accepted as to be above the need of any support from reason, and to be as difficult to destroy as it was originally difficult of construction. Less than twenty years ago, we never met with, or heard of, any one who accepted evolution; we did not even know that such a doctrine had been ever broached; unless it was that some one now and again said that there was a very dreadful book going about like a rampant lion, called "Vestiges of Creation," whereon we said that we would on no account read it, lest it should shake our faith; then we would shake our heads and talk of the preposterous folly and wickedness of such shallow speculations. Had not the book of Genesis been written for our learning? Yet, now, who seriously disputes the main principles of evolution? I cannot believe that there is a bishop on the bench at this moment who does not accept them; even the "holy priests" themselves bless evolution as their predecessors blessed Cleopatra—when they ought not. It is not he who first conceives an idea, nor he who sets it on its legs and makes it go on all fours, but he who makes other people accept the main conclusion, whether on right grounds or on wrong ones, who has done the greatest work as regards the promulgation of an opinion. And this is what Mr. Darwin has done for evolution. He has made us think that we know the origin of species, and so of genera, in spite of his utmost efforts to assure us that we know nothing of the causes from which the vast majority of modifications have arisen—that is to say, he has made us think we know the whole road, though he has almost ostentatiously blindfolded us at every step of the journey. But to the end of time, if the question be asked, "Who taught people to believe in evolution?" there can only be one answer—that it was Mr. Darwin.

Mr. Mivart urges with much force the difficulty of *starting* any modification on which "natural selection" is to work, and of getting a creature to vary in any definite direction. Thus, after quoting from Mr. Wallace some of the wonderful cases of "mimicry" which are to be found among insects, he writes:-

"Now, let us suppose that the ancestors of these various animals were all destitute of the very special protection they at present possess, as on the Darwinian hypothesis we must do. Let it be also conceded that small deviations from the antecedent colouring or form would tend to make some of their ancestors escape destruction, by causing them more or less frequently to be passed over or mistaken by their persecutors. Yet the deviation must, as the event has shown, in each case, be in some definite direction, whether it be towards some other animal or plant, or towards some dead or inorganic matter. But as, according to Mr. Darwin's theory, there is a constant tendency to indefinite variation, and as the minute incipient variations will be *in all directions,* they must tend to neutralise each other, and at first to form such unstable modifications, that it is difficult, if not impossible, to see how such indefinite modifications of insignificant beginnings can ever build up a sufficiently appreciable resemblance to a leaf, bamboo, or other object for "natural selection," to seize upon and perpetuate. This difficulty is augmented when we consider —a point to be dwelt upon hereafter—how necessary it is that many individuals should be similarly modified simultaneously. This has been insisted on in an able article in the 'North British Review' for June 1867, p. 286, and the consideration of the article has occasioned Mr. Darwin" ("Origin of Species," 5th ed., p. 104) "to make an important modification in his views ("Genesis of Species," p. 38).

To this Mr. Darwin rejoins:-

"But in all the foregoing cases the insects in their original state, no doubt, presented some rude and accidental resemblance to an object commonly found in the stations frequented by them. Nor is this improbable, considering the almost infinite number of surrounding objects, and the diversity of form and colour of the host of insects that exist" ("Natural Selection," p. 182, ed. 1876).

Mr. Mivart has just said: "It is difficult to see how such indefinite modifications of insignificant beginnings *can ever build up a sufficiently appreciable resemblance to a leaf, bamboo, or other object, for 'natural selection' to work upon.*"

The answer is, that "natural selection" did not begin to work *until, from unknown causes, an appreciable resemblance had nevertheless been presented.* I think the reader will agree with me that the development of the lowest life into a creature which bears even "a rude resemblance" to the objects commonly found in the station in which it is moving in its present differentiation, requires more explanation than is given by the word "accidental."

Mr. Darwin continues: "As some rude resemblance is necessary for the first start," &c.; and a little lower he writes: "Assuming that an insect originally happened to resemble in some degree a dead twig or a decayed leaf, and that it varied slightly in many ways, then all the variations which rendered the insect at all more like any such object, and thus favoured its escape, would be preserved, while other variations would be neglected, and ultimately lost, or if they rendered the insect at all less like the imitated object, they would be eliminated."

But here, again, we are required to begin with Natural Selection when the work is already in great part done, owing to causes about which we are left completely in the dark; we may, I think, fairly demur to the insects *originally* happening to resemble in some degree a dead twig or a decayed leaf. And when we bear in mind that the variations, being supposed by Mr. Darwin to be indefinite, or devoid of aim, will appear in every direction, we cannot forget what Mr. Mivart insists upon, namely, that the chances of many favourable variations being counteracted by other unfavourable ones in the same creature are not inconsiderable. Nor, again, is it likely that the favourable variation would make its mark upon the race, and escape being absorbed in the course of a few generations, unless—as Mr. Mivart elsewhere points out, in a passage to which I shall call the reader's attention presently—a larger number of similarly varying creatures made their appearance at the same time than there seems sufficient reason to anticipate, if the variations can be called fortuitous.

"There would," continues Mr. Darwin, "indeed be force in Mr. Mivart's objection if we were to attempt to account for the above resemblances, independently of 'natural selection,' through mere fluctuating variability; but as the case stands, there is none."

This comes to saying that, if there was no power in nature which operates so that of all the many fluctuating variations, those only are preserved which tend to the resemblance which is beneficial to the creature, then indeed there would be difficulty in understanding how the resemblance could have come about; but that as there is a beneficial resemblance to start with, and as there is a power in nature which would preserve and accumulate further beneficial resemblance, should it arise from this cause or that, the difficulty is removed. But Mr. Mivart does not, I take it, deny the existence of such a power in nature, as Mr. Darwin supposes, though, if I understand him rightly, he does not see that its operation *upon small fortuitous variations* is at all the simple and obvious process, which on a superficial view of the case it would appear to be. He thinks—and I believe the reader will agree with him—that this process is too slow and too risky. What he wants to know is, how the insect came even rudely to resemble the object, and how, if its variations are indefinite, we are ever to get into such a condition as to be able to report progress, owing to the constant liability of the creature which has varied favourably, to play the part of Penelope and undo its work, by varying in some one of the infinite number of other directions which are open to it—all of which, except this one, tend to destroy the resemblance, and yet may be in some other respect even more advantageous to the creature, and so tend to its preservation. Moreover, here, too, I think (though I cannot be sure), we have a recurrence of the original fallacy in the words—"If we were to account for the above resemblances, independently of 'natural selection,' through mere fluctuating variability." Surely Mr. Darwin does, after all, "account for the resemblances through mere fluctuating variability," for "natural selection" does not account for one single variation in the whole list of them from first to last, other than indirectly, as shewn in the preceding chapter.

It is impossible for me to continue this subject further; but I would beg the reader to refer to other paragraphs in the neighbourhood of the one just quoted, in which he may—though I do not think he will - see reason to think that I should have given Mr. Darwin's answer more fully. I do not quote Mr. Darwin's next paragraph, inasmuch as I see no great difficulty about "the last touches of perfection in mimicry," provided Mr. Darwin's theory will account for any mimicry at all. If it could do this, it might as well do more; but a strong impression is left on my mind, that without the help of something over and above the power to vary, which should give a definite aim to variations, all the "natural selection" in the world would not have prevented stagnation and self-stultification, owing to the indefinite tendency of the variations, which thus could not have developed either a preyer or a preyee, but would have gone round and round and round the primordial cell till they were weary of it.

As against Mr. Darwin, therefore, I think that the objection just given from Mr. Mivart is fatal. I believe, also, that the reader will feel the force of it much more strongly if he will turn to Mr. Mivart's own pages. Against the view which I am myself supporting, the objection breaks down entirely, for grant "a little dose of judgement and reason" on the part of the creature itself—grant also continued personality and memory—and a definite tendency is at once given to the variations. The process is thus started, and is kept straight, and helped forward through every stage by "the little dose of reason," &c., which enabled it to take its first step. We are, in fact, no longer without a helm, but can steer each creature that is so discontented with its condition, as to make a serious effort to better itself, into *some*— and into a very distant—harbour.

It has been objected against Mr. Darwin's theory that if all species and genera have come to differ through the accumulation of minute but— as a general rule—fortuitous variations, there has not been time enough, so far as we are able to gather, for the evolution of all existing forms by so slow a process. On this subject I would again refer the reader to Mr. Mivart's book, from which I take the following:-

"Sir William Thompson has lately advanced arguments from three distinct lines of inquiry agreeing in one approximate result. The three lines of inquiry are—(1) the action of the tides upon the earth's rotation; (2) the probable length of time during which the sun has illuminated this planet; and (3) the temperature of the interior of the earth. The result arrived at by these investigations is a conclusion that the existing state of things on the earth, life on the earth, all geological history showing continuity of life, must be limited within some such period of past time as one hundred million years. The first question which suggests itself, supposing Sir W. Thompson's views to be correct, is: Has this period been anything like enough for the evolution of all organic forms by 'natural selection'? The second is: Has the period been anything like enough for the deposition of the strata which must have been deposited if all organic forms have been evolved by minute steps, according to the Darwinian theory?" ("Genesis of Species," p. 154).

Mr. Mivart then quotes from Mr. Murphy—whose work I have not seen - the following passage:-

"Darwin justly mentions the greyhound as being equal to any natural species in the perfect co-ordination of its parts, 'all adapted for extreme fleetness and for running down weak prey.' Yet it is an artificial species (and not physiologically a species at all) formed by a long-continued selection under domestication; and there is no reason to suppose that any of the variations which have been selected to form it have been other than gradual and almost imperceptible. Suppose that it has taken five hundred years to form the greyhound out of his wolf-like ancestor. This is a mere guess, but it gives the order of magnitude. Now, if so, how long would it take to obtain an elephant from a protozoon or even from a tadpole-like fish? Ought it not to take much more than a million times as long?" ("Genesis of Species," p. 155).

I should be very sorry to pronounce any opinion upon the foregoing data; but a general impression is left upon my mind, that if the differences between an elephant and a tadpole-like fish have arisen from the accumulation of small variations that have had no direction given them by intelligence and sense of needs, then no time conceivable by man would suffice for their development. But grant "a little dose of reason and judgement," even to animals low down in the scale of nature, and grant this, not only during their later life, but during their embryological existence, and see with what infinitely greater precision of aim and with what increased speed the variations would arise. Evolution entirely unaided by inherent intelligence must be a very slow, if not quite inconceivable, process. Evolution helped by intelligence would still be slow, but not so desperately slow. One can conceive that there has been sufficient time for the second, but one cannot conceive it for the first.

I find from Mr. Mivart that objection has been taken to Mr. Darwin's views, on account of the great odds that exist against the appearance of any given variation at one and the same time, in a sufficient number of individuals, to prevent its being obliterated almost as soon as produced by the admixture of unvaried blood which would so greatly preponderate around it; and indeed the necessity for a nearly simultaneous and similar variation, or readiness so to vary on the part of many individuals, seems almost a postulate for evolution at all. On this subject Mr. Mivart writes:-

"The 'North British Review' (speaking of the supposition that species is changed by the survival of a few individuals in a century through a similar and favourable variation) says—

"'It is very difficult to see how this can be accomplished, even when the variation is eminently favourable indeed; and still more, when the advantage gained is very slight, as must generally be the case. The advantage, whatever it may be, is utterly outbalanced by numerical inferiority. A million creatures are born; ten thousand survive to produce offspring. One of the million has twice as good a chance as any other of surviving, but the chances are fifty to one against the gifted individuals being one of the hundred survivors. No doubt the chances are twice as great against any other individual, but this does not prevent their being enormously in favour of *some* average individual. However slight the advantage may be, if it is shared by half the individuals produced, it will probably be present in at least fifty-one of the survivors, and in a larger proportion of their offspring; but the chances are against the preservation of any one "sport" (*i.e.*, sudden marked variation) in a numerous tribe. The vague use of an imperfectly-understood doctrine of chance, has led Darwinian supporters, first, to confuse the two cases above distinguished, and secondly, to imagine that a very slight balance in favour of some individual sport must lead to its perpetuation. All that can be said is that in the above example the favoured sport would be preserved once in fifty times. Let us consider what will be its influence on the main stock when preserved. It will breed and have a progeny of say 100; now this progeny will, on the whole, be intermediate between the average individual and the sport. The odds in favour of one of this generation of the new breed will be, say one and a half to one, as compared with the average individual; the odds in their favour will, therefore, be less than that of their parents; but owing to their greater number the chances are that about one and a half of them would survive. Unless these breed together—a most improbable event—their progeny would again approach the average individual; there would be 150 of them, and their superiority would be, say in the ratio of one and a quarter to one; the probability would now be that nearly two of them would survive, and have 200 children with an eighth superiority. Rather more than two of these would survive; but the superiority would again dwindle; until after a few generations it would no longer be observed, and would count for no more in the struggle for life than any of the hundred trifling advantages which occur in the ordinary organs.

"'An illustration will bring this conception home. Suppose a white man to have been wrecked on an island inhabited by negroes, and to have established himself in friendly relations with a powerful tribe, whose customs he has learnt. Suppose him to possess the physical strength, energy, and ability of a dominant white race, and let the food of the island suit his constitution; grant him every advantage which we can conceive a white to possess over the native; concede that in the struggle for existence, his chance of a long life will be much superior to that of the native chiefs;

yet from all these admissions there does not follow the conclusion, that after a limited or unlimited number of generations, the inhabitants of the island will be white. Our shipwrecked hero would probably become king; he would kill a great many blacks in the struggle for existence; he would have a great many wives and children . . . In the first generation there will be some dozens of intelligent young mulattoes, much superior in average intelligence to the negroes. We might expect the throne for some generations to be occupied by a more or less yellow king; but can any one believe that the whole island will gradually acquire a white, or even a yellow population? . . . Darwin says, that in the struggle for life a grain may turn the balance in favour of a given structure, which will then be preserved. But one of the weights in the scale of nature is due to the number of a given tribe. Let there be 7000 A's and 7000 B's representing two varieties of a given animal, and let all the B's, in virtue of a slight difference of structure, have the better chance by one-thousandth part. We must allow that there is a slight probability that the descendants of B will supplant the descendants of A; but let there be 7001 A's against 7000 B's at first, and the chances are once more equal, while if there be 7002 A's to start, the odds would be laid on the A's. Thus they stand a greater chance of being killed; but, then, they can better afford to be killed. The grain will only turn the scales when these are very nicely balanced, and an advantage in numbers counts for weight, even as an advantage in structure. As the numbers of the favoured variety diminish, so must its relative advantages increase, if the chance of its existence is to surpass the chance of its extinction, until hardly any conceivable advantage would enable the descendants of a single pair to exterminate the descendants of many thousands, if they and their descendants are supposed to breed freely with the inferior variety, and so gradually lose their ascendancy,'" ("North British Review," June 1867, p. 286 "Genesis of Species," p. 64, and onwards).

Against this it should be remembered that there is always an antecedent probability that several specimens of a given variation would appear at one time and place. This would probably be the case even on Mr. Darwin's hypothesis, that the variations are fortuitous; if they are mainly guided by sense of need and intelligence, it would almost certainly be so, for all would have much the same idea as to their well-being, and the same cause which would lead one to vary in this direction would lead not a few others to do so at the same time, or to follow suit. Thus we see that many human ideas and inventions have been conceived independently but simultaneously. The chances, moreover, of specimens that have varied successfully, intermarrying, are, I think, greater than the reviewer above quoted from would admit. I believe that on the hypothesis that the variations are fortuitous, and certainly on the supposition that they are intelligent, they might be looked for in members of the same family, who would hence have a better chance of finding each other out. Serious as is the difficulty advanced by the reviewer as against Mr. Darwin's theory, it may be in great measure parried without departing from Mr. Darwin's own position, but the "little dose of judgement and reason" removes it, absolutely and entirely. As for the reviewer's shipwrecked hero, surely the reviewer must know that Mr. Darwin would no more expect an island of black men to be turned white, or even perceptibly whitened after a few generations, than the reviewer himself would do so. But if we turn from what "might" or what "would" happen to what "does" happen, we find that a few white families have nearly driven the Indian from the United States, the Australian natives from Australia, and the Maories from New Zealand. True, these few families have been helped by immigration; but it will be admitted that this has only accelerated a result which would otherwise, none the less surely, have been effected.

There is all the difference between a sudden sport, or even a variety introduced from a foreign source, and the gradual, intelligent, and, in the main, steady, growth of a race towards ends always a little, but not much, in advance of what it can at present compass, until it has reached equilibrium with its surroundings. So far as Mr. Darwin's variations are of the nature of "sport," *i.e.*, rare, and owing to nothing that we can in the least assign to any known cause, the reviewer's objections carry much weight. Against the view here advocated, they are powerless.

I cannot here go into the difficulties of the geologic record, but they too will, I believe, be felt to be almost infinitely simplified by supposing the development of structure and instinct to be guided by intelligence and memory, which, even under unstable conditions, would be able to meet in some measure the demands made upon them.

When Mr. Mivart deals with evolution and ethics, I am afraid that I differ from him even more widely than I have done from Mr. Darwin. He writes ("Genesis of Species," p. 234): "That 'natural selection' could not have produced from the sensations of pleasure and pain experienced by brutes a higher degree of morality than was useful; therefore it could have produced any amount of 'beneficial habits,' but not abhorrence of certain acts as impure and sinful."

Possibly "natural selection" may not be able to do much in the way of accumulating variations that do not arise; but that, according to the views supported in this volume, all that is highest and most beautiful in the soul, as well as in the body, could be, and has been, developed from beings lower than man, I do not greatly doubt. Mr. Mivart and myself should probably differ as to what is and what is not beautiful. Thus he writes of "the noble virtue of a Marcus Aurelius" (p. 235), than whom, for my own part, I know few respectable figures in history to whom I am less attracted. I cannot but think that Mr. Mivart has taken his estimate of this emperor at second-hand, and without reference to the writings which happily enable us to form a fair estimate of his real character.

Take the opening paragraphs of the "Thoughts" of Marcus Aurelius, as translated by Mr. Long:-

"From the reputation and remembrance of my father [I learned] modesty and a manly character; from my mother, piety and beneficence, abstinence not only from evil deeds, but even from evil thoughts. . . . From my great-grandfather, not to have frequented public schools, and to have had good teachers at home, and to know that on such things a man should spend liberally . . . From Diognetus . . . [I learned] to have become intimate with philosophy, . . . and to have written dialogues in my youth, and to have desired a plank bed and skin, and whatever else of the kind belongs to the Greek discipline. . . . From Rusticus I received the impression that my character required improvement and discipline;" and so on to the end of the chapter, near which, however, it is right to say that there appears a redeeming touch, in so far as that he thanks the gods that he could not write poetry, and that he had never occupied himself about the appearance of things in the heavens.

Or, again, opening Mr. Long's translation at random I find (p. 37):-

"As physicians have always their instruments and knives ready for cases which suddenly require their skill, so do thou have principles ready for the understanding of things divine and human, and for doing everything, even the smallest, with a recollection of the bond that unites the divine and human to one another. For neither wilt thou do anything well which pertains to man without at the same time having a reference to things divine; nor the contrary."

Unhappy one! No wonder the Roman empire went to pieces soon after him. If I remember rightly, he established and subsidised professorships in all parts of his dominions. Whereon the same befell the arts and literature of Rome as befell Italian painting after the Academic system had taken root at Bologna under the Caracci. Mr. Martin Tupper, again, is an amiable and well-meaning man, but we should hardly like to see him in Lord Beaconsfield's place. The Athenians poisoned Socrates; and Aristophanes —than whom few more profoundly religious men have ever been born— did not, so far as we can gather, think the worse of his countrymen on that account. It is not improbable that if they had poisoned Plato too, Aristophanes would have been well enough pleased; but I think he would have preferred either of these two men to Marcus Aurelius.

I know nothing about the loving but manly devotion of a St. Lewis, but I strongly suspect that Mr. Mivart has taken him, too, upon hearsay.

On the other hand, among dogs we find examples of every heroic quality, and of all that is most perfectly charming to us in man.

As for the possible development of the more brutal human natures from the more brutal instincts of the lower animals, those who read a horrible story told in a note, pp. 233, 234 of Mr. Mivart's "Genesis of Species," will feel no difficulty on that score. I must admit, however, that the telling of that story seems to me to be a mistake in a philosophical work, which should not, I think, unless under compulsion, deal either with the horrors of the French Revolution—or of the Spanish or Italian Inquisition.

For the rest of Mr. Mivart's objections, I must refer the reader to his own work. I have been unable to find a single one, which I do not believe to be easily met by the Lamarckian view, with the additions (if indeed they are additions, for I must own to no very profound knowledge of what Lamarck did or did not say), which I have in this volume proposed to make to it. At the same time I admit, that as against the Darwinian view, many of them seem quite unanswerable.

CHAPTER XV—CONCLUDING REMARKS

Here, then, I leave my case, though well aware that I have crossed the threshold only of my subject. My work is of a tentative character, put before the public as a sketch or design for a, possibly, further endeavour, in which I hope to derive assistance from the criticisms which this present volume may elicit. Such as it is, however, for the present I must leave it.

We have seen that we cannot do anything thoroughly till we can do it unconsciously, and that we cannot do anything unconsciously till we can do it thoroughly; this at first seems illogical; but logic and consistency are luxuries for the gods, and the lower animals, only. Thus a boy cannot really know how to swim till he can swim, but he cannot swim till he knows how to swim. Conscious effort is but the process of rubbing off the rough corners from these two contradictory statements, till they eventually fit into one another so closely that it is impossible to disjoin them.

Whenever, therefore, we see any creature able to go through any complicated and difficult process with little or no effort—whether it be a bird building her nest, or a hen's egg making itself into a chicken, or an ovum turning itself into a baby—we may conclude that the creature has done the same thing on a very great number of past occasions.

We found the phenomena exhibited by heredity to be so like those of memory, and to be so utterly inexplicable on any other supposition, that it was easier to suppose them due to memory in spite of the fact that we cannot remember having recollected, than to believe that because we cannot so remember, therefore the phenomena cannot be due to memory.

We were thus led to consider "personal identity," in order to see whether there was sufficient reason for denying that the experience, which we must have clearly gained somewhere, was gained by us when we were in the persons of our forefathers; we found, not without surprise, that unless we admitted that it might be so gained, in so far as that we once *actually were* our remotest ancestor, we must change our ideas concerning personality altogether.

We therefore assumed that the phenomena of heredity, whether as regards instinct or structure were mainly due to memory of past experiences, accumulated and fused till they had become automatic, or quasi automatic, much in the same way as after a long life—

.. "Old experience do attain
To something like prophetic strain."

After dealing with certain phenomena of memory, but more especially with its abeyance and revival, we inquired what the principal corresponding phenomena of life and species should be, on the hypothesis that they were mainly due to memory.

I think I may say that we found the hypothesis fit in with actual facts in a sufficiently satisfactory manner. We found not a few matters, as, for example, the sterility of hybrids, the phenomena of old age, and puberty as generally near the end of development, explain themselves with more completeness than I have yet heard of their being explained on any other hypothesis.

We considered the most important difficulty in the way of instinct as hereditary habit, namely, the structure and instincts of neuter insects; these are very unlike those of their parents, and cannot apparently be transmitted to offspring by individuals of the previous generation, in whom such structure and instincts appeared, inasmuch as these creatures are sterile. I do not say that the difficulty is wholly removed, inasmuch as some obscurity must be admitted to remain as to the manner in which the structure of the larva is aborted; this obscurity is likely to remain till we know more of the early history of civilisation among bees than I can find that we know at present; but I believe the difficulty was reduced to such proportions as to make it little likely to be felt in comparison with that of attributing instinct to any other cause than inherited habit, or inherited habit modified by changed conditions.

We then inquired what was the great principle underlying variation, and answered, with Lamarck, that it must be "sense of need;" and though not without being haunted by suspicion of a vicious circle, and also well aware that we were not much nearer the origin of life than when we started, we still concluded that here was the truest origin of species, and hence of genera; and that the accumulation of variations, which in time amounted to specific and generic differences, was due to intelligence and memory on the part of the creature varying, rather than to the operation of what Mr. Darwin has called "natural selection." At the same time we admitted that the course of nature is very much as Mr. Darwin has represented it, in this respect, in so far as that there is a struggle for existence, and that the weaker must go to the wall. But we denied that this part of the course of nature would lead to much, if any, accumulation of variation, unless the variation was directed mainly by intelligent sense of need, with continued personality and memory.

We conclude, therefore, that the small, structureless, impregnate ovum from which we have each one of us sprung, has a potential recollection of all that has happened to each one of its ancestors prior to the period at which any such ancestor has issued from the bodies of its progenitors—provided, that is to say, a sufficiently deep, or sufficiently often-repeated, impression has been made to admit of its being remembered at all.

Each step of normal development will lead the impregnate ovum up to, and remind it of, its next ordinary course of action, in the same way as we, when we recite a well-known passage, are led up to each successive sentence by the sentence which has immediately preceded it.

And for this reason, namely, that as it takes two people "to tell" a thing —a speaker and a comprehending listener, without which last, though much may have been said, there has been nothing told—so also it takes two people, as it were, to "remember" a thing—the creature remembering, and the surroundings of the creature at the time it last remembered. Hence, though the ovum immediately after impregnation is instinct with all the memories of both parents, not one of these memories can normally become active till both the ovum itself, and its surroundings, are sufficiently like what they respectively were, when the occurrence now to be remembered last took place. The memory will then immediately return, and the creature will do as it did on the last occasion that it was in like case as now. This ensures that similarity of order shall be preserved in all the stages of development, in successive generations.

Life, then, is faith founded upon experience, which experience is in its turn founded upon faith—or more simply, it is memory. Plants and animals only differ from one another because they remember different things; plants and animals only grow up in the shapes they assume because this shape is their memory, their idea concerning their own past history.

Hence the term "Natural History," as applied to the different plants and animals around us. For surely the study of natural history means only the study of plants and animals themselves, which, at the moment of using the words "Natural History," we assume to be the most important part of nature.

A living creature well supported by a mass of healthy ancestral memory is a young and growing creature, free from ache or pain, and thoroughly acquainted with its business so far, but with much yet to be reminded of. A creature which finds itself and its surroundings not so unlike those of its parents about the time of their begetting it, as to be compelled to recognise that it never yet was in any such position, is a creature in the heyday of life. A creature which begins to be aware of itself is one which is beginning to recognise that the situation is a new one.

It is the young and fair, then, who are the truly old and the truly experienced; it is they who alone have a trustworthy memory to guide them; they alone know things as they are, and it is from them that, as we grow older, we must study if we would still cling to truth. The whole charm of youth lies in its advantage over age in respect of experience, and where this has for some reason failed, or been misapplied, the charm is broken. When we say that we are getting old, we should say rather that we are getting new or young, and are suffering from inexperience, which drives us into doing things which we do not understand, and lands us, eventually, in the utter impotence of death. The kingdom of heaven is the kingdom of little children.

A living creature bereft of all memory dies. If bereft of a great part of memory, it swoons or sleeps; and when its memory returns, we say it has returned to life.

Life and death, then, should be memory and forgetfulness, for we are dead to all that we have forgotten.

Life is that property of matter whereby it can remember. Matter which can remember is living; matter which cannot remember is dead.

Life, then, is memory. The life of a creature is the memory of a creature. We are all the same stuff to start with, but we remember different things, and if we did not remember different things we should be absolutely like each other. As for the stuff itself of which we are made, we know nothing save only that it is "such as dreams are made of."

I am aware that there are many expressions throughout this book, which are not scientifically accurate. Thus I imply that we tend towards the centre of the earth, when, I believe, I should say we tend towards to the centre of gravity of the earth. I speak of "the primordial cell," when I mean only the earliest form of life, and I thus not only assume a single origin of life when there is no necessity for doing so, and perhaps no evidence to this effect, but I do so in spite of the fact that the amba, which seems to be "the simplest form of life," does not appear to be a cell at all. I have used the word "beget," of what, I am told, is asexual generation, whereas the word should be confined to sexual generation only. Many more such errors have been pointed out to me, and I doubt not that a larger number remain of which I know nothing now, but of which I may perhaps be told presently.

I did not, however, think that in a work of this description the additional words which would have been required for scientific accuracy were worth the paper and ink and loss of breadth which their introduction would entail. Besides, I know nothing about science, and it is as well that there should be no mistake on this head; I neither know, nor want to know, more detail than is necessary to enable me to give a fairly broad and comprehensive view of my subject. When for the purpose of giving this, a matter importunately insisted on being made out, I endeavoured to make it out as well as I could; otherwise—that is to say, if it did not insist on being looked into, in spite of a good deal of snubbing, I held that, as it was blurred and indistinct in nature, I had better so render it in my work.

Nevertheless, if one has gone for some time through a wood full of burrs, some of them are bound to stick. I am afraid that I have left more such burrs in one part and another of my book, than the kind of reader whom I alone wish to please will perhaps put up with. Fortunately, this kind of reader is the best-natured critic in the world, and is long suffering of a good deal that the more consciously scientific will not tolerate; I wish, however, that I had not used such expressions as "centres of thought and action" quite so often.

As for the kind of inaccuracy already alluded to, my reader will not, I take it, as a general rule, know, or wish to know, much more about science than I do, sometimes perhaps even less; so that he and I shall commonly be wrong in the same places, and our two wrongs will make a sufficiently satisfactory right for practical purposes.

Of course, if I were a specialist writing a treatise or primer on such and such a point of detail, I admit that scientific accuracy would be *de rigueur*; but I have been trying to paint a picture rather than to make a diagram, and I claim the painter's license *"quidlibet audendi."* I have done my utmost to give the spirit of my subject, but if the letter interfered with the spirit, I have sacrificed it without remorse.

May not what is commonly called a scientific subject have artistic value which it is a pity to neglect? But if a subject is to be treated artistically— that is to say, with a desire to consider not only the facts, but the way in which the reader will feel concerning those facts, and the way in which he will wish to see them rendered, thus making his mind a factor of the intention, over and above the subject itself—then the writer must not be denied a painter's license. If one is painting a hillside at a sufficient distance, and cannot see whether it is covered with chestnut-trees or walnuts, one is not bound to go across the valley to see. If one is painting a city, it is not necessary that one should know the names of the streets. If a house or tree stands inconveniently for one's purpose, it must go without more ado; if two important features, neither of which can be left out, want a little bringing together or separating before the spirit of the place can be well given, they must be brought together, or separated. Which is a more truthful view, of Shrewsbury, for example, from a spot where St. Alkmund's spire is in parallax with St. Mary's—a view which should give only the one spire which can be seen, or one which should give them both, although the one is hidden? There would be, I take it, more representation in the misrepresentation than in the representation - "the half would be greater than the whole," unless, that is to say, one expressly told the spectator that St. Alkmund's spire was hidden behind St. Mary's—a sort of explanation which seldom adds to the poetical value of any work of art. Do what one may, and no matter how scientific one may be, one cannot attain absolute truth. The question is rather, how do people like to have their error? than, will they go without any error at all? All truth and no error cannot be given by the scientist more than by the artist; each has to sacrifice truth in one way or another; and even if perfect truth could be given, it is doubtful whether it would not resolve itself into unconsciousness pure and simple, consciousness being, as it were, the clash of small conflicting perceptions, without which there is neither intelligence nor recollection possible. It is not, then, what a man has said, nor what he has put down with actual paint upon his canvass, which speaks to us with living language—*it is what he has thought to us* (as is so well put in the letter quoted on page 83), by which our opinion should be guided;—what has he made us feel that he had it in him, and wished to do? If he has said or painted enough to make us feel that he meant and felt as we should wish him to have done, he has done the utmost that man can hope to do.

I feel sure that no additional amount of technical accuracy would make me more likely to succeed, in this respect, if I have otherwise failed; and as this is the only success about which I greatly care, I have left my scientific inaccuracies uncorrected, even when aware of them. At the same time, I should say that I have taken all possible pains as regards anything which I thought could materially affect the argument one way or another.

It may be said that I have fallen between two stools, and that the subject is one which, in my hands, has shown neither artistic nor scientific value. This would be serious. To fall between two stools, and to be hanged for a lamb, are the two crimes which—

"Nor gods, nor men, nor any schools allow."

Of the latter, I go in but little danger; about the former, I shall know better when the public have enlightened me.

The practical value of the views here advanced (if they be admitted as true at all) would appear to be not inconsiderable, alike as regards politics or the well-being of the community, and medicine which deals with that of the individual. In the first case we see the rationale of compromise, and the equal folly of making experiments upon too large a scale, and of not making them at all. We see that new ideas cannot be fused with old, save gradually and by patiently leading up to them in such a way as to admit of a sense of continued identity between the old and the new. This should teach us moderation. For even though nature wishes to travel in a certain direction, she insists on being allowed to take her own time; she will not be hurried, and will cull a creature out even more surely for forestalling her wishes too readily, than for lagging a little behind them. So the greatest musicians, painters, and poets owe their greatness rather to their fusion and assimilation of all the good that has been done up to, and especially near about, their own time, than to any very startling steps they have taken in advance. Such men will be sure to take some, and important, steps forward; for unless they have this power, they will not be able to assimilate well what has been done already, and if they have it, their study of older work will almost indefinitely assist it; but, on the whole, they owe their greatness to their completer fusion and assimilation of older ideas; for nature is distinctly a fairly liberal conservative rather than a conservative liberal. All which is well said in the old couplet -

"Be not the first by whom the new is tried,
Nor yet the last to throw the old aside."

Mutatis mutandis, the above would seem to hold as truly about medicine as about politics. We cannot reason with our cells, for they know so much more than we do that they cannot understand us;—but though we cannot reason with them, we can find out what they have been most accustomed to, and what, therefore, they are most likely to expect; we can see that they get this, as far as it is in our power to give it them, and may then generally leave the rest to them, only bearing in mind that they will rebel equally against too sudden a change of treatment, and no change at all.

Friends have complained to me that they can never tell whether I am in jest or earnest. I think, however, it should be sufficiently apparent that I am in very serious earnest, perhaps too much so, from the first page of my book to the last. I am not aware of a single argument put forward which is not a *bonâ fide* argument, although, perhaps, sometimes admitting of a humorous side. If a grain of corn looks like a piece of chaff, I confess I prefer it occasionally to something which looks like a grain, but which turns out to be a piece of chaff only. There is no lack of matter of this description going about in some very decorous volumes; I have, therefore, endeavoured, for a third time, to furnish the public with a book whose fault should lie rather in the direction of seeming less serious than it is, than of being less so than it seems.

At the same time, I admit that when I began to write upon my subject I did not seriously believe in it. I saw, as it were, a pebble upon the ground, with a sheen that pleased me; taking it up, I turned it over and over for my amusement, and found it always grow brighter and brighter the more I examined it. At length I became fascinated, and gave loose rein to self-illusion. The aspect of the world seemed changed; the trifle which I had picked up idly had proved to be a talisman of inestimable value, and had opened a door through which I caught glimpses of a strange and interesting transformation. Then came one who told me that the stone was not mine, but that it had been dropped by Lamarck, to whom it belonged rightfully, but who had lost it; whereon I said I cared not who was the owner, if only I might use it and enjoy it. Now, therefore, having polished it with what art and care one who is no jeweller could bestow upon it, I return it, as best I may, to its possessor.

What am I to think or say? That I tried to deceive others till I have fallen a victim to my own falsehood? Surely this is the most reasonable conclusion to arrive at. Or that I have really found Lamarck's talisman, which had been for some time lost sight of?

Will the reader bid me wake with him to a world of chance and blindness? Or can I persuade him to dream with me of a more living faith than either he or I had as yet conceived as possible? As I have said, reason points remorselessly to an awakening, but faith and hope still beckon to the dream.